SUNDOWN SLIM

HENRY HERBERT KNIBBS

1st WORLD
LIBRARY
Literary Society

Sundown Slim

Henry Hubert Knibbs

© 1st World Library, 2007
PO Box 2211
Fairfield, IA 52556
www.1stworldlibrary.com
First Edition

LCCN: 2007930794

Softcover ISBN: 978-1-4218-4837-2
Hardcover ISBN: 978-1-4218-4740-5
eBook ISBN: 978-1-4218-4934-8

Purchase *"Sundown Slim"*
as a traditional bound book at:
www.1stWorldLibrary.com/purchase.asp?ISBN=978-1-4218-4837-2

1st World Library is a literary, educational organization
dedicated to:

- Creating a free internet library of downloadable ebooks

- Hosting writing competitions and offering book publishing
scholarships.

Interested in more 1st World Library books? contact:
literacy@1stworldlibrary.com
Check us out at: www.1stworldlibrary.com

1st World Library Literary Society

Giving Back to the World

"If you want to work on the core problem, it's early school literacy."

- James Barksdale, former CEO of Netscape

"No skill is more crucial to the future of a child, or to a democratic and prosperous society, than literacy."

- Los Angeles Times

"Literacy... means far more than learning how to read and write... The aim is to transmit... knowledge and promote social participation."

- UNESCO

"Literacy is not a luxury, it is a right and a responsibility. If our world is to meet the challenges of the twenty-first century we must harness the energy and creativity of all our citizens."

- President Bill Clinton

"Parents should be encouraged to read to their children, and teachers should be equipped with all available techniques for teaching literacy, so the varying needs and capacities of individual kids can be taken into account."

- Hugh Mackay

DEDICATED TO

EVERETT E. HARASZTHY

CONTENTS

ARIZONA..9

I. SUNDOWN IN ANTELOPE 11

II. THE JOKE 21

III. THIRTY MILES TO THE CONCHO 29

IV. PIE; AND SEPTEMBER MORN......................................38

V. ON THE CANON TRAIL 52

VI. THE BROTHERS......................................64

VII. FADEAWAY'S HAND....................................73

VIII. AT "THE LAST CHANCE" 82

IX. SUNDOWN'S FRIEND....................................94

X. THE STORM 105

XI. CHANCE--CONQUEROR............................. 112

XII. A GIFT 123

XIII. SUNDOWN, VAQUERO........................... 133

XIV. ON THE TRAIL TO THE BLUE............................. 143

XV. THEY KILLED THE BOSS!..................... 151

XVI. SUNDOWN ADVENTURES 158

XVII. THE STRANGER 165

XVIII. THE SHERIFF--AND OTHERS 180

XIX. THE ESCAPE....................................... 194

XX. THE WALKING MAN................................. 204

XXI. ON THE MESA... 215

XXII. WAIT! 222

XXIII. THE PEACEMAKER 234

XXIV. AN UNEXPECTED VISIT 245

XXV. VAMOSE, EH?.. 253

XXVI. THE INVADERS... 261

XXVII. "JUST ME AND HER" 277

XXVIII. IMPROVEMENTS 285

XXIX. A MAN'S COUNTRY 296

ARIZONA

Across the wide, sun-swept mesas the steel trail of the railroad runs east and west, diminishing at either end to a shimmering blur of silver. South of the railroad these level immensities, rich in their season with ripe bunch-grass and grama-grass roll up to the barrier of the far blue hills of spruce and pine. The red, ragged shoulders of buttes blot the sky-line here and there; wind-worn and grotesque silhouettes of gigantic fortifications, castles and villages wrought by some volcanic Cyclops who grew tired of his labors, abandoning his unfinished task to the weird ravages of wind and weather.

In the southern hills the swart Apache hunts along historic trails o'er which red cavalcades once swept to the plundering of Sonora's herds. His sires and their flashing pintos have vanished to other hunting-grounds, and he rides the boundaries of his scant heritage, wrapped in sullen imaginings.

The canons and the hills of this broad land are of heroic mould as are its men. Sons of the open, deep-chested, tall and straight, they ride like conquerors and walk—like bears. Slow to anger and quick to act, they carry their strength and health easily and with a dignity which no worn trappings, faded shirt, or flop-brimmed hat may obscure. Speak to one of them and his level gaze will travel to your feet and back again to your eyes. He may not know what you are, but he assuredly knows what you are not. He will answer you quietly and to the point. If you have been fortunate enough to have ridden range, hunted or camped with him or his kind, ask him, as he stands with thumb in belt and wide Stetson tilted back, the trail to heaven. He will smile and point toward the mesas and the mountains of his home. Ask him the trail to that other place with which he so frequently garnishes his conversation, and he will gravely point to the mesas and the hills again. And there you have Arizona.

Henry Hubert Knibbs

CHAPTER I

SUNDOWN IN ANTELOPE

Sundown Slim, who had enjoyed the un-upholstered privacy of a box-car on his journey west from Albuquerque, awakened to realize that his conveyance was no longer an integral part of the local freight which had stopped at the town of Antelope, and which was now rumbling and grumbling across the Arizona mesas. He was mildly irritated by a management that gave its passengers such negligent service. He complained to himself as he rolled and corded his blankets. However, he would disembark and leave the car to those base uses for which corporate greed, and a shipper of baled hay, intended it. He was further annoyed to find that the door of the car had been locked since he had taken possession. Hearing voices, he hammered on the door. After an exchange of compliments with an unseen rescuer, the door was pushed back and he leaped to the ground. He was a bit surprised to find, not the usual bucolic agent of a water-plug station, but a belted and booted rider of the mesas; a cowboy in all the glory of wide Stetson, wing chaps, and Mexican spurs.

"Thought you was the agent. I couldn't see out," apologized the tramp.

The cowboy laughed. "He was scared to open her up, so I took a chanct, seein' as I'm agent for the purvention of crulty to Hoboes."

"Well, you got a fine chance to make a record this evening" said Sundown, estimating with experienced eye the possibilities of Antelope and its environs. "I et at Albuquerque."

"Ain't a bad town to eat in," commented the puncher, gazing at the sky.

"I never seen one that was," the tramp offered, experimentally.

The cowboy grinned. "Well, take a look at this pueblo, then. You can see her all from here. If the station door was open you could see clean through to New Mexico. They got about as much use for a Bo in these parts as they have for raisin' posies. And this ain't no garden."

"Well, I'm raised. I got me full growth," said Sundown, straightening his elongated frame,—he stood six-feet-four in whatever he could get to stand in,—"and I raised meself."

"Good thing you stopped when you did," commented the puncher. "What's your line?"

"Me line? Well, the Santa Fe, jest now. Next comes cookin'. I been cook in everything from a hotel to a gradin'-camp. I cooked for high-collars and swalley-tails, and low-brows and jeans—till it come time to go. Incondescent to that I been poet select to the T.W.U."

"Temperance?"

"Not exactly. T.W.U. is Tie Walkers' Union. I lost me job

account of a long-hair buttin' in and ramblin' round the country spielin' high-toned stuff about 'Art for her own sake'—and such. Me pals selected him animus for poet, seein' as how I just writ things nacheral; no high-fluted stuff like him. Why, say, pardner, I believe in writin' from the ground up, so folks can understand. Why, this country is sufferin' full of guys tryin' to pull all the G strings out of a harp to onct—when they ought to be practicin' scales on a mouth-organ. And it's printed ag'in' 'em in the magazines, right along. I read lots of it. But speakin' of eats and *thinkin'* of eats, did you ever listen to 'Them Saddest Words,'—er—one of me own competitions?"

"Not while I was awake. But come on over to 'The Last Chance' and lubricate your works. I don't mind a little po'try on a full stummick."

"Well, I'm willin', pardner."

The process of lubrication was brief; and "Have another?" queried the tramp. "I ain't all broke—only I ain't payin' dividen's, bein' hard times."

"Keep your two-bits," said the puncher. "This is on me. You're goin' to furnish the chaser, Go to it and cinch up them there 'saddest.'"

"Bein' just two-bits this side of bein' a socialist, I guess I'll keep me change. I ain't a drinkin' man—regular, but I never was scared of eatin'."

Sundown gazed about the dingy room. Like most poets, he was not averse to an audience, and like most poets he was quite willing that such audience should help defray his incidental expenses—indirectly, of course. Prospects were pretty thin just then. Two Mexican herders loafed at the other end of the bar. They appeared anything but susceptible to the blandishments of Euterpe. Sundown gazed at the ceiling, which was fly-specked and uninspiring,

"Turn her loose!" said the puncher, winking at the bartender.

Sundown folded his long arms and tilted one lean shoulder as though defying the elements to blast him where he stood:—

"Lives there a gent who has not heard,
Before he died, the saddest word?

"'What word is that?' the maiden cried;
'I'd like to hear it before I died.'"

"'Then come with me,' her father said,
As to the stockyards her he led;

"Where layin' on the ground so low
She seen a tired and weary Bo.

"But when he seen her standin' 'round,
He riz up from the cold, cold ground.

"'Is this a hold-up game?' sez he.
And then her pa laughed wickedly.

"'This ain't no hold-up!' loud he cried,
As he stood beside the fair maiden's side.

"'But this here gal of mine ain't heard
What you Boes call the saddest word.'"

"'The Bo, who onct had been a gent,
Took off his lid and low he bent.

"He saw the maiden was fed up good,
So her father's wink he understood.

"'The saddest word,' the Bo he spoke,
'Is the dinner-bell, when you are broke.'"

And Sundown paused, gazing ceilingward, that the moral might seep through.

"You're ridin' right to home!" laughed the cow-boy. "You just light down and we'll trail over to Chola Charley's and prospect a tub of frijoles. The dinner-bell when you are broke is plumb correct. Got any more of that po'try broke to ride gentle?"

"Uhuh. Say, how far is it to the next town?"

"Comin' or goin'?"

"Goin'."

"'Bout seventy-three miles, but there's nothin' doin' there. Worse'n this."

"Looks like me for a job, or the next rattler goin' west. Any chanct for a cook here?"

"Nope. All Mexican cooks. But say, I reckon you *might* tie up over to the Concho. Hearn tell that Jack Corliss wants a cook. Seems his ole stand-by Hi Wingle's gone to Phoenix on law business. Jack's a good boss to tie to. Worked for him myself."

"How far to his place?" queried Sundown.

"Sixty miles, straight south."

"Gee Gosh! Looks like the towns was scared of each other in this here country. Who'd you say raises them frijoles?"

The cowboy laughed and slapped Sundown on the back. "Come on, Bud! You eat with me this trip."

Western humor, accentuated by alcohol, is apt to broaden rapidly in proportion to the quantity of liquor consumed. After a given quantity has been consumed—varying with the individual—Western humor broadens without regard to proportion of any kind.

The jovial puncher, having enjoyed Sundown's society to the extent of six-bits' worth of Mexican provender, suggested a return to "The Last Chance," where the tramp was solemnly introduced to a newly arrived coterie of thirsty riders of the mesas. Gaunt and exceedingly tall, he loomed above the heads of the group in the barroom "like a crane in a frog-waller," as one cowboy put it. "Which ain't insinooatin' that our hind legs is good to eat, either," remarked another. "He keeps right on smilin'," asserted the first speaker. "And takin' his smile," said the other. "Wonder what's his game? He sure is the lonesomest-lookin' cuss this side of that dead pine on Bald Butte, that I ever seen." But conviviality was the order of the evening, and the punchers grouped together and told and listened to jokes, old and new, talked sagebrush politics, and threw dice for the privilege of paying rather than winning. "Says he's scoutin' for a job cookin'," remarked a young cowboy to the main group of riders. "Heard him tell Johnny."

Meanwhile, Sundown, forgetful of everything save the congeniality of the moment, was recounting, to an amused audience of three, his experiences as assistant cook in an Eastern hotel. The rest of the happy and irresponsible punchers gravitated to the far end of the bar and proposed

Henry Hubert Knibbs

that they "have a little fun with the tall guy." One of them drew his gun and stepped quietly behind the tramp. About to fire into the floor he hesitated, bolstered his gun and tiptoed clumsily back to his companions. "Got a better scheme," he whispered.

Presently Sundown, in the midst of his recital, was startled by a roar of laughter. He turned quickly. The laughter ceased. The cowboy who had released him from the box-car stated that he must be going, and amid protests and several challenges to have as many "one-mores," swung out into the night to ride thirty miles to his ranch. Then it was, as has been said elsewhere and oft, "the plot thickened."

A rider, leaning against the bar and puffing thoughtfully at a cigar of elephantine proportions, suddenly took his cigar from his lips, held it poised, examined it with the eye of a connoisseur—of cattle—and remarked slowly: "Now, why didn't I think of it? Wonder you fellas didn't think of it. They need a cook bad! Been without a cook for a year—and everybody fussin' 'round cookin' for himself."

Sundown caught the word "cook" and turned to, face the speaker. "I was lookin' for a job, meself," he said, apologetically. "Did you know of one?"

"You was!" exclaimed the cowboy. "Well, now, that's right queer. I know where a cook is needed bad. But say, can you honest-to-Gosh *cook*?"

"I cooked in everything from a hotel to a gradin'-camp. All I want is a chanct."

The cowboy shook his head. "I don' know. It'll take a pretty good man to hold down this job."

"Where is the job?" queried Sundown.

Several of the men grinned, and Sundown, eager to be friendly, grinned in return.

"Mebby you *could* hold it down," continued the cowboy. "But say, do you eat your own cookin'?"

"Guess you're joshin' me." And the tramp's face expressed disappointment. "I eat my own cookin' when I can't get any better," he added, cheerfully.

"Well, it ain't no joke—cookin' for that hotel," stated the puncher, gazing at the end of his cigar and shaking his head. "Is it, boys?"

"Sure ain't," they chorused.

"A man's got to shoot the good chuck to hold the trade," he continued.

"Hotel?" queried Sundown. "In this here town?"

"Naw!" exclaimed the puncher. "It's one o' them swell joints out in the desert. Kind o' what folks East calls a waterin'-place. Eh, boys?"

"That's her!" volleyed the group.

"Kind o' select-like," continued the puncher.

"Sure is!" they chorused.

"Do you know what the job pays?" asked Sundown.

"U-m-m-m, let's see. Don't know as I ever heard. But there'll be no trouble about the pay. And you'll have things your own way, if you can deliver the goods."

"That's right!" concurred a listener.

Sundown looked upon work of any kind too seriously to suspect that it could be a subject for jest. He gazed hopefully at their hard, keen faces. They all seemed interested, even eager that he should find work. "Well, if it's a job I can hold down," he said, slowly, "I'll start for her right now. I ain't afraid to work when I got to."

"That's the talk, pardner! Well, I'll tell you. You take that road at the end of the station and follow her south right plumb over the hill. Over the hill you'll see a ranch, 'way on. Keep right on fannin' it and you'll come to a sign that reads 'American Hotel.' That's her. Good water, fine scenery, quiet-like, and just the kind of a place them tourists is always lookin' for. I stopped there many a time. So has the rest of the boys."

"You was tellin' me it was select-like—" ventured Sundown.

The men roared. Even Sundown's informant relaxed and grinned. But he became grave again, flicked the ashes from his cigar and waved his hand. "It's this way, pardner. That there hotel is run on the American style; if you got the price, you can have anything in the house. And tourists kind o' like to see a bunch of punchers settin' 'round smokin' and talkin' and tellin' yarns. Why, they was a lady onct—"

"But she went back East," interrupted a listener.

"That's the way with them," said the cowboy. "They're always stickin' their irons on some other fella's stock. Don't you pay no 'tention to them."

Sundown shook hands with his informant, crossed to the corner of the room, and slung his blanket-roll across his back. "Much obliged to you fellas," he said, his lean, timorous face beaming with gratitude. "It makes a guy feel happy when a bunch of strangers does him a good turn. You see I ain't got the chanct to get a job, like you fellas, me bein' a Bo. I had a pal onct—but He crossed over. He was the only one that ever done me a good turn without my askin'. He was a college guy. I wisht he was here so he could say thanks to you fellas classy-like. I'm feeling them kind of thanks, but I can't say 'em."

The grins faded from some of the faces. "You ain't goin' to fan it to-night?" asked one.

"Guess I will. You see, I'm broke, now. I'm used to travelin' any old time, and nights ain't bad—believe me. It's mighty hot daytimes in this here country. How far did you say?"

"Just over the hill—then a piece down the trail. You can't miss it," said the cowboy who had spoken first.

"Well, so-long, gents. If I get that job and any of you boys come out to the hotel, I'll sure feed you good."

An eddy of smoke followed Sundown as he passed through the doorway. A cowboy snickered. The room became silent.

"Call the poor ramblin' lightnin'-rod back," suggested a kindly puncher.

"He'll come back fast enough," asserted the perpetrator of the "joke." "It's thirty dry and dusty miles to the water-hole ranch. When he gets a look at how far it is to-morrow mornin' he'll sure back into the fence and come flyin' for Antelope with reins draggin'. Set 'em up again, Joe."

Henry Hubert Knibbs

CHAPTER II

THE JOKE

Owing to his unaccustomed potations Sundown was perhaps a trifle over-zealous in taking the road at night. He began to realize this after he had journeyed along the dim, starlit trail for an hour or so and found no break in the level monotony of the mesa. He peered ahead, hoping to see the blur of a hill against the southern stars. The air was cool and clear and sweet. He plodded along, happy in the prospect of work. Although he was a physical coward, darkness and the solitudes held no enemies for him. He felt that the world belonged to him at night. The moon was his lantern and the stars were his friends. Circumstance and environment had wrought for him a coat of cheerful effrontery which passed for hardihood; a coat patched with slang and gaping with inconsistencies, which he put on or off at will. Out on the starlit mesas he had metaphorically shed his coat. He was at home. Here there were no men to joke about his awkwardness and his ungainly height. A wanderer by nature, he looked upon space as his kingdom. Great distances were but the highways of his heritage, each promising new vistas, new adventuring. His wayside fires were his altars, their smoke the incense to his gods. A true adventurer, albeit timid, he journeyed not knowing why, but rather because he knew no reason for not journeying. Wrapped in his vague imaginings he swung along, peering ahead from time to time until at last he saw upon the far background of the night a darker something shaped like a tiny mound. "That's her!" he exclaimed, joyously, and quickened his pace. "But Gee Gosh! I guess them fellas forgot I was afoot. That hill looks turruble far off. Mebby because it's dark." The distant hill seemed to keep pace ahead of him, sliding away into the southern night as he advanced. Having that stubbornness so frequently associated with timidity, he plodded on, determined to top the hill before morning. "Them fellas as rides don't know how far things are," he commented. "But, anyhow, the folks at that hotel will sure know I want the job, walkin' all night for it."

Gradually the outline of the hill became bolder. Sundown estimated that he had been traveling several hours, when the going stiffened to a slow grade. Presently the grade became steep and rocky. Thus far the road had led straight south. Now it swung to the west and skirted the base of the hill in a gradual ascent. Then it swung back again following a fairly easy slope to the top. His optimism waned as he saw no light ahead. The night grew colder. The stars flickered as the wind of the dawn, whispering over the grasses, touched his face. He paused for a moment on the crest of the hill, turned to look back, and then started down the slope. It was steep and rutted. He had not gone far when he stumbled and fell. His blanket-roll had pitched ahead of him. He fumbled about for it and finally found it. "Them as believes in signs would say it was about time to go to roost," he remarked, nursing his knee that had been cut on a fragment of ragged tufa. A coyote wailed. Sundown started up. "Some lonesome. But she sure is one grand old night! Guess I'll turn in."

He rolled in his blankets. Hardly had he adjusted his length of limb to the unevenness of the ground when he fell asleep. He had come twenty-five miles across the midnight mesas. Five miles below him was his destination, shrouded by the night, but visioned in his dreams as a palatial summer resort, aglow with lights and eagerly awaiting the coming of the new cook.

The dawn, edging its slow way across the mesas, struck palely on the hillside where he slept. A rabbit, huddled beneath a scrub-cedar, hopped to the middle of the road and sat up, staring with moveless eyes at the motionless hump of blanket near the road. In a flash the wide mesas were tinged with gold as the smouldering red sun rose, to march unclouded to the western sea.

Midway between the town of Antelope and the river Concho is the water-hole. The land immediately surrounding the water-hole is enclosed with a barb-wire fence. Within the enclosure is a ranch-house painted white, a scrub-cedar corral, a small stable, and a lean-to shading the water-hole from the desert sun. The place is altogether neat and habitable. It is rather a surprise to the chance wayfarer to find the ranch uninhabited. As desolate as a stranded steamer on a mud bank, it stands in the center of several hundred acres of desert, incapable, without irrigation, of producing anything more edible than lizards and horned toads. Why a homesteader should have chosen to locate there is a mystery. His reason for abandoning the place is glaringly obvious. Though failure be written in every angle and nook of the homestead, it is the failure of large-hearted enterprise, of daring to attempt, of striving to make the desert bloom, and not the failure of indolence or sloth.

Western humor like Western topography is apt to be more or less rugged. Between the high gateposts of the yard enclosure there is a great, twelve-foot sign lettered in black. It reads: "American Hotel." A band of happy cowboys appropriated the sign when on a visit to Antelope, pressed a Mexican freighter to pack it thirty miles across the desert, and nailed it above the gateway of the water-hole ranch. It is a standing joke among the cattle- and sheep-men of the Concho Valley.

Sundown sat up and gazed about. The rabbit, startled out of its ordinary resourcefulness, stiffened. The delicate nostrils ceased twitching. "Good mornin', little fella! You been travelin' all night too?" And Sundown yawned and stretched. Down the road sped a brown exclamation mark with a white dot at its visible end. "Guess he don't have to travel nights to get 'most anywhere," laughed Sundown. He kicked back his blankets and rose stiffly. The luxury of his yawn was stifled as he saw below him the ranchhouse with some strange kind of a sign above its gate. "If that's the hotel," he said as he corded his blankets, "she don't look much bigger than me own. But distances is mighty deceivin' in this here open-face country." For a moment he stood on the hillside, a gaunt, lonely figure, gazing out across the limitless mesas. Then he jogged down the grade, whistling.

As he drew near the ranch his whistling ceased and his expression changed to one of quizzical uncertainty. "That's the sign, all right,—'American Hotel,'—but the hotel part ain't livin' up to the sign. But some hotels is like that; mostly front."

He opened the ranch-house gate and strode to the door. He knocked timidly. Then he dropped his blanket-roll and stepped to a window. Through the grimy glass he saw an empty, board-walled room, a slant of sunlight across the floor, and in the sunlight a rusted stove. He walked back to the gateway and stood gazing at the sign. He peered round helplessly. Then a slow grin illumined his face. "Why," he exclaimed, "it's—it's a joke. Reckon the proprietor must be out huntin' up trade. And accordin' to that he won't be back direct."

He wandered about the place like a stray cat in a strange attic, timorous and curious. Ordinarily he would have considered himself fortunate. The house offered shelter and seclusion. There was clear cold water to drink and a stove on which to cook. As he thought of the stove the latitude and longitude of the "joke" dawned upon him with full significance. He drank at the water-hole and, gathering a few sticks, built a fire. From his blankets he took a tin can, drew a wad of newspaper from it, and made coffee. Then he cast about for something to eat. "Now, if I was a cow—" he began, when he suddenly remembered the rabbit. "Reckon he's got relations hoppin' around in them bushes." He picked up a stick and started for the gate.

Not far from the ranch he saw a rabbit crouched beneath a clump of brush. He flung his stick and missed. The rabbit ran to another bush and stopped. Encouraged by the little animal's nonchalance, he dashed after it with a wild and startling whoop. The rabbit circled the brush and set off at right angles to his pursuer's course. Sundown made the turn, but it was "on one wheel" so to speak. His foot caught in a prairie-dog hole and he dove headlong with an exclamation that sounded as much like "Whump!" as anything else. He uttered another and less forced exclamation when he discovered in the tangle of brush that had broken his fall, another rabbit that had not survived his sudden visitation. He picked up the limp, furry shape. "Asleep at the switch," he said. "He ain't much bigger than a whisper, but he's breakfast."

Rabbit, fried on a stove-lid, makes a pretty satisfying meal when eating ceases to be a pleasure and becomes a necessity. Sundown wisely reserved a portion of his kill for future consumption.

As the morning grew warmer, he fell asleep in the shade of

the ranch-house. Late in the afternoon he wakened, went into the house and made coffee. After the coffee he came out, rolled a cigarette, and sat smoking and gazing out across the afternoon mesas. "I feel it comin'," he said to himself. "And it's a good one, so I guess I'll put her in me book."

He rummaged in his blankets and unearthed a grimy, tattered notebook. Lubricating the blunt point of a stubby pencil he set to work. When he had finished, the sun was close to the horizon. He sat back and gazed sideways at his effort. "I'll try her on meself," he said, drawing up his leg and resting the notebook against his lean knee. "Wish I could stand off and listen to meself," he muttered. "Kind o' get the defect better." Then he read laboriously:—

> "Bo, it's goin' to be hot all right;
> Sun's a floodin' the eastern range.
> Mebby it was kind o' cold last night,
> But there's nothin' like havin' a little change.
> Money? No. Only jest room for me;
> Mountings and valleys and plains and such.
> Ain't I got eyes that was made to see?
> Ain't I got ears? But they don't hear much:
> Only a kind of a inside song,
> Like when the grasshopper quits his sad,
> And says: 'Rickety-chick! Why, there is nothin' wrong!'
> And after the coffee, things ain't so bad."

"Huh! Sounds all right for a starter. Ladies and them as came with you, I will now spiel the next section."

> "The wind is makin' my bed for me,
> Smoothin' the grass where I'm goin' to flop,
> When the quails roost up in the live-oak tree,
> And my legs feel like as they want to stop.
> Pal or no pal, it's about the same,

Henry Hubert Knibbs

For nobody knows how you feel inside.
Hittin' the grit is a lonesome game,—
But quit it? No matter how hard I tried.
But mebby I will when that inside song
Stops a-buzzin' like bees that's mad,
Grumblin' together: 'There's nothin' wrong!'
And—after the coffee things ain't so bad."

"Bees ain't so darned happy, either. They're too busy. Guess it's a good thing I went back to me grasshopper in the last verse. And now, ladies and gents, this is posituvely the last appearance of the noted electrocutionist, Sundown Slim; so, listen."

"Ladies, I've beat it from Los to Maine.
And, gents, not knowin' jest what to do,
I turned and slippered it back again,
Wantin' to see, jest the same as you.
Ridin' rods and a-dodgin' flies;
Eatin' at times when me luck was good.
Spielin' the con to the easy guys,
But never jest makin' it understood,
Even to me, why that inside song
Kep' a-handin' me out the glad,
Like the grasshopper singin': 'There's nothin' wrong!'
And—after the coffee things ain't so bad."

Sundown grinned with unalloyed pleasure. His mythical audience seemed to await a few words, so he rose stiffly, and struck an attitude somewhat akin to that of Henry Irving standing beside a milk-can and contemplating the village pump. "It gives me great pleasure to inform you"—he hesitated and cleared his throat—"that them there words of mine was expired by half a rabbit—small—and two cans of coffee. Had I been fed up like youse"—and he bowed grandly—"there's no tellin' what I might 'a' writ. Thankin' you for the box-office receipts, I am yours to demand, Sundown Slim, of Outdoors, Anywhere, till further notice."

Then he marched histrionically to the ranchhouse and made a fire in the rusted stove.

CHAPTER III

THIRTY MILES TO THE CONCHO

John Corliss rode up to the water-hole, dismounted, and pushed through the gate. His horse "Chinook" watched him with gently inquisitive eyes. Chinook was not accustomed to inattention when he was thirsty. He had covered the thirty miles from the Concho Ranch in five long, dry, and dusty hours. He nickered. "In a minute," said Corliss. Then he knocked at the ranch-house door. Riders of the Concho usually strode jingling into the ranch-house without formality. Corliss, however, had been gazing at the lean stovepipe for hours before he finally decided that there was smoke rising from it. He knocked a second time.

"She ain't locked," came in a rusty, smothered voice.

Corliss shoved the door open with his knee. The interior was heavy with smoke. Near the stove knelt Sundown trying to encourage the smoke to more perpendicular behavior. He coughed. "She ain't good in her intentions, this here stove. One time she goes and the next time she stays and takes a smoke. Her innards is out of gear. Whew!"

"The damper has slipped down," said Corliss.

"Her little ole chest-pertector is kind o' worked down toward her stummick. There, now she feels better a'ready."

"Cooking chuck?" queried Corliss, glancing round the bare room.

"Rabbit," replied Sundown. "When I hit this here hotel I was hungry. I seen a rabbit—not this here one, but the other one. This one was settin' in a bunch of-brush on me right-of-way. I was behind and runnin' to make up time. I kind o' seen the leetle prairie-dog give me the red to slow down, but it was too late. Hit his cyclone cellar with me right driver, and got wrecked. This here leetle wad o' cotton was under me steam-chest. No other passengers hurt, except the engineer."

Corliss laughed. "You're a railroad man, I take it. Belong in this country?"

Sundown rose from his knees and backed away from the stove. "Nope. Don't belong anywhere, I guess. My address when I'm to home is Sundown Slim, Outdoors, Anywhere, speakin' general."

"Come in afoot?"

"Uhuh. Kind o' thought I'd get a job. Fellas at Antelope told me they wanted a cook at this hotel. I reckon they do—and some boarders and somethin' to cook."

"That's one of their jokes. Pretty stiff joke, sending you in here afoot."

"Oh, I ain't sore, mister. They stole me nanny, all right, but I feel jest as good here as anywhere."

Corliss led Chinook to the water-hole. Sundown followed.

Henry Hubert Knibbs

"Ever think how many kinds of water they was?" queried Sundown. "Some is jest water; then they's some got a taste; then some's jest wet, but this here is fine! Felt like jumpin' in and drinkin' from the bottom up when I lit here. Where do you live?"

"On the Concho, thirty miles south."

"Any towns in between?"

Corliss smiled. "No, there isn't a fence or a house from here to the ranch."

"Gee Gosh! Any cows in this country?"

"Yes. The Concho runs ten thousand head on the range."

"Had your supper?"

"No. I was late getting away from the ranch. Expected to make Antelope, but I guess I'll bush here to-night."

"Well, seein' you're the first boarder at me hotel, I'll pass the hash." And Sundown stepped into the house and returned with the half rabbit. "I got some coffee, too. I can cook to beat the band when I got somethin' to cook. Help yourself, pardner. What's mine is anybody's that's hungry. I et the other half."

"Don't mind if I do. Thanks. Say, you can cook?"

"Next to writin' po'try it's me long suit."

"Well, I'm no judge of poetry," said Corliss. "This rabbit tastes pretty good."

"You ain't a cop, be you?" queried Sundown.

"No. Why?"

"Nothin'. I was jest wonderin'."

"You have traveled some, I take it."

"Me? Say! I'm the ramblin' son with the nervous feet. Been round the world and back again on them same feet, and some freights. Had a pal onct. He was a college guy. Run on to him on a cattle-boat. He writ po'try that was the real thing! It's ketchin' and I guess I caught it from him. He was a good little pal."

"What became of him?"

"I dunno, pardner. They was a wreck—but guess I'll get that coffee."

"How did you cross the Beaver Dam?" inquired Corliss as Sundown reappeared with his can of coffee.

"So that's what you call that creek back there? Well, it don't need no Beaver hitched on to it to say what I'd call it. I come through last night, but I'm dry now."

The cattle-man proffered Sundown tobacco and papers. They smoked and gazed at the stars. "Said your friend was a college man. What was his name?" queried Corliss, turning to glance at Sundown.

"Well, his real name was Billy Corliss, but I called him jest Bill."

"Corliss! When did you lose track of him?"

"In that wreck, 'bout a year ago. We was ridin' a fast freight goin' west. He said he was goin' home, but he never said where it was. Hit a open switch—so they said after—and when they pulled the stitches, and took that plaster dingus off me leg, I starts out huntin' for Billy. Nobody knowed anything about him. Wasn't no signs in the wreck,—so they said. You see I was in that fadeaway joint six weeks."

"What did he look like?"

"Billy? More like a girl than a man. Slim-like, with blue eyes and kind o' bright, wavy-like hair. He never said nothin' about his folks. He was a awful quiet kid."

John Corliss studied Sundown's face. "You say he was killed in a wreck?"

"I ain't sure. But I reckon he was. It was a bad one. He was ridin' a empty, just ahead of me. Then the whole train buckled up and somethin' hit me on the lid. That's all I remember, till after."

"What are you going to do now? Go back to Antelope?"

"Me? Guess I will. I was lookin' for a job cooking but the pay ain't right here. What you lookin' at me that way for?"

"Sit still. I'm all right. My brother Will left home three years ago. Didn't say a word to any one. He'd been to school East, and he wrote some things for the magazines—poetry. I was wondering—"

"Say, mister, what's your name?"

"John Corliss."

"Gee Gosh! I knowed when I et that rabbit this mornin' that somethin' was goin' to happen. Thought it was po'try, but I was mistook."

"So you ate your half of the rabbit this morning, eh?"

"Sure!!—"

"And you gave me the rest. You sure are loco."

"Mebby I be. Anyhow, I'm used to bein' hungry. They ain't so much of me to keep as you—crossways, I mean. Of course, up and down—"

"Well, I'm right sorry," said Corliss. "You're the queerest Hobo I ever saw."

"That's what they all say," said Sundown, grinning. "I ain't no common hand-out grabber, not me! I learnt things from Bill. He had class!"

"You sure Will never said anything about the Concho, or his brother, or Chance?"

"Chance? Who's he?"

"Wolf-dog that belonged to Will."

"Gee Gosh! Big, and long legs, and kind of long, rough hair, and deep in the chest and—"

"That's Chance; but how did you know?"

"Why, Billy writ a pome 'bout him onct. Sold it and we lived high—for a week. Sure as you live! It was called 'Chance of the Concher.' Gee Gosh! I thought it was jest one of them poetical dogs, like."

Corliss, who was not given to sentiment, smoked and pondered the possibility of his brother's whereabouts. He had written to all the large cities asking for information from the police as to the probability of their being able to locate his brother. The answers had not been encouraging. At the end of three years he practically gave up making inquiry and turned his whole attention to the management of the Concho. There had been trouble between the cattle and sheep interests and time had passed more swiftly than he had realized. His meeting with Sundown had awakened the old regret for his brother's uncalled-for disappearance. Had he been positive that his brother had been killed in the wreck he would have felt a kind of relief. As it was, the uncertainty as to his whereabouts, his welfare, worried and perplexed him, especially in view of the fact that he was on his way to Antelope to present to the Forest Service a petition from the cattle-men of the valley for grazing allotments. The sheep had been destroying the grazing on the west side of the river. There had been bickerings and finally an open declaration of war against David Loring, the old sheep-man of the valley. Corliss wished to avoid friction with David Loring. Their ranches were opposite each other. And as Corliss was known as level-headed and shrewd, it devolved upon him to present in person the complaint and petition of his brother cattle-men. Argument with David Loring, as he had passed the latter's homestead that morning, had delayed him on his journey to Antelope. Presently he got up and entered the ranch-house. Sundown followed and poked about in the corners of the room. He found a bundle of gunny-sacks and spreading them on the floor, laid his blankets on them.

Corliss stepped out and led Chinook to the distant mesa and picketed him for the night. As he returned, he considered the advisability of hiring the tramp to cook until his own cook returned from Phoenix. He entered the house, kicked off his leather chaps, tossed his spurs into a corner, and made a bed of his saddle-blankets and saddle. "I'll be starting early," he said as he drew off his boots. "What are you intending to do next?"

"Me? Well, I ain't got no plans. Beat it back to Antelope, I guess. Say, mister, do you think my pal was your brother?"

"I don't know. From your description I should say so. See here. I don't know you, but I need a cook. The Concho is thirty miles in. I'm headed the other way, but if you are game to walk it, I'll see if I can use you."

"Me! You ain't givin' me another josh, be you?"

"Never a josh. You won't think so when you get to punchin' dough for fifteen hungry cowboys. Want to try it?"

"Say, mister, I'm just comin' to. A guy told me in Antelope that they was a John Corliss—only he said Jack—what was needin' a cook. Just thunk of it, seein' as I was thinkin' of Billy most ever since I met you. Are you the one?"

"Guess I am," said Corliss, smiling. "It's up to you."

"Say, mister, that listens like home more'n anything I heard since I was a kid. I can sure cook, but I ain't no rider."

"How long would it take you to foot it to the Concho?"

"Oh, travelin' easy, say 'bout eight hours."

"Don't see that you need a horse, then, even if there was one handy."

"Nope. I don't need no horse. All I need is a job."

"All right. You'd have to travel thirty miles either way—to get out of here. I won't be there, but you can tell my foreman, Bud Shoop, that I sent you in."

"And I'll jest be tellin' him that 'bout twelve, to-morrow. I sure wisht Billy was here. He'd sure be glad to know his ole pal was cookin' for his brother. Me for the shavin's. And say, thanks, pardner. Reckon they ain't all jokers in Arizona."

"No. There are a few that can't make or take one," said Corliss. "Hope you'll make the ranch all right."

"I'm there! Next to cookin' and writin' po'try, walkin' is me long suit."

CHAPTER IV

PIE; AND SEPTEMBER MORN

When a Westerner, a native-born son of the outlands, likes a man, he likes him. That is all there is to it. His horses, blankets, money, provender, and even his saddle are at his friend's disposal. If the friend prove worthy,—and your Westerner is shrewd,—a lifelong friendship is the result. If the friend prove unworthy, it is well for him to seek other latitudes, for the average man of the outlands has a peculiar and deep-seated pride which is apt to manifest itself in prompt and vigorous action when touched by ridicule or ingratitude. There are many Davids and Jonathans in the sagebrush country. David may have flocks and herds, and Jonathan may have naught but the care of them. David may possess lands and water-rights, and Jonathan nothing more than a pick, a shovel, a pan, and an incurable itch for placering. A Westerner likes a man for what he is and not because of his vocation. He usually proceeds cautiously in the matter of friendship, but sudden and instinctive friendships are not infrequent. It so happened that John Corliss had taken a liking to the Hobo, Sundown Slim. Knowing a great deal more about cattle than about psychology, the rancher wasted no time in trying to analyze his feelings. If the tramp had courage enough to walk another thirty miles across the mesas to get a job cooking, there must be something to him

Henry Hubert Knibbs

besides legs. Possibly the cattle-man felt that he was paying a tribute to the memory of his brother. In any event, he greeted Sundown next morning as the latter came to the water-hole to drink. "You can't lose your way," he said, pointing across the mesa. "Just keep to the road. The first ranch on the right is the Concho. Good luck!" And he led Chinook through the gateway. In an hour he had topped the hill. He reined Chinook round. He saw a tiny figure far to the south. Half in joke he waved his sombrero. Sundown, who had glanced back from time to time, saw the salute and answered it with a sweeping gesture of his lean arm. "And now," he said, "I got the whole works to meself. That Concho guy is a mighty fine-lookin' young fella, but he don't look like Billy. Rides that hoss easy-like jest as if he was settin' in a rockin'-chair knittin' socks. But I reckon he could flash up if you stepped on his tail. I sure ain't goin' to."

It was mid-afternoon, when Sundown, gaunt and weary, arrived at the Concho. He was faint for lack of food and water. The Mexican cook, or rather the cook's assistant, was the only one present when Sundown drifted in, for the Concho was, in the parlance of the riders, "A man's ranch from chuck to sunup, and never a skirt on the clothes-line."

Not until evening was Sundown able to make his errand known, and appreciated. A group of riders swung in in a swirl of dust, dismounted, and, as if by magic, the yard was empty of horses.

The riders disappeared in the bunk-house to wash and make ready for supper. One of the men, who had spoken to him in passing, reappeared.

"Lookin' for the boss?" he asked.

"Nope. I seen him. I'm lookin' for Mr. Shoop."

"All right, pardner. Saw off the mister and size me up. I'm him."

"The boss said I was to be cook," said Sundown, rather awed by the personality of the bluff foreman.

"Meet him at Antelope?"

"No. It was the American Hotel. He said for me to tell you if I walked in I could get a job cookin'."

"All right. What he says goes. Had anything to eat recent?"

"I et a half a rabbit yesterday mornin'."

"Well, sufferin' shucks! You fan it right in here!"

Later that evening, Sundown straggled out to the corral and stood watching the saddle-stock of the Concho pull hay from the long feed-rack and munch lazily. Suddenly he jerked up his hand and jumped round. The men, loafing in front of the bunk-house, laughed. Chance, the great wolf-dog, was critically inspecting the tramp's legs.

Sundown was a self-confessed coward, physically. Above all things he feared dogs. His reception by the men, aside from Bud Shoop's greeting, had been cool. Even the friendship of a dog seemed acceptable at that moment. Plodding along the weary miles between the water-hole and the ranch, he had, in his way, decided to turn over a new leaf: to ignore the insistent call of the road and settle down to something worth while. Childishly egotistical, he felt in a vague way that his virtuous intent was not appreciated, not reasoning that the men knew nothing of his wanderings, nor cared to know anything other than as to his ability to cook. So he timidly stroked the long muzzle of the wolf-dog, and was agreeably surprised to find that Chance seemed to like it. In fact, Chance, having an instinct superior to that of his men companions of the Concho, recognized in the gaunt and lonely figure a kindred spirit; a being that had the wander-fever in its veins; that was forever searching for the undiscoverable, the something just beyond the visible boundaries of day. The dog, part Russian wolf-hound and part Great Dane, deep-chested, swift and powerful, shook his shaggy coat and sneezed. Sundown jumped. Again the men laughed. "You and me's built about alike—for speed," he said, endeavoring to convey his friendly intent through compliment. "Did you ever ketch a rabbit?"

Chance whined. Possibly he understood. In any event, he leaped playfully against Sundown's chest and stood with his paws on the tramp's shoulders. Sundown shrunk back against the corral bars. "Go to it," he said, trying to cover his fear with a jest, "if you like bones."

From behind him came a rush of feet. "Great Scott!" exclaimed Shoop. "Come 'ere, Chance. I sure didn't know he was loose."

The dog dropped to his feet and wagged his tail inquiringly.

"Chance—there—he don't cotton to strangers," explained Shoop, slipping his hand in the wolf-dog's collar. "Did he nip you?"

"Nope. But me and him ain't strangers, mister. You see, I knowed the boss's brother Billy, what passed over in a wreck. He used to own Chance, so the boss says."

"You knew Billy! But Chance don't know that. I'll chain him up till he gets used to seein' you 'round."

Shoop led the dog to the stable. Sundown felt relieved. The solicitude of the foreman, impersonal as it was, made him happier.

Next morning he was installed as cook. He did fairly well, and the men rode away joking about the new "dough-puncher."

Then it was that Sundown had an inspiration—not to write verse, but to manufacture pies. He knew that the great American appetite is keen for pies. Finding plenty of material,—dried apples, dried prunes, and apricots,—he set to work, having in mind former experiences on the various "east-sides" of various cities. Determined that his reputation should rest not alone upon flavor, he borrowed a huge Mexican spur from his assistant and immersed it in a pan of boiling water. "And speakin' of locality color," he murmured, grinning at the possibilities before him, "how's that, Johnny?" And he rolled out a thin layer of pie-dough and taking the spur for a "pattern-wheel," he indented a free-hand sketch of the Concho brand on the immaculate dough. Next he wheeled out a rather wobbly cayuse, then an equally wobbly and ferocious cow. Each pie came from the oven with some symbol of the range printed upon it, the general effect being enhanced by the upheaval of the piecrust in the process of baking. When the punchers rode in that evening and entered the messroom, they sniffed knowingly. But not until the psychological moment did Sundown parade his pies. Then he stepped to the kitchen and, with the lordly gesture of a Michael Angelo unveiling a statue for the approval of Latin princes, commanded the assistant to "Bring forth them pies." And they were "brung."

Each astonished puncher was gravely presented with a whole pie—bubbling kine, dimpled cayuses, and sprawling spurs. Silence—as silence is wont to do in dramatic moments—

reigned supreme. Then it was that the purveyor of spontaneous Western exclamations missed his opportunity, being elsewhere at the time.

"Whoop! Let 'er buck!" exclaimed Bud Shoop, swinging an imaginary hat and rocking from side to side.

"So-o, Boss!" exclaimed a puncher from the Middle West.

"Hand-made and silver mounted," remarked another. "Hate to eat 'em."

"Trade you my pinto for a steer," offered still another.

"Nothin' doin'! That hoss of yours has got colic—bad."

"Swap this here goat for that rooster of yours," said "Sinker," a youth whose early education in art had been neglected.

"Goat? You box-head! That's a calf. Kind 'a' mired down, but it's sure a calf. And this ain't no rooster. This here's a eagle settin' on his eggs. You need specs."

"Noah has sure been herdin' 'em in," said another puncher.

Meanwhile, "Noah" stood in the messroom doorway, arms folded and face beaming. His attitude invited applause, and won it. Eventually his reputation as a "pie-artist" spread far and wide. When it leaked out that he had wrought his masterpieces with a spur, there was some murmuring. Being assured by the assistant that the spur had been previously boiled, the murmuring changed to approval. "That new cook was sure a original cuss! Stickin' right to the range in his picture-work. Had them there old Hopi picture-writin's on the rocks beat a mile." And the like.

Inspired by a sense of repletion, conducive to generosity and humor, the boys presented Sundown with a pair of large-rowelled Mexican spurs, silver-mounted and altogether formidable. Like many an historic adventurer, he had won his spurs by a *tour-de-force* that swept his compatriots off their feet; innuendo if you will—but the average cowboy is capable of assimilating much pie.

Although Sundown was offered the use of a bunk in the men's quarters, he chose to sleep in a box-stall in the stable, explaining that he was accustomed to sleep in all kinds of places, and that the unused box-stall with fresh clean straw and blankets would make a very comfortable bedroom. His reason for declining a place with the men became apparent about midnight.

Bud Shoop had, in a bluff, offhand way, given him a flannel shirt, overalls, an old flop-brimmed Stetson, and, much to Sundown's delight, a pair of old riding-boots. Hitherto, Sundown had been too preoccupied with culinary matters to pay much attention to his clothing. Incidentally he was spending not a little time in getting accustomed to his spurs, which he wore upon all occasions, clinking and clanking about the cook-room, a veritable Don Quixote of the (kitchen) range.

The arrival of Corliss, three days after Sundown's advent, had a stimulating effect on the new cook. He determined to make the best appearance possible.

The myriad Arizona stars burned with darting radiance, in thin, unwavering shafts of splintered fire. The moon, coldly brilliant, sharp-edged and flat like a disk of silver paper, touched the twinkling aspens with a pallid glow and stamped a distorted silhouette of the low-roofed ranch-buildings on the hard-packed earth. In the corral the shadow of a restless pony drifted back and forth. Chance, chained to a post near the bunk-house, shook himself and sniffed the keen air, for just at that moment the stable door had opened and a ghostly figure appeared; a figure that shivered in the moonlight. The dog bristled and whined. "S-s-s-h!" whispered Sundown. "It's me, ain't it?"

With his bundle of clothes beneath his arm, he picked a hesitating course across the yard and deposited the bundle beside the water-trough. Chance, not altogether satisfied with Sundown's assurance, proclaimed his distrust by a long nerve-reaching howl. Some one in the bunkhouse muttered. Sundown squatted hastily in the shadow of the trough. Bud Shoop rose from his bunk and crept to the door. He saw nothing unusual, and was about to return to his bed when an apparition rose slowly from behind the water-trough. The foreman drew back in the shadow of the doorway and watched.

Sundown's bath was extensive as to territory but brief as to duration. He dried himself with a gunny-sack and slipped shivering into his new raiment. "That there September Morn ain't got nothin' on me except looks," he spluttered. "And she is welcome to the looks. Shirts and pants for mine!"

Then he crept back to his blankets and slept the sleep of one who has atoned for his sins of omission and suffered righteously in the ordeal.

Bud Shoop wanted to laugh, but forgot to do it. Instead he padded back to his bunk and lay awake pondering. "Takin' a bath sure does make a fella feel like the fella he wants to feel like—but in the drinkin'-trough, at night . . .! I reckon that there Hobo ain't right in his head."

Sundown dreamed that he was chasing an elusive rabbit over

endless wastes of sand and greasewood. With him ran a phantom dog, a lean, shaggy shape that raced tirelessly. When Sundown wanted to give up the dream-hunt and rest, the dog would urge him on with whimperings and short, explosive barks of impatience. Presently the dream-dog ran ahead and disappeared beyond a rise. Sundown sank to the desert and slept. He dreamed within his dream that the dog was curled beside him. He put out his hand and stroked the dog's head. Presently a side of the box-stall took outline. A ray of sunlight filtered in; sunlight flecked with fine golden dust. The straw rustled at his side and he sat up quickly. Chance, stretching himself and yawning, showed his long, white fangs in an elaborated dog-smile. "Gee Gosh!" exclaimed Sundown, eyeing the dog sideways, "so it's you, eh? You wasn't foolin' me, then, when you said we'd be pals?"

Chance settled down in the straw again and sighed contentedly.

From the corral came the sound of horses running. The boys were catching up their ponies for the day's work. Chance pricked his ears. "I guess it's up to me and you to move lively," said Sundown, stretching and groaning. "We're sleepin' late, account of them midnight abolitions."

He rose and limped to the doorway. Chance followed him, evidently quite uninterested in the activities outside. Would this queer, ungainly man-thing saddle a horse and ride with the others, or would he now depart on foot, taking the trail to Antelope? Chance knew quite as well as did the men that something unusual was in the air. Hi Wingle, the cook, had returned unexpectedly that night. Chance had listened gravely while his master had told Bud Shoop that "the outfit" would move over to Bald Knoll in the morning. Then the dog had barked and capered about, anticipating a break in the monotony of ranch-life.

Sundown hurried to the cook-room. Chance at his heels. Hi Wingle was already installed in his old quarters, but he greeted Sundown heartily, and set him to work helping.

After breakfast, Bud Shoop, in heavy wing chaps and trailing his spurs, swaggered up to Sundown. "How you makin' it this mornin'?" he inquired. There was a note of humorous good-fellowship in his voice that did not escape Sundown.

"Doin' fine without crutches," replied Sundown, grinning.

"Well, you go eat now, and I'll catch up a cayuse for you. We're goin' to fan it for Bald Knoll in about ten minutes."

"Do I go, too?"

"Sure! Do you think we don't eat pie only onct a year? You bet you go—helpin' Hi. Boss's orders."

"Thanks—but I ain't no rider."

Shoop glanced questioningly at Sundown's legs. "Mebby not. But if I owned them legs I'd contract to ride white-lightnin' bareback. I'd just curl 'em 'round and grab holt of my feet when they showed up on the other side. Them ain't legs; them's *cinchas*."

"Mebby they ain't," sighed Sundown. "It's the only pair I got, and I'm kind of used to 'em."

"Did you let Chance loose?" queried the foreman.

"Me? Nix. But he was sleepin' in the stall with me this mornin'."

"Heard him goin' on last night. Thought mebby a coyote or a wolf had strayed in to get a drink."

"Get a drink! Can't they get a drink up in them hills?"

"Sure! But they kind of fancy the flavor of the water-trough. They come in frequent. But you better fan it for chuck. See you later."

Sundown hurried through breakfast. He was anxious to hear more about the habits of coyotes and wolves. When he again came to the corral, many of the riders had departed. Shoop stood waiting for John Corliss.

"You said them wolves and coyotes—" began Sundown.

"Yes, ding 'em!" interrupted Shoop. "Looks like they come down last night. Somethin' 's been monkeyin' with the water."

"Did you ever see one—at night?" queried Sundown, nervously.

"See 'em? Why, I shot droves of 'em right from the bunk-house door. I never miss a chance. Cut loose every time I see one standin' with his front paws on the trough. Get 'em every time."

"Wisht I'd knowed that."

"So?"

"Uhuh. I'd 'a' borrowed a gun off you and set up and watched for 'em myself."

Bud Shoop made a pretense of tightening a cinch on Sundown's pony, that he might "blush unseen," as it were.

Henry Hubert Knibbs

Presently Corliss appeared and motioned to Shoop. "How's the new cook doing?" he asked.

"Fine!"

Sundown retired modestly to the off-side of the pony.

"Got a line on him already," said Shoop. "First thing, Chance, here, took to him. Then, next thing, he manufactures a batch of pies that ain't been matched on the Concho since she was a ranch. Then, next thing after that, Chance slips his collar and goes and bushes with the Bo—sleeps with him till this mornin'. And you can rope me for a parson if that walkin' wish-bone didn't get to ramblin' in his sleep last night and come out and take a *bath* in the *drinkin'*-trough! He's got on them clothes I give him, this mornin'. Can you copper that?"

"Bad dream, Bud."

"You wait!" said the grinning foreman. "You watch him. Don't pay no 'tention to me."

Corliss smiled. Shoop's many and devious methods of estimating character had their humorous angles. The rancher appreciated a joke quite as much as did any of his employees, but usually as a spectator and not a participant. Bud Shoop had served him well and faithfully, tiding over many a threatened quarrel among the men by a humorous suggestion or a seemingly impersonal anecdote anent disputes in general. So Corliss waited, meanwhile inspecting the ponies in the corral. He noticed a pinto with a saddle-gall and told Shoop to turn the horse out on the range.

"It's one of Fadeaway's string," said Shoop.

"I know it. Catch him up."

Shoop, who felt that his opportunity to confirm his dream-like statement about Sundown's bathing, was slipping away, suddenly evolved a plan. He knew that the horses had all been watered. "Hey!" he called to Sundown, who stood gravely inspecting his own mount. "Come over here and make this cayuse drink. He won't for me."

Shoop roped the horse and handed the rope to Sundown, who marched to the water-trough. The pony sniffed at the water and threw up his head. "I reckoned that was it!" said Shoop.

"What?" queried Corliss, meanwhile watching Sundown's face.

"Oh, some dam' coyote's been paddlin' in that trough again. No wonder the hosses won't drink this mornin'. I don't blame 'em."

Sundown rolled a frightened eye and tried to look at everything but his companions. Corliss and Shoop exploded simultaneously. Slowly the light of understanding dawned, rose, and radiated in the dull red of the new cook's face. He was hurt and a bit angry. The anticipating and performing of his midnight ablutions had cost Slim a mighty struggle, mentally and otherwise.

"If you think it's any early mornin' joke to take a wash-up in that there Chinese coffin—why, try her yourself, about midnight." Then he addressed Shoop singly. "If I was *you*, and you got kind of absent-minded and done likewise, and I seen *you*, do you think I'd go snitch to the boss? Nix, for it might set him to worryin'."

Shoop accepted the compliment good-naturedly, for he knew

he had earned it. He swaggered up to Sundown and slapped him on the back. "Cheer up, pardner, and listen to the good news. I'm goin' to have that trough made three foot longer so it'll be more comfortable."

"Thanks, but never again at night. Guess if I hadn't been feelin' all-to-Gosh happy at havin' a home and a job, I'd 'a' froze stiff."

CHAPTER V

ON THE CANON TRAIL

The Loring homestead, a group of low-roofed adobe buildings blending with the abrupt red background of the hill which sheltered it from the winter winds, was a settlement in itself, providing shelter and comfort for the wives and children of the herders. Each home maintained a small garden of flowers and vegetables. Across the somber brown of the 'dobe walls hung strings of chiles drying in the sun. Gay blossoms, neatly kept garden rows, red ollas hanging in the shade of cypress and acacia, the rose-bordered plaza on which fronted the house of the patron, the gigantic windmill purring lazily and turning now to the right, now to the left, to meet the varying breeze, the entire prospect was in its pastoral quietude a reflection of Senora Loring's sweet and placid nature. Innuendo might include the windmill, and justly so, for the Senora in truth met the varying breeze of circumstance and invariably turned it to good uses, cooling the hot temper of the patron with a flow of soft Spanish utterances, and enriching the simple lives of the little colony with a charity as free and unvarying as the flow of the clear, cool water.

Far to the east, where the mesas sloped gently to the hills, grazed the sheep, some twenty bands of a thousand each, and each band guarded and cared for by a herder and an assistant who cooked and at times journeyed with the lazy burros to and from the hacienda for supplies and provisions.

David Loring, erstwhile plainsman and scout, had drifted in the early days from New Mexico to Arizona with his small band of sheep, and settled in the valley of the Concho. He had been tolerated by the cattle-men, as his flock was but a speck on the limitless mesas. As his holdings increased, the ranchers awakened to the fact that he had come to stay and that some boundary must be established to protect their grazing. The Concho River was chosen as the dividing line, which would have been well enough had Loring been a party to the agreement. But he declined to recognize any boundary. The cattle-men felt that they had given him fair warning in naming the Concho as the line of demarcation. He, in turn, considered that his right to graze his sheep on any part or all of the free range had not been circumscribed.

His neighbor—if cattle-men and sheep-men may under any circumstances be termed neighbors—was John Corliss. The Corliss rancho was just across the river opposite the Loring homestead. After the death of their parents the Corliss boys, John and his younger brother Will, had been constant visitors at the sheep-man's home, both of them enjoying the vivacious companionship of Eleanor Loring, and each, in his way, in love with the girl. Eventually the younger brother disappeared without any apparent reason. Then it was that John Corliss's visits to the Loring rancho became less frequent and the friendliness which had existed between the rival ranches became a kind of tolerant acquaintanceship, as that of neighbors who have nothing in common save the back fence.

Fernando, the oldest herder in Loring's employ, stood shading his eyes from the glare of noon as he gazed toward the distant rancho. His son was with the flock and the old man had just risen from preparing the noon meal. "The Senorita," he murmured, and his swart features were lighted by a wrinkled smile. He stepped to his tent, whipped a gay bandanna from his blankets and knotted it about his lean throat. Then he took off his hat, gazing at it speculatively. It was beyond reconstruction as to definite shape, so he tossed it to the ground, ran his fingers through his silver-streaked hair, and stepped out to await his Senorita's arrival.

The sunlight flashed on silver spur and bit as the black-and-white pinto "Challenge" swept across the mesa toward the sheep-camp. Into the camp he flung, fretting at the curb and pivoting. His rider, Eleanor Loring, about to dismount, spoke to him sharply. Still he continued to pivot uneasily. "Morning, Fernando! Challenge is fussy this morning. I'll be right back!" And she disciplined Challenge with bit and spur, wheeling him and loping him away from the camp. Down the trail she checked him and brought him around on his hind feet. Back they came, with a rush. Fernando's deep-set eyes glowed with admiration as the girl "set-up" the pinto and swung to the ground with a laugh. "Made him do it all over again, si. He is the big baby, but he pretends he is bronco. Don't you, Challenge?" She dropped the reins and rubbed his nose. The pony laid back his ears in simulated anger and nipped at her sleeve. "Straighten your ears up, pronto!" she commanded, nevertheless laughing. Then a strain of her father's blood was apparent as she seized the reins and stood back from the horse. "Because you're bluffing this morning, I'm going to make you do your latest trick. Down!" she commanded. The pony extended his foreleg and begged to shake hands. "No! Down!" With a grunt the horse dropped to his knees, rolled to his side, but still kept his head raised. "Clear down! Dead, Challenge!" The horse lay with extended neck, but switched his tail significantly. "Don't you dare roll!" she said, as he gave evidence of getting up. Then, at her gesture, he heaved himself to his feet and shook himself till the stirrups clattered. The girl dropped the reins and turned to the old herder. "I taught him that, Fernando. I didn't make him do it just to show off. He understands now, and he'll behave."

Old Fernando grinned. "He always have the good manner, being always with the Senorita," he said bowing.

"Thanks, Fernando. You always say something nice. But I can't let you get ahead of me. What a pretty scarf. It's just right. Do you wear it always, Fernando?"

"It is—I know—what the vaquero of the Concho call the 'josh' that you give me, but I am yet not too old to like it. It is muy pleasure, si! to be noticed when one is old—by the Senorita of especial."

The girl's dark eyes flashed and she laughed happily. "It's lots of fun, isn't it—to 'josh'? But I came to see if you needed anything."

"Nothing while still the Senorita is at thees camp."

"Well, you'd better think up something, for I'm going in a minute. Have to make the rounds. Dad is down with the rheumatism and as cross as a grizzly. I was glad to get away. And then, there's Madre."

Fernando smiled and nodded. He was not unfamiliar with the patron's temper when rheumatism obliged him to be inactive. "He say nothing, the patron—that we cross the sheep to the west of the river, Senorita?"

"No. Not lately. I don't know why he should want to. The feed is good here."

"I have this morning talk with the vaquero Corlees. He tell me that the South Fork is dry up."

"John Corliss is not usually interested in our sheep," said the girl.

"No. Of the sheep he knows nothing." And the old herder smiled. "But many times he look out there," he added, pointing toward the Loring rancho.

"He was afraid father would catch him talking to one of the herders," laughed the girl.

"The vaquero Corlees he afraid of not even the bear, I think, Senorita."

Eleanor Loring laughed. "Don't you let father catch you calling him a bear!" she cautioned, provoking the old herder to immediate apology and a picturesque explanation of the fact that he had referred not to the patron, but the grizzly.

"All right, Fernando. I'll not forget to tell the patron that you called him a bear."

The old herder grinned and waved farewell as she mounted and rode down the trail. Practical in everyday affairs, he untied his bandanna and neatly folded and replaced it among his effects. As he came out of the tent he picked up his hat. He was no longer the cavalier, but a stoop-shouldered, shriveled little Mexican herder. He slouched out toward the flock and called his son to dinner. No, it was not so many years—was not the Senorita but twenty years old?—since he had wooed the Senora Loring, then a slim dark girl of the people, his people, but now the wealthy Senora, wife of his patron. Ah, yes! It was good that she should have the comfortable home and the beautiful daughter. He had nothing but his beloved sheep, but did they not belong to his Senorita?

At the ford the girl took the trail to the uplands, deciding to visit the farthest camp first, and then, if she had time, to call at one or two other camps on her way back to the rancho. As the trail grew steeper, she curbed the impatient Challenge to a steadier pace and rode leisurely to the level of the timber. On the park-like level, clean-swept between the boles of the great pines, she again put Challenge to a lope until she came to the edge on the upper mesa. Then she drew up suddenly and held the horse in.

Far out on the mesa was the figure of a man, on foot. Toward him came a horse without bridle or saddle. She recognized the figure as that of John Corliss, and she wondered why he was on foot and evidently trying to coax a stray horse toward him. Presently she saw Corliss reach out slowly and give the horse something from his hand. Still she was puzzled, and urging Challenge forward, drew nearer. The stray, seeing her horse, pricked up its ears, swung round stiffly, and galloped off. Corliss turned and held up his hand, palm toward her. It was their old greeting; a greeting that they had exchanged as boy and girl long before David Loring had become recognized as a power to be reckoned with in the Concho Valley.

"Peace?" she queried, smiling, as she rode up.

"Why not, Nell?"

"Oh, cattle and sheep, I suppose. There's no other reason, is there?"

Corliss was silent, thinking of his brother Will.

"Unless—Will—" she said, reading his thought.

He shook his head, "That would be no reason for—for our quarreling, would it?"

She laughed. "Why, who has quarreled? I'm sure I haven't."

"But you don't seem the same—since Will left."

"Neither do you, John. You haven't called at the rancho for—well, about a year."

"And then I was told to stay away even longer than that."

"Oh, you mustn't mind Dad. He growls—but he won't bite."

Corliss glanced up at her. His steady gray eyes were smiling, but his lips were grave. "Would it make any difference if I did come?"

The girl's dark face flushed and her eyes sparkled. "Lots! Perhaps you and Dad could agree to stop growling altogether. But we won't talk about it. I'd like to know what you are doing up here afoot?"

"Wouldn't tell you for a dollar," he replied, smiling. "My horse is over there—near the timber. The rest of the band are at the waterhole."

"Oh, but you will tell me!" she said. "And before we get back to the canon."

"I wasn't headed that way—" he began; but she interrupted quickly.

"Of course. I'm not, either." Then she glanced at him with

mischief scintillating in her dark eyes. "Fernando told me you were talking with him this morning. I don't see that it has done you much good."

His perplexity was apparent in his silence.

"Fernando is—is polite," she asserted, wheeling her horse.

Corliss stood gazing at her unsmilingly. "I want to be," he said presently.

"Oh, John! I—you always take things so seriously. I was just 'joshing' you, as Fernando says. Of course you do! Won't you shake hands?"

He strode forward. The girl drew off her gauntlet and extended her hand. "Let's begin over again," she said as he shook hands with her. "We've both been acting."

Before she was aware of his intent, he bowed his head and kissed her fingers. She drew her hand away with a little cry of surprise. She was pleased, yet he mistook her expression.

He flushed and, confused, drew back. "I—I didn't mean it," he said, as though apologizing for his gallantry.

The girl's eyes dilated for an instant. Then she laughed with all the joyous *abandon* of youth and absolute health. "You get worse and worse," she said, teasingly. "Do go and have another talk with Fernando, John. Then come and tell me all about it."

Despite her teasing, Corliss was beginning to enjoy the play. As a rule undemonstrative, he was when moved capable of intense feeling, and the girl knew it. She saw a light in his eyes that she recognized; a light that she remembered well, for once when they were boy and girl together she had dared him to kiss her, and had not been disappointed.

"You are cross this morning," she said, making as though to go.

"Well, I've begun over again, Nell. You wait till I get Chinook and we'll ride home together."

"Oh, but I'm—you're not going that way," she mocked.

"Yes, I am—and so are you. If you won't wait, I'll catch you up, anyway. You daren't put Challenge down the canon trail faster than a walk."

"I daren't? Then, catch me!"

She wheeled her pony and sped toward the timber. Corliss, running heavily in his high-heeled boots, caught up his own horse and leaped to the saddle as Chinook broke into a run. The young rancher knew that the girl would do her best to beat him to the canon level. He feared for her safety on the ragged trail below them.

Chinook swung down the trail taking the turns without slackening his speed and Corliss, leaning in on the curves, dodged the sweeping branches.

Arrived at the far edge of the timber, he could see the girl ahead of him, urging Challenge down the rain-gutted trail at a lope. As she pulled up at an abrupt turn, she waved to him. He accepted the challenge and, despite his better judgment, set spurs to Chinook.

Round the next turn he reined up and leaped from his horse. Below him he saw Challenge, riderless, and galloping along the edge of the hillside. On the trail lay Eleanor Loring, her black hair vivid against the gray of the shale. He plunged toward her and stooping caught her up in his arms. "Nell! Nell!" he cried, smoothing back her hair from her forehead. "God, Nell! I—I didn't mean it."

Her eyelids quivered. Then she gasped. He could feel her trembling. Presently her eyes opened and a faint smile touched her white lips. "I'm all right. Challenge fell—and I jumped clear. Struck my head. Don't look at me like that! I'm not going to die."

"I'm—I'm mighty glad, Nell!" he said, helping her to a seat on the rock against which she had fallen.

Her hands were busy with her hair. He found her hat and handed it to her. "If my head wasn't just splitting, I'd like to laugh. You are the funniest man alive! I couldn't speak, but I heard you call to me and tell me you didn't mean it! Then you say you are mighty glad I'm alive. Doesn't that sound funny enough to bring a person to life again?"

"No, it's not funny. It was a close call."

She glanced at his grave, white face. "Guess you were scared, John. I didn't know you could be scared at anything. Jack Corliss as white as a sheet and trembling like a—a girl!"

"On account of a girl," said Corliss, smiling a little.

"Now, *that* sounds better. What were you doing up on the mesa this afternoon?"

"I took some lump-sugar up for my old pony, Apache. He likes it."

"Well, I'll never forget it!" she exclaimed. "How the boys would laugh if they heard *you'd* been feeding sugar to an old broken-down cow-pony! You! Why, I feel better already."

"I'm right glad you do, Nell. But you needn't say anything about the sugar. I kind of like the old hoss. Will you promise?"

"I don't know. Oh, my head!" She went white and leaned against him. He put his arm around her, and her head lay back against his shoulder. "I'll be all right—in a minute," she murmured.

He bent above her, his eyes burning. Slowly he drew her close and kissed her lips. Her eyelids quivered and lifted. "Nell!" he whispered.

"Did you mean it?" she murmured, smiling wanly.

He drew his head back and gazed at her up-turned face. "I'm all right," she said, and drew herself up beside him. "Serves me right for putting Challenge down the trail so fast."

As they rode homeward Corliss told her of the advent of Sundown and what the latter had said about the wreck and the final disappearance of his "pal," Will Corliss.

The girl heard him silently and had nothing to say until they parted at the ford. Then she turned to him. "I don't believe Will was killed. I can't say why, but if he had been killed I think I should have known it. Don't ask me to explain, John. I have always expected that he would come back. I have been thinking about him lately."

"I can't understand it," said Corliss. "Will always had what he wanted. He owns a half-interest in the Concho. I can't do as I want to, sometimes. My hands are tied, for if I made a bad move and lost out, I'd be sinking Will's money with mine."

"I wouldn't make any bad moves if I were you," said the girl, glancing at the rancher's grave face.

"Business is business, Nell. We needn't begin that old argument. Only, understand this: I'll play square just as long as the other side plays square. There's going to be trouble before long and you know why. It won't begin on the west side of the Concho."

"Good-bye, John," said the girl, reining her pony around.

He raised his hat. Then he wheeled Chinook and loped toward the ranch.

Eleanor Loring, riding slowly, thought of what he had said. "He won't give in an inch," she said aloud. "Will would have given up the cattle business, or anything else, to please me." Then she reasoned with herself, knowing that Will Corliss had given up all interest in the Concho, not to please her but to hurt her, for the night before his disappearance he had asked her to marry him and she had very sensibly refused, telling him frankly that she liked him, but that until he had settled down to something worth while she had no other answer for him.

She was thinking of Will when she rode in to the rancho and turned her horse over to Miguel. Suddenly she flushed, remembering John Corliss's eyes as he had held her in his arms.

CHAPTER VI

THE BROTHERS

As Corliss rode up to the ranch gate he took the mail from the little wooden mail-box and stuffed it into his pocket with the exception of a letter which bore the postmark of Antelope and his address in a familiar handwriting. He tore the envelope open hastily and glanced at the signature, "Will."

Then he read the letter. It told of his brother's unexpected arrival in Antelope, penniless and sick. Corliss was not altogether surprised except in regard to the intuition of Eleanor, which puzzled him, coming as it had so immediately preceding the letter.

He rode to the rancho and ordered one of the men to have the buckboard at the gate early next morning. He wondered why his brother had not driven out to the ranch, being well known in Antelope and able to command credit. Then he thought of Eleanor, and surmised that his brother possibly wished to avoid meeting her. And as it happened, he was not mistaken.

On the evening of the following day he drove up to the Palace Hotel and inquired for his brother. The proprietor drew him to one side. "It's all right for you to see him, John, but I been tryin' to keep him in his room. He's—well, he ain't just feelin' right to be on the street. Sabe?"

Corliss nodded, and turning, climbed the stairs. He knocked at a door. There was no response. He knocked again.

"What you want?" came in a muffled voice.

"It's John," said Corliss. "Let me in."

The door opened, and Corliss stepped into the room to confront a dismal scene. On the washstand stood several empty whiskey bottles and murky glasses. The bedding was half on the floor, and standing with hand braced against the wall was Will Corliss, ragged, unshaven, and visibly trembling. His eyelids were red and swollen. His face was white save for the spots that burned on his emaciated cheeks.

"John!" he exclaimed, and extended his hand.

Corliss shook hands with him and then motioned him to a chair. "Well, Will, if you're sick, this isn't the way to get over it."

"Brother's keeper, eh? Glad to see me back, eh, Jack?"

"Not in this shape. What do you suppose Nell would think?"

"I don't know and I don't care. I'm sick. That's all."

"Where have you been—for the last three years?"

"A whole lot you care. Been? I have been everywhere from heaven to hell—the whole route. I'm in hell just now."

"You look it. Will, what can I do for you? You want to quit

the booze and straighten up. You're killing yourself."

"Maybe I don't know it! Say, Jack, I want some dough. I'm broke."

"All right. How much?"

"A couple of hundred—for a starter."

"What are you going to do with it?"

"What do you suppose? Not going to eat it."

"No. And you're not going to drink it, either. I'll see that you have everything you need. You're of age and can do as you like. But you're not going to kill yourself with whiskey."

Will Corliss stared at his brother; then laughed.

"Have one with me, Jack. You didn't used to be afraid of it."

"I'm not now, but I'm not going to take a drink with you."

"Sorry. Well, here's looking." And the brother poured himself a half-tumblerful of whiskey and gulped it down. "Now, let's talk business."

Corliss smiled despite his disgust. "All right. You talk and I'll listen."

The brother slouched to the bed and sat down. "How's the Concho been making it?" he asked.

"We've been doing pretty fair. I've been busy."

"How's old man Loring?"

"About the same."

"Nell gone into mourning?"

Corliss frowned and straightened his shoulders.

"See here, Will, you said you'd talk business. I'm waiting."

"Touched you that time, eh? Well, you can have Nell and be damned. No Mexican blood for mine."

"If you weren't down and out—" began Corliss; then checked himself. "Go ahead. What do you want?"

"I told you—money."

"And I told you—no."

The younger man started up. "Think because I'm edged up that I don't know what's mine? You've been piling it up for three years and I've been hitting the road. Now I've come to get what belongs to me and I'm going to get it!"

"All right, Will. But don't forget that I was made guardian of your interest in the Concho until you got old enough to be responsible. The will reads, until you come of age, providing you had settled down and showed that you could take care of yourself. Father didn't leave his money to either of us to be drunk up, or wasted."

"Prodigal son, eh, Jack? Well, I'm it. What's the use of getting sore at me? All I want is a couple of hundred and I'll get out of this town mighty quick. It's the deadest burg I've struck yet."

John Corliss gazed at his brother, thinking of the bright-faced, blue-eyed lad that had ridden the mesas and the hills with him. He was touched by the other's miserable condition, and even more grieved to realize that this condition was but the outcome of a rapid lowering of the other's moral and physical well-being. He strode to him and sat beside him. "Will, I'll give anything I have to help you. You know that. Anything! You're so changed that it just makes me sick to realize it. You needn't have got where you are. I would have helped you out any time. Why didn't you write to me?"

"Write? And have you tell Nell Loring how your good little brother was whining for help? She would have enjoyed that—after what she handed me."

"I don't know what she said to you," said Corliss, glancing at his brother. "But I know this: she didn't say anything that wasn't so. If that's the reason you left home, it was a mighty poor one. You've always had your own way, Will."

"Why shouldn't I? Who's got anything to say about it? You seem to think that I always need looking after—you and Nell Loring. I can look after myself."

"Doesn't look like it," said Corliss, gesturing toward the washstand. "Had anything to eat to-day?"

"No, and I don't want anything."

"Well, wash up and we'll go and get some clothes and something to eat. I'll wait."

"You needn't. Just give me a check—and I won't bother you after that."

"No. I said wash up! Get busy now!"

The younger man demurred, but finally did as he was told. They went downstairs and out to the street. In an hour they returned, Will Corliss looking somewhat like his former self in respectable raiment. "John," he said as they entered the room again, "you've always been a good old stand-by, ever since we were kids. I guess I got in bad this time, but I'm going to quit. I don't want to go back to the Concho—you know why. If you'll give me some dough I'll take care of myself. Just forget what I said about my share of the money."

"Wait till morning," said Corliss. "I'll take the room next, here, and if you get to feeling bad, call me."

"All right, Jack. I'll cut it out. Maybe I will go back to the Concho; I don't know."

"Wish you would, Will. You'll get on your feet. There's plenty to do and we're short-handed. Think it over."

"Does—Nell—ever say anything?" queried the brother.

"She talks about you often. Yesterday we were talking about you. I told her what Sundown said about—"

"Sundown?"

"Forgot about him. He drifted in a few months ago. I met up with him at the water-hole ranch. He was broke and looking for work. Gave him a job cooking, and he made good. He told me that he used to have a pal named Will Corliss—"

"And Sundown's at the Concho! I never told him where I lived."

"He came into Antelope on a freight. Got side-tracked and had to stay. He didn't know this used to be your country till I told him."

"Well, that beats me, Jack! Say, Sun was just an uncle to me when we were on the road. We made it clear around, freights, cattle-boats, and afoot. I didn't hit the booze then. Funny thing: he used to hit it, and I kind of weaned him. Now it's me. . ."

"He's straight, all right," said Corliss. "He 'tends right to business. The boys like him."

"Everybody liked him," asserted Will Corliss. "But he is the queerest Hobo that ever hit the grit."

"Some queer, at that. It's after nine now, Will. You get to bed. I want to see Banks a minute. I'll be back soon."

When John Corliss had left the room, something intangible went with him. Will felt his moral stamina crumbling. He waited until he heard his brother leave the hotel. Then he went downstairs and returned with a bottle of whiskey. He drank, hid the bottle, and went to bed. He knew that without the whiskey he would have been unable to sleep.

The brothers had breakfast together next morning. After breakfast Corliss went for the team and returned to the hotel, hoping to induce his brother to come home with him. Will Corliss, however, pleaded weariness, and said that he would stay at the Palace until he felt better.

"All right, Will. I'll leave some cash with Banks. He'll give you what you need as you want it."

"Banks? The sheriff?"

"Yes."

"Oh, all right. Suppose you think I'm not to be trusted."

"No. But we'll leave it that way till I see you again. Write in if you need me—and take care of yourself. When you get ready to settle down, I'll turn over your share of the Concho to you. So long, Will."

Will Corliss watched his brother drive away. When the team had disappeared up the road he walked down the street to the sheriff's office. The sheriff greeted him cordially.

"I came for that money, Jim."

"Sure! Here you are," and the sheriff handed him a five-dollar gold-piece.

"Quit kidding and come across," said Corliss, ignoring the significance of the allowance.

"Can't, Will. John said to give you five any time you wanted it, but only five a day."

"He did, eh? John's getting mighty close in his old age, ain't he?"

"Mebby. I don't know."

"How much did he leave for me?"

"Five a day, as I said."

"Oh, you go to hell!"

The sheriff smiled pleasantly. "Nope, Billy! I'm goin' to stay right to home. Have a cigar?"

The young man refused the proffered cigar, picked up the gold-piece and strolled out.

The sheriff leaned back in his chair. "Well if Billy feels that way toward folks, reckon he won't get far with John, or anybody else. Too dinged bad. He used to be a good kid."

Henry Hubert Knibbs

CHAPTER VII

FADEAWAY'S HAND

Fadeaway, one of the Concho riders, urged his cayuse through the ford, reined short, and turned to watch Chance, who accompanied him. The dog drew back from the edge of the stream and bunching himself, shot up and over the muddy water, nor did the jump break his stride as he leaped to overtake the rider, who had spurred out of his way. Fadeaway cursed joyously and put his pony to a lope. Stride for stride Chance ran beside him. The cowboy, swaying easily, turned and looked down upon the dog. Chance was enjoying himself. "Wonder how fast the cuss *can* run?" And Fadeaway swung his quirt. The stride quickened to the rhythmic beat of the cow-horse at top speed. The dog kept abreast without apparent effort. A half-mile beyond the ford the pace slackened as the pony took the hill across which the trail led to the open mesas. As they topped the rise Fadeaway again urged his cayuse to a run, for the puncher had enjoyed the hospitality of his companions of "The Blue," a distant cattle ranch, a day longer than had been set for his return to the Concho. Just then a startled jack rabbit leaped up and bounced down the trail ahead of them. Fadeaway jerked his horse to a stop. "Now we'll see some real speed!" he said. There was a flash of the dog's long body, which grew smaller and smaller in the distance; then a puff of dust spurted up.

Fadeaway saw the dog turn end over end, regain his feet and toss something in the air.

"The fastest dog in Arizona," remarked the cowboy. "And you, you glass-eyed son of a mistake, you're about as fast as a fence-post!" This to his patient and willing pony, that again swung into a run and ran steadily despite his fatigue, for he feared the instant slash of the quirt should he slacken pace.

Round a bend in the trail, where an arm of the distant forest ran out into the mesa. Fadeaway again set his horse up viciously. Chance stopped and looked up at the rider. The cowboy pointed through the thin rim of timber beyond which a herd of sheep was grazing. "Take 'em!" he whispered. Chance hesitated, not because he was unfamiliar with sheep, but because he had been punished for chasing and worrying them. "Go to it! Take 'em, Chance!"

The dog slunk through the timber and disappeared. The cowboy rode slowly, peering through the timber. Presently came the trample of frightened sheep—a shrill bleating, and then silence. Fadeaway loped out into the open. The sheep were running in all directions. He whistled the dog to him. Chance's muzzle dripped red. The dog slunk round behind the horse, knowing that he had done wrong, despite the fact that he had been set upon the sheep.

From the edge of the timber some one shouted. The cowboy turned and saw a herder running toward him. He reined around and sat waiting grimly. When the herder was within speaking distance. Fadeaway's hand dropped to his hip and the herder stopped. He gesticulated and spoke rapidly in Spanish. Fadeaway answered, but in a kind of Spanish not taught in schools or heard in indoor conversation.

The herder pressed forward. "Why, how! Fernando. Now

what's bitin' you?"

"The sheep! He kill the lamb!" cried the herder.

Fadeaway laughed. "Did, eh? Well, I tried to call him off. Reckon you heard me whistle him, didn't you?"

The cowboy's assertion was so palpably an insult that old Fernando's anger overcame his caution. He stepped forward threateningly. Fadeaway's gun was out and a splash of dust leaped up at Fernando's feet. The herder turned and ran. Fadeaway laughed and swung away at a lope.

When he arrived at the Concho he unsaddled, turned his pony into the corral, and called to Chance. He was at the water-trough washing the dog's muzzle when John Corliss appeared. Fadeaway straightened up. He knew what was coming and knew that he deserved it. The effects of his conviviality at the Blue had worn off, leaving him in an ugly mood.

Corliss looked him over from head to heel. Then he glanced at the dog. Chance turned his head down and sideways, avoiding his master's eye. Fadeaway laughed.

"You get your time!" said Corliss.

"You're dam' right!" retorted Fadeaway.

"And you're damned wrong! Chance knows better than to tackle sheep unless he's put up to it. You needn't explain. Bud will give you your time."

Then Corliss turned to Shoop who had just ridden in.

"Chain that dog up and keep him chained up! And give

Fadeaway his time, right up to the minute!"

Shoop dropped easily from the saddle, led his horse toward the corral, and whistled a sprightly ditty as he unsaddled him.

Fadeaway rolled a cigarette and strolled over to the bunk-house where he retailed his visit and its climax to a group of interested punchers.

"So he tied the can onto you, eh? And for settin' Chance on the sheep? He ought to be much obliged to you, Fade. They ain't room for sheep and cattle both on this here range. We're gettin' backed plumb into the sunset."

Fadeaway nodded to the puncher who had spoken.

"And ole man Loring's just run in twenty thousand head from New Mex.," continued the puncher. "Wonder how Corliss likes that?"

"Don' know—and dam' 'f I care. If a guy can't have a little sport without gettin' fired for it, why, that guy don't work for the Concho. The Blue's good enough for me and I can get a job ridin' for the Blue any time I want to cinch up."

"Well, Fade, I reckon you better cinch up pronto, then," said Shoop who had just entered. "Here's your time. Jack's some sore, believe me!"

"Sore, eh? Well, before he gets through with me he'll be sorer. You can tell him for me."

"'Course I *can*—but I ain't goin' to. And I wouldn't if I was you. No use showin' your hand so early in the game." And Shoop laughed.

Henry Hubert Knibbs

"Well, she's full—six aces," said Fadeaway, touching his holster significantly.

"And Jack throws the fastest gun on the Concho," said Shoop, his genial smile gone; his face flushed. "I been your friend, if I do say it, Fade. But don't you go away with any little ole idea that I ain't workin' for Jack Corliss."

"What's that to me? I'm fired, ain't I?"

"Correct. Only I was thinkin' your cayuse is all in. You couldn't get out of sight on him tonight. But you can take one of my string and send it back when you get ready."

"Oh, I ain't sweatin' to hit the trail," said Fadeaway, for the benefit of his audience.

"All right, Fade. But the boss is. It's up to you."

After he had eaten, Fadeaway rolled his few belongings in his slicker and tied it to the saddle. He was not afraid of Corliss, but like men of his stamp he wanted Corliss to know that he was not alone unafraid, but willing to be aggressive. He mounted and rode up to the ranch-house. Corliss, who had seen him approach through the window, sat at his desk, waiting for the cow-boy to dismount and come in. But Fadeaway sat his horse, determined to make the rancher come outside.

Corliss understood, and pushing back his chair, strode to the doorway. "Want to see me?" he asked.

Fadeaway noticed that Corliss was unarmed, and he twisted the circumstance to suit a false interpretation of the fact. "Playin' safe!" he sneered.

Corliss flushed and the veins swelled on his neck, but he kept silent. He looked the cowboy in the eye and was met by a gaze as steady as his own; an aggressive and insolent gaze that had for its backing sheer physical courage and nothing more. It became a battle of mental endurance and Corliss eventually won.

After the lapse of several seconds, the cowboy spoke to his horse. "Come on, Doc! The son-of-a—is loco."

Corliss heard, but held his peace. He stood watching the cowboy until the latter was out on the road. He noticed that he took the northern branch, toward Antelope. Then the rancher entered the house, picked up his hat, buckled on his gun, and hastened to the corral. He saddled Chinook and took the trail to the Loring rancho.

He rode slowly, trying to arrive at the best method of presenting his side of the sheep-killing to Loring. He hoped that Eleanor Loring would not be present during the interview with her father. He was disappointed, for she came from the wide veranda as he rode up and greeted him.

"Won't you come in?" she asked.

"I guess not. I'd like to see your father."

She knew that her father had forbidden Corliss the house, and, indeed, the premises. She wondered what urgency brought him to the rancho. "I'll call him, then."

Corliss answered the grave questioning in her eyes briefly. "The sheep," he said.

"Oh!" She turned and stepped to the veranda. "Dad, John is here."

Henry Hubert Knibbs

David Loring came to the doorway and stood blinking at Corliss. He did not speak.

"Mr. Loring, one of my men set Chance on a band of your sheep. My foreman tells me that Chance killed a lamb. I want to pay for it."

Loring had expected something of the kind. "Mighty proud of it, I reckon?"

"No, I'm not proud of it. I apologize—for the Concho."

"You say it easy."

"No, it isn't easy to say—to you. I'll pay the damage. How much?"

"Your dog, eh? Well, if you'll shoot the dam' dog the lamb won't cost you a cent."

"No, I won't shoot the dog. He was put up to it. I fired the man that set him on to the sheep."

"That's your business. But that don't square you with me."

"I'll settle, if you'll fix the price," said Corliss.

"You will, eh? Then, mebby you'd think you was square with ole man Loring and come foolin' around here like that tramp brother of yours. Fine doin's in Antelope, from what I hear."

"Dad!" exclaimed the girl, stepping to her father. "Dad!"

"You go in the house, Nellie! We'll settle this."

Corliss dismounted and strode up to Loring. "If you weren't

an old man I'd give you the licking of your life! I've offered to settle with you and I've apologized. You don't belong in a white man's country."

"I got a pup that barks jest like that—and he's afraid of his own bark," said Loring.

"Have it your way. I'm through." And Corliss stepped to his horse.

"Well, I ain't!" cried Loring. "I'm jest startin' in! You better crawl your cayuse and eat the wind for home, Mr. Concho Jack! And lemme tell you this: they's twenty thousand head of my sheep goin' to cross the Concho, and the first puncher that runs any of my sheep is goin' to finish in smoke!"

"All right, Loring. Glad you put me on to your scheme. I don't want trouble with you, but if you're set on having trouble, you can find it."

The old man straightened and shook his fist at the rancher. "Fust time you ever talked like a man in your life. Nex' thing is to see if you got sand enough to back it up. There's the gate."

Corliss mounted and wheeled his horse. The girl, who stood beside her father, started forward as though to speak to the rancher. Loring seized her arm. Her face flamed and she turned on her father. "Dad! Let me go!"

He shrunk beneath her steady gaze. He released her arm and she stepped up to Corliss. "I'm sorry, John," she said, and offered her hand.

"You heard it all, Nell. I'd do anything to save you all this, if I could."

Henry Hubert Knibbs

"Anything?"

"Yes."

"Well, try and get Will—to—stop drinking. He—I heard all about it. I can't do anything to help. You ought to look after him. He's your brother. He's telling folks in Antelope that you refused to help him. Is that so?"

"I refused to give him two hundred dollars to blow in if that's what you mean."

"Did you quarrel with Will?"

"No. I asked him to come home. I knew he wouldn't."

"Yes. And I think I know how you went at it. I wish I could talk to him."

"I wish you would. You can do more with him than anybody."

Loring strode toward Corliss. The girl turned to her father. He raised his arm and pointed toward the road. "You git!" he said. She reached up and patted his grizzled cheek. Then she clung to him, sobbing.

CHAPTER VIII

AT "THE LAST CHANCE"

The afternoon following the day of his discharge from the Concho, Fadeaway rode into Antelope, tied his pony to the hitching-rail in front of "The Last Chance," and entered the saloon. Several men loafed at the bar. The cowboy, known as "a good spender when flush," was made welcome. He said nothing about being out of employment, craftily anticipating the possibility of having to ask for credit later, as he had but a half-month's pay with him. He was discussing the probability of early rains with a companion when Will Corliss entered the place.

Fadeaway greeted him with loud, counterfeit heartiness, and they drank together. Their talk centered on the Concho. Gradually they drew away from the group at the bar. Finally Corliss mentioned his brother. Fadeaway at once became taciturn.

Corliss noticed this and questioned the puncher. "Had a row with Jack?" he asked.

"Between you and me, I did. He fired me, couple of days ago."

"Full?"

"Nope. Chance killed one of Loring's sheep. John hung it onto me, seein' Chance was with me. Guess John's gettin' religion."

Corliss laughed, and his lips twisted to a sneer. "Guess he is. I tried to touch him for two hundred of my own money and he turned me down. Maybe I like it."

"Turned you down, eh! That's what I call nerve! And you been away three year and more. Reckon, by the way the Concho is makin' good, you got more'n two hundred comin'. She's half yours, ain't she?"

"Yes. And I'm going to get my share. He told me I could have a job—that he was short-handed. What do you think of that! And I own half the Concho! I guess I'd like to ride range with a lot of—well, you understand, Fade. I never liked the Concho and I never will. Let's have another. No. This is on me."

Again they drank and Corliss became more talkative. He posed as one wronged by society in general and his brother especially.

As his talk grew louder, Fadeaway cautioned him. "Easy, Billy. No use advertisin'. Come on over here." And Fadeaway gestured toward one of the tables in the rear of the room.

Corliss was about to retort to the other's apparently good-natured interference with his right to free speech, when he caught Fadeaway's glance. "Well?" he exclaimed.

The cowboy evidently had something to say in confidence. Corliss followed him to one of the tables.

"It's this way," began the cowboy. "You're sore at Jack. Now Jack's got friends here and it won't help you any to let 'em know you're sore at him. I ain't feelin' like kissin' him myself—right now. But I ain't advertisin' it. What you want to do is—"

"What's that got to do with me?" interrupted Corliss.

Fadeaway laughed. "Nothin'—if you like. Only there's been doin's since you lit out." And he paused to let the inference sink in.

"You mean—?"

"Look here, Billy. I been your friend ever since you was a kid. And seein' you're kind of out of luck makes me sore—when I think what's yours by rights. Mebby I'm ridin' over the line some to say it, but from what I seen since you been gone, Jack ain't goin' to cry any if you never come back. Old man Loring ain't goin' to live more'n a thousand years. Mebby Jack don't jest love him—but Jack ain't been losin' any time since you been gone."

Corliss flushed. "I suppose I don't know that! But he hasn't seen the last of me yet."

"If I had what's comin' to you, you bet I wouldn't work on no cattle-ranch, either. I'd sure hire a law-shark and find out where I got off."

Fadeaway's suggestion had its intended effect. The younger man knew that an appeal to the law would be futile so long as he chose to ignore that clause in the will which covered the contingency he was illustrating by his conduct. Fadeaway again cautioned him as he became loud in his invective against his brother. The cowboy, while posing as friend and

Henry Hubert Knibbs

adviser, was in reality working out a subtle plan of his own, a plan of which Corliss had not the slightest inkling.

"And the Concho's makin' good," said Fadeaway, helping himself to a drink. He shoved the bottle toward Corliss. "Take a little 'Forget-it,' Billy. That's her! Here's to what's yours!" They drank together. The cowboy rolled a cigarette, tilted back his chair, and puffed thoughtfully. "Yes, she's makin' good. Why, Bud is gettin' a hundred and twenty-five, now. Old Hi Wingle's drawin' down eighty—Jack's payin' the best wages in this country. Must of cleaned up four or five thousand last year. And here you're settin', broke."

"Well, you needn't rub it in," said Corliss, frowning.

Fadeaway grinned. "I ain't, Billy. I'm out of a job myself: and nothin' comin'—like you."

Corliss felt that there was something in his companion's easy drift that had not as yet come to the surface. Fadeaway's hard-lined face was unreadable. The cowboy saw a question in the other's eyes and cleverly ignored it. Since meeting the brother he had arrived at a plan to revenge himself on John Corliss and he intended that the brother should take the initiative.

He got up and proffered his hand. "So long, Billy. If you ever need a friend, you know where to find him."

"Hold on, Fade. What's your rush?"

"Got to see a fella. Mebby I'll drop in later."

Corliss rose.

Fadeaway leaned across the table. "I'm broke, and you're

broke. The Concho pays off Monday, next week. The boys got three months comin'—close to eighteen hundred—and gold."

"Gold? Thought John paid by check?"

"He's tryin' to keep the boys from cashin' in, here. Things are goin' to be lively between Loring and the Concho before long. Jack needs all the hands he's got."

"But I don't see what that's got to do with it, Fade."

"Nothing 'ceptin' I'm game to stand by a pal—any time."

"You mean—?"

"Jest a josh, Billy. I was only thinkin' what *could* be pulled off by a couple of wise ones. So-long!"

And the cowboy departed wondering just how far his covert suggestion had carried with Will Corliss. As for Will Corliss, Fadeaway cared nothing whatever. Nor did he intend to risk getting caught with a share of the money in his possession, provided his plan was carried to a conclusion. He anticipated that John Corliss would be away from the ranch frequently, owing to the threatened encroachment of Loring's sheep on the west side of the Concho River. Tony, the Mexican, would be left in charge of the ranch. Will Corliss knew the combination of the safe—of that Fadeaway was pretty certain. Should they get the money, people in the valley would most naturally suspect the brother. And Fadeaway reasoned that John Corliss would take no steps to recover the money should suspicion point to his brother having stolen it. Meanwhile he would wait.

Shortly after Fadeaway had gone out, Will Corliss got up and sauntered to the street. He gazed up and down the straggling length of Antelope and cursed. Then he walked across to the sheriff's office.

The sheriff motioned him to a chair, which he declined. "Better sit down, Billy. I want to talk to you."

"Haven't got time," said Corliss. "You know what I came for."

"That's just what I want to talk about. See here, Billy, you've been hitting it up pretty steady this week. Here's the prospect. John told me to hand you five a day for a week. You got clothes, grub, and a place to sleep and all paid for. You could go out to the ranch if you wanted to. The week is up and you're goin' it just the same. If you want any more money you'll have to see John. I give you all he left with me."

"By God, that's the limit!" exclaimed Corliss.

"I guess it is, Billy. Have a cigar?"

Corliss flung out of the office and tramped across to the saloon. He called for whiskey and, seating himself at one of the tables, drank steadily. Fadeaway wasn't such a fool, after all. But robbery! Was it robbery? Eighteen hundred dollars would mean San Francisco . . . Corliss closed his eyes. Out of the red mist of remembrance a girl's face appeared. The heavy-lidded eyes and vivid lips smiled. Then other faces, and the sound of music and laughter. He nodded to them and raised his glass. . . . As the raw whiskey touched his lips the red mist swirled away. The dingy interior of the saloon, the booted and belted riders, the grimy floor littered with cigarette-ends, the hanging oil-lamp with its blackened chimney, flashed up and spread before him like the speeding film of a picture, stationary upon the screen of his vision, yet trembling toward a change of scene. A blur appeared in the doorway. In the nightmare of his intoxication he welcomed the change. Why didn't some one say something or do something? And the figure that had appeared, why should it pause and speak to one of the men at the bar, and not come at once to him. They were laughing. He grew silently furious. Why should they laugh and talk and keep him waiting? He knew who had come in. Of course he knew! Did Fadeaway think to hide himself behind the man at the bar? Then Fadeaway should not wear chaps with silver conchas that glittered and gleamed as he shifted his leg and turned his back. "Said he was my friend," mumbled Corliss. "My friend! Huh!" Was it a friend that would leave him sitting there, alone?

He rose and lurched to the bar. Some one steadied him as he swayed. He stiffened and struck the man in the face. He felt himself jerked backward and the shock cleared his vision. Opposite him two men held Fadeaway, whose mouth was bleeding. The puncher was struggling to get at his gun.

Corliss laughed. "Got you that time, you thief!"

"He's crazy drunk," said one of the men. "Don't get het up, Fade. He ain't packin' a gun."

Fadeaway cursed and wiped the blood from his mouth. He was playing his part well. Accident had helped him. To all intents and purposes they were open enemies.

Still, he was afraid Corliss would talk, so he laughed and extended his hand. "Shake, Billy. I guess you didn't know what you were doin'. I was tryin' to keep you from fallin'."

Corliss stared at the other with unwinking eyes.

Fadeaway laughed and turned toward the bar. "Ought to hand him one, but he's all in now, I reckon. That's what a fella gets for mixin' up with kids. Set 'em up, Joe."

Left to himself Corliss stared about stupidly. Then he started for the doorway.

As he passed Fadeaway, the latter turned and seized his arm. "Come on up and forget it, Billy. You and me's friends, ain't we?"

The cowboy, by sheer force of his personality, dominated the now repentant Corliss, whose stubbornness had given way to tearful retraction and reiterated apology. Of course they were friends!

They drank and Fadeaway noticed the other's increasing pallor. "Jest about one more and he'll take a sleep," soliloquized the cowboy. "In the mornin' 's when I ketch him, raw, sore, and ready for anything."

One of the cowboys helped Corliss to his room at the Palace. Later Fadeaway entered the hotel, asked for a room, and clumped upstairs. He rose early and knocked at Corliss's door, then entered without waiting for a response.

He wakened Corliss, who sat up and stared at him stupidly. "Mornin', Billy. How's the head?"

"I don't know yet. Got any cash, Fade? I'm broke."

"Sure. What you want?"

Corliss made a gesture, at which the other laughed. "All right, pardner. I'll fan it for the medicine."

When he returned to the room, Corliss was up and dressed. Contrary to Fadeaway's expectations, the other was apparently himself, although a little too bright and active to be normal.

"Guess I got noisy last night," said Corliss, glancing at Fadeaway's swollen lip.

"Forget it! Have some of this. Then I got to fan it."

"Where are you going?"

"Me? Over to the Blue. Got a job waitin' for me."

Corliss's fingers worked nervously. "When did you say the Concho paid off?" he queried, avoiding the other's eye.

Fadeaway's face expressed surprise. "The Concho? Why, next Monday. Why?"

"Oh—nothing. I was just wondering . . ."

"Want to send any word to Jack?" asked the cowboy.

"No, I don't. Thanks, just the same, Fade."

"Sure! Well, I guess I'll be goin'."

"Wait a minute. Don't be in a rush. I was thinking . . ."

Fadeaway strode to the window and stood looking out on the street. His apparent indifference was effective.

"Say, Fade, do you think we could—could get away with it?"

"With what?" exclaimed the cowboy, turning.

"Oh, you know! What you said yesterday."

"Guess I said a whole lot yesterday that I forgot this mornin'. I get to joshin' when I'm drinkin' bug-juice. What you gettin' at?"

"The money—at the Concho."

"Oh, that! Why, Billy, I was jest stringin' you! Supposin' somebody was to make a try for it; there's Chance like to be prowlin' around and the safe ain't standin' open nights. Besides, Jack sleeps next to the office. That was a josh."

"Well, I could handle Chance," said Corliss. "And I know the combination to the safe, if it hasn't been changed. You said Jack was likely to be away nights, now."

Fadeaway shook his head. "You're dreamin', Bill. 'Sides, I wouldn't touch a job like that for less'n five hundred."

"Would you—for five hundred?"

"I dunno. Depends on who I was ridin' with."

"Well, I'll divvy up—give you five hundred if you'll come in on it."

Again Fadeaway shook his head. "It's too risky, Billy. 'Course you mean all right—but I reckon you ain't got nerve enough to put her through."

"I haven't!" flashed Corliss. "Try me!"

"And make a get-away," continued the cowboy. "I wouldn't want to see you pinched."

"I'll take a chance, if you will," said Corliss, now assuming, as Fadeaway had intended, the role of leader in the proposed robbery.

"How you expect to get clear—when they find it out?"

"I could get old man Soper to hide me out till I could get to Sagetown. He'll do anything for money. I could be on the Limited before the news would get to Antelope."

"And if you got pinched, first thing you'd sing out 'Fadeaway,' and then me for over the road, eh?"

"Honest, Fade. I'll swear that I won't give you away, even if I get caught. Here's my hand on it."

"Give me nine hundred and I'll go you," said Fadeaway, shaking hands with his companion.

Corliss hesitated. Was the risk worth but half the money involved? "Five's a whole lot, Fade."

"Well, seein' you're goin' to do the gettin' at it, why, mebby I'd risk it for five hundred. I dunno."

"You said you'd stand by a pal, Fade. Now's your chance."

"All right. See here, Bill. You cut out the booze all you can to-day. Foot it out to the Beaver Dam to-night and I'll have a hoss for you. We can ride up the old canon trail. Nobody takes her nowadays, so we'll be under cover till we hit the ford. We can camp there back in the brush and tackle her next evenin'. So-long."

Fadeaway was downstairs and out on the street before Corliss realized that he had committed himself to a desperate and dangerous undertaking. He recalled the expression in Fadeaway's eyes when they had shaken hands. Unquestionably the cowboy meant business.

CHAPTER IX

SUNDOWN'S FRIEND

Bud Shoop was illustrating, with quaint and humorous gestures and adjectives, one of his early experiences as Ranger on the Apache Reservation. The men, grouped around the night-fire, smoked and helped the tale along with reminiscent suggestions and ejaculations of interest and curiosity. In the midst of a vivid account of the juxtaposition of a telephone battery and a curious yet unsuspicious Apache, Shoop paused in the recital and gazed out across the mesa. "It's the boss," he said, getting to his feet. "Wonder what's up?"

Corliss rode into camp, swung from the saddle, and called to Shoop. The men gazed at each other, nodded, and the words "Loring" and "sheep," punctuated their mutterings.

Shoop and Corliss talked together. Then the foreman called to Hi Wingle, asking him how the "chuck" was holding out.

"Runnin' short on flour and beans, Bud. Figured on makin' the Concho to-morrow."

Corliss and his foreman came to the fire. "Boss says we're goin' to bush here the rest of this week," and Corliss nodded.

"I'm expecting company on the west side," explained Corliss,

The men gazed at each other knowingly.

"All right," said Wingle. "Four sacks of flour and a sack of frijoles'll see us through. Got enough other stuff."

"Send some one in for it," ordered Corliss. "I'm going to stay with the outfit, from now on."

The men cheered. That was the kind of a boss to work for! No settin' back and lettin' the men do the fightin'! Some style to Jack Corliss! All of which was subtly expressed in their applause, although unspoken.

"To see that you boys don't get into mischief," continued Corliss, smiling.

"Which means keepin' other folks out of mischief, eh, patron?" said a cow-puncher.

At the word "patron" the men laughed. "They're talkin' of turnin' this outfit into a sheep-camp," remarked another. "Ba-a-ah!" And again they laughed.

Shoop motioned to Sundown who rose from beside the fire. "You can saddle up, Sun."

Sundown caught up his horse and stood waiting while one of the men saddled two pack-animals. "Tony has the keys. He'll pack the stuff for you," said Corliss. "Keep jogging and you ought to be back here by sunup."

The assistant cook mounted and took the lead-rope of the pack-horses. He was not altogether pleased with the prospect of an all-night ride, but he knew that he had been chosen as the one whose services could most easily be dispensed with at the camp. Silently he rode away, the empty kyacks clattering as the pack-horses trotted unwillingly behind him. Too busy with the unaccustomed lead-rope to roll cigarettes, he whistled, and, in turn, recited verse to keep up his spirits.

About midnight he discerned the outline of the low ranch-buildings and urged his horse to a faster gait. As he passed a clump of cottonwoods, his horse snorted and shied. Sundown reined him in and leaned peering ahead. The pack-animals tugged back on the rope. Finally he coaxed them past the cottonwoods and up to the gate. It was open, an unusual circumstance which did not escape his notice. He drifted through the shadows toward the corral, where he tied the horses. Then he stepped to the bunk-house, found a lantern and lighted it. He hallooed. There was no response. He stalked across to the ranch-house. He found the door unlocked. "Hi! Tony!" he called. No one answered. He pushed the door open and entered. Holding the lantern above his head he peered around the room.

In the dim light of the lantern vague outlines took shape. He noticed that the small safe in the corner was open. He became alarmed and again called. He heard a slight movement behind him and turned to see the door close. From behind stepped a figure, a slender figure that seemed unreal, yet familiar. With a cry of surprise he jumped back and stood facing his old friend and companion of the road, Will Corliss.

"Billy!" he ejaculated, backing away and staring.

"Yes, it's Billy." And Corliss extended his hand.

"But—what, where—?" Sundown hesitated and glanced at the safe. His eyes widened and he lowered the lantern.

"Billy!" he said, ignoring the other's proffered hand, "what you doin' here?"

Corliss assumed a nonchalant air. "Shake, pal! It's a long time since we been in a wreck, eh?"

Sundown was silent, studying the other's hardened features. "Billy!" he reiterated, "what you doin' here?"

Corliss laughed nervously. "What are you doing here?" he retorted,—"in the office of the Concho, at midnight?"

"I was comin' to get flour and beans for the camp—" he began.

Corliss interrupted him. "Sounds good, that! But they don't keep the grub here. Guess you made a mistake."

Sundown's face was expressionless. "Guess you made the mistake, Billy. I thought you was—dead."

"Not on your tin-type, Sun."

"I never thought you was crooked, Billy."

"Crooked!" flashed Corliss. "Say, you—you forget it. I'm here to get what's coming to me. Jack turned me down, so I'm going to take what's mine."

"Mebby it's yours, but you ain't gettin' it right," said Sundown. "I—I—never thought you was—"

"Oh, cut that out! You didn't used to be so dam' particular."

"I never swiped a cent in me life, Billy."

"Well, forget it. I'm in a hurry. You go ahead and get the chuck. Here are the keys to the store-room—and beat it. Just forget that you saw me; that's all."

Sundown shook his head. "I ain't forgettin' that easy, Billy. 'Sides, I'm workin' for the Concho, now. They're treatin' me fine—and I reckon I got to be square."

"You mean you're going to squeal—going back on your old pal, eh?"

Sundown's face expressed conflicting emotions. He straightened his lean shoulders. "I tell you, Billy; if you beat it now, they won't be nothin' to squeal about."

"I'm going to." And Corliss stepped toward the safe. "Just hold that light this way a minute."

Sundown complied, and Corliss thought that the other had overcome his scruples. Corliss hastily drew a small canvas sack from the safe and stuffed it into his pocket. Sundown backed toward the door.

Corliss got to his feet. "Well, so-long, Sun. Guess I'll light out."

"Not with that," said Sundown. "I ain't no preacher, but I ain't goin' to see you go straight to hell and me do nothin'. Mebby some of that dough is yourn. I dunno. But somebody's goin' to get pinched for takin' it. Bein' a Bo, it'll be me."

"So that's what's worrying you, eh? Scared you'll get sent over for this. Well, you won't. You haven't got anything on you."

"'T ain't that, Billy. It's you."

Corliss laughed. "You're getting religion, too. Well, I never thought you'd go back on me."

"I ain't. I was always your friend, Billy."

Corliss hesitated. The door behind Sundown moved ever so little. Corliss's eyes held Sundown with unwinking gaze. Slowly the door swung open. Sundown felt rather than heard a presence behind him. Before he could turn, something crashed down on his head. The face of his old friend, intense, hard, desperate, was the last thing imaged upon his mind as the room swung round and he dropped limply to the floor.

"Just in time," said Fadeaway, bending over the prostrate figure. "Get a move, Bill. I followed him from the cotton-woods and heard his talk. I was waitin' to get him when he come out, but I seen what he was up to and I fixed him."

Corliss backed against the wall, trembling and white. "Is he—did you—?"

Fadeaway grinned. "No, just chloroformed him. Get a move, Bill. No tellin' who'll come moseyin' along. Got the stuff?"

Corliss nodded.

Fadeaway blew out the light. "Come on, Bill. She worked slick."

"But—he knows me," said Corliss. "He'll squeal."

"And I reckon Jack'll believe him. Why, it's easy, Bill. They find the Bo on the job and the money gone. Who did it? Ask me."

At the cottonwoods they mounted. "Now, you fan it for

Soper's," said Fadeaway. "I'll keep on for the Blue. To-morrow evenin' I'll ride over and get my divvy."

Corliss hesitated.

"You better travel," said Fadeaway, reining his horse around. "So-long."

Chance, a prisoner in the stable, whined and gnawed at the rope with which Corliss had tied him. The rope was hard-twisted and tough. Finally the last strand gave way. The dog leaped through the doorway and ran sniffing around the enclosure. He found Sundown's trail and followed it to the ranch-house. At the threshold the dog stopped. His neck bristled and he crooked one foreleg. Slowly he stalked to the prone figure on the floor. He sniffed at Sundown's hands and pawed at him. Slowly Sundown's eyes opened. He tried to rise and sank back groaning. Chance frisked around him playfully coaxing. Finally Sundown managed to sit up. With pain-heavy eyes he gazed around the room. Slowly he got to his feet and staggered to the doorway. He leaned against the lintel and breathed deeply of the fresh morning air. The clear cold tang of the storm that had passed, lingered, giving a keen edge to the morning. "We're sure in wrong," he muttered, gazing at Chance, who stood watching him with head cocked and eyes eager for something to happen—preferably action. Sundown studied the dog dully. "Say, Chance," he said finally, "do you think you could take a little word to the camp? I heard of dogs doin' such things. Mebby you could. Somebody's got to do 'somethin' and I can't." Painfully he stooped and pointed toward the south. "Go tell the boss!" he commanded. Chance whined. "No, that way. The camp!"

Chance nosed across the yard toward the gate. Then he stopped and looked back. Sundown encouraged him by waving his arm toward the south. "Go ahead, Chance. The boss wants you."

Chance trotted toward the cottonwood, nosed among them, and finally took Sundown's trail to the knoll.

Sundown crept to the bunk-house, wondering what had become of the Mexican, Tony. He determined to search for him, but became dizzy, and, crawling to a bunk, lay back groaning as the dull pain in his head leaped intermittently to blinding stabs of agony. It seemed ages before he heard the quick staccato of hoofs on the road. He raised himself on his elbow as Shoop and Corliss rode up on their mud-spattered and steaming ponies. Sundown called as they dismounted at the corral.

Corliss and Shoop stamped in, breathing hard. "What's up?" questioned Corliss.

"They—they got the money," muttered Sundown, pointing toward the office.

"Who? See what's up, Bud."

Shoop swung out and across the enclosure.

Corliss stooped over Sundown. "What's wrong, Sun? Why, Great God, you're hurt!"

The rancher brought water and bathed Sundown's head. "Who did it?" he questioned.

"I dunno, boss. I come and caught 'em at it. Two of 'em, I guess. I was tryin' to stop one fella from takin' it when the other slips me one on the head, and I takes a sleep. I was lookin' for Tony in the office."

"Where's Tony?"

"I dunno. I was goin' to see—but—my head . . ."

"That's all right. You take it easy as you can. I'll find out."

And Corliss left the room. With Chance he explored the outbuildings and finally discovered the Mexican bound and gagged in the stable. He released him, but could make nothing of his answers save that some one had come at night, tied his hands and feet, and carried him from the ranch-house.

Corliss returned to Sundown. In the bunkhouse he encountered Shoop.

"They robbed the safe," said Shoop, and he spoke with a strange quietness. "Better come and take a look, Jack."

"Didn't blow her," said Shoop, pointing toward the corner as they entered the office.

Corliss knelt and examined the safe. "The man that did it knew the combination," he said. "There isn't a mark on the door."

He rose, and Shoop met his eye. Corliss shook his head. "I don't know," he said, as if in answer to a silent questioning. Then he told Shoop to look for tracks.

"The rain's fixed the tracks," said Shoop, turning in the doorway. "But it ain't drowned out my guess on this proposition."

"Well, keep guessing, Bud, till I talk to Sundown." And Corliss walked slowly to the bunkhouse. He sat on the edge of the bunk and laid his hand on Sundown's sleeve. "Look here, Sun, if you know anything about this, just tell me. The money's gone and you didn't get that cut on the head trying to take it. I guess you're straight, all right, but I think you know something."

Sundown blinked and set his jaw.

Corliss observed and wisely forbore to threaten or command. "Did you recognize either of the men?" he asked, presently.

"No!" lied Sundown. "Wasn't I hit in the back of me head?"

Corliss smiled grimly. "What were you doing when you got hit?"

"Tryin' to stop the other guy—"

"What did he look like?"

"I dunno. Me lantern was on the floor. He was a hefty guy, bigger 'n you. Mebby six feet and pow'ful built. Had whiskers so's I couldn't pipe his face. Big puncher hat down over his eyes and a handkerchief tied like a mask. I was scared of him, you bet!"

Corliss slowly drew a sack of tobacco and papers from his pocket. He rolled a cigarette and puffed reflectively. Then he laughed. "I'm out about eighteen hundred. That's the first thing. Next, you're used up pretty bad and we're short-handed. Then, we're losing time trying to track the thieves. But I'm not riled up a little bit. Don't think I'm mad at you. I'm mighty glad you didn't get put out in this deal. That's where I stand. I want to find out who took the money. I don't say that I'll lift a rein to follow them. Depends on who did it."

Sundown winced, and gazed up helplessly. He felt oppressed by the broad-chested figure near him. He felt that he could not get away from—what? Not Corliss, for Corliss was undoubtedly friendly. In a flash he saw that he could not get away from the truth. Yet he determined to shield his old pal of the road. "You're sure givin' me the third degree," he said with an attempt at humor. "I reckon I got to come through. Boss, are you believin' I didn't take the cash?"

"Sure I am! But that isn't enough. Are you working for the Concho, Sun, or for some other outfit?"

"The Concho," muttered Sundown stubbornly.

"And I'm the Concho. You're working for me. Listen. I've got a yarn to spin. The man that took the money—or one of them—was short, and slim, and clean-shaved, and he didn't wear a puncher hat. You weren't scared of him because he was a coward. You tried to get him to play square and he talked to you while the other man got you from behind. That's just a guess, but you furnished the meat for it."

"Me hands are up," said Sundown.

"All right. I'm not going to get after Billy for this. You lied to me, but you lied to save your pal. Shake!"

CHAPTER X

THE STORM

Will Corliss, riding through the timberlands toward the west, shivered as a drop of rain touched his hand. He glanced up through the trees. The sky seemed clouded to the level of the pine-tops. He spurred his horse as he again felt a spatter of rain. Before him lay several miles of rugged trail leading to an open stretch across which he would again enter the timber on the edge of the hollow where Soper's cabin was concealed. When Corliss had suggested Soper's place as a rendezvous, Fadeaway had laughed to himself, knowing that old man Soper had been driven from the country by a committee of irate ranchers. The illicit sale of whiskey to the cowboys of the Concho Valley had been the cause of Soper's hurried evacuation. The cabin had been burned to the ground. Fadeaway knew that without Soper's assistance Corliss would be unable to get to the railroad—would be obliged either to return to the Concho or starve on the empty mesas.

Corliss bent his head as the rain drove faster. When he arrived at the edge of the mesa, the storm had increased to a steady dull roar of rushing rain. He hesitated to face the open and reined up beneath a spruce. He was drenched and shivered. The fever of drink had died out leaving him unstrung and strangely fearful of the night. His horse stood with lowered head, its storm-blown mane whipping in the wind like a wet cloth. A branch riven from a giant pine crashed down behind him. Corliss jerked upright in the saddle, and the horse, obeying the accidental touch of the spurs, plodded out to the mesa with head held sideways.

The rider's hands grew numb and he dropped the reins over the horn and shoved his hands in his pockets. Unaccustomed to riding he grew weary and, despite the storm, he drowsed, to awaken with a start as gusts of wind swept against his face. He raised his dripping hat and shook the water from it. Then he crouched shivering in the saddle. He cursed himself for a fool and longed for shelter and the warmth of a fire. Slowly a feeling of helplessness stole over him and he pictured himself returning to the Concho and asking forgiveness of his brother. Yet he kept stubbornly on, glancing ahead from time to time until at last he saw the dim edge of the distant timber—a black line against the darkness. He urged his horse to a trot, and was all but thrown as the animal suddenly avoided a prairie-dog hole. The sweep of the storm was broken as he entered the farther timber. Then came the muffled roll of thunder and an instant white flash. The horse reared as a bolt struck a pine. Came the ghastly whistle of flying splinters as the tree was shattered. Corliss grabbed the saddle-horn as the horse bolted through the timberlands, working against the curb to reach the open. Once more on the trail the animal quieted. They topped a gentle rise. Corliss breathed his relief. Soper's cabin was in the hollow below them.

Cautiously the horse worked sideways down the ridge, slipping and checking short as the loose stones slithered beneath his feet. At the bottom of the hollow Corliss reined up and shouted. The wind whipped his call to a thin shred of sound that was swept away in the roar of the storm. Again he shouted. As though in answer there came a burning flash of blue. The dripping trees surrounding the hollow jumped into view to be blotted from sight as the succeeding crash of thunder diminished to far titanic echoes. Where Soper's cabin had stood there was a wet, glistening heap of fallen logs and rafters, charred and twisted. The lightning flash had revealed more to the rider than the desolation of the burned and abandoned homestead. He saw with instant vividness the wrecked framework of his own plans. He heard the echo of Fadeaway's sneering laugh in the fury of the wind. He told himself that he had been duped and that he deserved it. Lacking physical strength to carry him through to a place of tentative safety, he gave up, and credited his sudden regret to true repentance rather than to weakness. He would return to the Concho, knowing that his brother would forgive him. He wept as he thought of his attitude of the repentant and broken son returning in sorrow to atone for his sin and shame. He magnified his wrongdoing to heroic proportions endeavoring to filch some sentimental comfort from the romantic. He it was that needed the sympathy of the world and not his brother John; John was a plodder, a clod, good enough, but incapable of emotion, or the finer feelings. And Eleanor Loring . . . she could have saved him from all this. He had begun well; had written acceptable verse . . . then had come her refusal to marry him. What a fool he had been through it all! The wind and rain chastised his emotional intoxication, and he turned shivering to look for shelter. Dismounting, he crept beneath a low spruce and shivered beneath the scant covering of his saddle-blanket. To-morrow the sun would shine on a new world. He would arise and conquer his temptation. As he drifted to troubled sleep he knew, deep in his heart, that despite his heroics he would at that moment have given the little canvas sack of his brother's money for the obliterating warmth of intoxication.

With the morning sun he rose and saddled. About to mount,

his stiffened muscles blundered. He slipped and fell. The horse, keen with hunger, jumped away from him and trotted down the trail. He followed shouting. His strength gave out and he gave up the chase, wondering where the horse would go. Stumbling along the slippery trail, he cursed his clumsiness. A chill sweat gathered on his face. His legs trembled and he was forced to rest frequently. Crossing a stream, he stooped and drank. Then he toiled on, eagerly scanning the hoof-prints in the rain-gutted trail.

The sun was high when he arrived at the wagon-road above the Concho. Dazed and weak, he endeavored to determine which direction the horse had taken. The heat of the sun oppressed him. He became faint, and, crawling beneath the shade of a wayside fir, he rested, promising himself that he would, when the afternoon shadows drifted across the road, make his way to the Concho. He had slept little more than an hour when the swift patter of hoofs wakened him. As he got to his feet, a buckboard, drawn by a pair of pinto range-ponies, drew up. Corliss started back. The Mexican driving the ponies turned toward the sweet-faced Spanish woman beside him as though questioning her pleasure. She spoke in quick, low accents. He cramped the wagon and she stepped to the road. The Senora Loring, albeit having knowledge of his recent return to Antelope, his drinking, and all the unsavory rumors connected with his return, greeted Corliss as a mother greets a wayward son. She set all this knowledge aside and spoke to him with the placid wisdom of her years and nature. Her gentle solicitude touched him. She had been his foster-mother in those years that he and his brother had known no other fostering hand than that of old Hi Wingle, the cook, whose efforts to "raise" the Corliss boys were more largely faithful than discriminating.

Senora Loring knew at a glance that he was in trouble of some kind. She asked no questions, but held out her hands.

Henry Hubert Knibbs

Corliss, blind with tears, dropped to his knee: "Madre! Madre!" he cried.

She patted his head. "You come with me. Then perhaps you have to say to me that which now you do not say."

He shook his head, but she paid no attention, leading the way to the buckboard. He climbed beside the driver, then with an ejaculation of apology, leaped to the road and helped her in.

"Where you would like to go?" she asked. "The Concho?"

Again he shook his head. "I can't. I—"

She questioned his hesitation with her eyes.

"I'll tell you when—when I feel better. Madre, I'm sick."

"I know," she said.

Then, turning to the driver, she gestured down the wagon-trail.

They drove through the morning woodlands, swung to the east, and crossed the ford. The clustered adobes of the Loring homestead glimmered in the sun. Corliss glanced across the river toward the Concho. Again the Senora Loring questioned him with a glance.

He shook his head. "Away—anywhere," he said, gesturing toward the horizon.

"You come home with me," she said quietly. "Nellie is not at the home to-day. You rest, and then perhaps you go to the Concho."

As they entered the gateway of the Loring rancho, Corliss made as though to dismount. The Senora Loring touched his arm. He shrugged his shoulders; then gazed ahead at the peaceful habitation of the old sheep-herder.

The Senora told the driver to tie the team and wait. Then she entered the house. Corliss gazed about the familiar room while she made coffee. Half starved, he ate ravenously the meal she prepared for him. Later, when she came and sat opposite, her plump hands folded in her lap, her whole attitude restful and assuring, he told her of the robbery, concealing nothing save the name of Fadeaway.

Then he drew the canvas sack from his pocket. "I thought I could go back and face it out, but now, I can't. Will you—return it—and—tell John?"

She nodded. "Si! If you wish it so, my son. You would not do that as I would tell you—so I say nothing. I can only—what you say—help, with my hands," and she gestured gracefully as though leading a child. "You have money to go away?"

"No, madre."

"Then I give you the money." And the Senora, ignoring his half-hearted protests, stepped to an adjoining room and returned. "Here is this to help you go. Some day you come back strong and like your father the big John Corliss. Then I shall be much glad."

"I'll pay it back. I'll do anything—"

But she silenced him, touching his lips with her fingers. "No. The promise to make is not so hard, but to keep . . . Ah! When you come back, then you promise; si?"

Not a word of reproof, not a glance or a look of disapproval, yet Corliss knew that the Senora's heart was heavy with sorrow for him. He strode to the doorway. Senora Loring followed and called to the driver. As Corliss shook hands with her, she kissed him.

An anger against himself flushed his cheek. "I don't know which road I'll take, madre,—after I leave here,—this country. But I shall always remember . . . And tell Nell . . . that . . ." he hesitated.

The Senora smiled and patted his arm. "Si! I understand."

"And, madre, there is a man—vaquero, or cook, a big man, tall, that they call Sundown, who works for the Concho. If you see him, please tell him—that I sent it back." And he gestured toward the table whereon lay the little canvas sack of gold. "Good-bye!"

He stepped hurriedly from the veranda, climbed to the seat of the buckboard, and spoke to the driver. For a long time the Senora stood in the doorway watching the glint of the speeding ponies. Then she went to her bedroom and knelt before the little crucifix. Her prayer was, strangely enough, not for Will Corliss. She prayed that the sweet Madonna would forgive her if she had done wrong.

CHAPTER XI

CHANCE—CONQUEROR

Sundown's return to the camp occasioned some indirect questioning and not a little comment. He told the story of his adventure at the Concho in detail up to the point of his conversation with Will Corliss. Then he lapsed into generalities, exhibiting with some little pride the wound on his head as evidence of his attempt to prevent the robbery and incidentally as a reason for being unable to discourse further upon the subject. His oft-repeated recital invariably concluded with, "I steps in and tries to stop the first guy when *Wham!* round goes the room and I takes a sleep."

The men seemed satisfied with Sundown's graphic account in the main. Hi Wingle, the cook, asked no questions, but did a great deal of thinking. He was aware that Will Corliss had returned to the Concho, and also, through rumor, that Corliss and Fadeaway had been together in Antelope. The fact that the robbers failed to get the money—so it was given out— left the drama unfinished, and as such it lacked sustained interest. There would be no bandits to capture; no further excitement; so the talk eventually drifted to other subjects.

The assistant cook's evident melancholy finally gave place to a happier mood as he realized that he had gained a modicum of respect in a camp where hitherto he had been more or less of a joke. While he grieved over the events which led up to his newly attained prestige as a man of nerve, he was not a little proud of the prestige itself, and principally because he lacked the very quality of courage that he was now accredited with. Perhaps the fact that he had "played square," as he saw it, was the true foundation of his attitude.

He discharged his duties as assistant cook with a new and professional flourish that amused the riders. When they rolled from their blankets in the crisp air of the morning, they were never kept waiting for their coffee, hot bread, and frijoles. Moreover, he always had a small fire going, around which he arranged the tin plates, cups, knives and forks. This additional fire was acceptable, as the cooking was done on a large sheet-iron camp-stove, the immediate territory of which was sacred to Hi Wingle. Wingle, who had been an old-timer when most of the Concho hands were learning the rudiments of the game, took himself and his present occupation seriously. His stove was his altar, though burnt offerings were infrequent. He guarded his culinary precincts with a watchful eye. His attitude was somewhat akin to that of Cardinal Richelieu in the handkerchief scene, "Take but one step within these sacred bounds and on our head I'll lunch the cuss of Rum," or something to that effect. He was short, ruddy, and bald, and his antithesis, Sundown, was a source of constant amazement to him. Wingle had seen many tall men, but never such an elongated individual as his assistant. It became the habit of one or another of the boys to ask the cook the way to the distant Concho, usually after the evening meal, when they were loafing by the camp-fire. Wingle would thereupon scratch his head and assume an air of intense concentration. "Well," he would invariably remark, "you take the trail along Sundown's shadder there, and keep a-fannin' it smart for about three hours. When you come to the end of the shadder, take the right fork of the river, and in another hour you'll strike the Concho. That's the quickest way." And this bit of attenuated humor never failed to produce an effect.

One morning, about a week after Sundown's return to his duties as assistant, while Wingle was drying his hands, preparatory to reading a few pages of his favorite novel, Sundown ambled into camp with an armful of greasewood, dumped it near the wagon, and, straightening up, rolled a cigarette.

Wingle, immersed in the novel, read for a while and then glanced up questioningly.

Sundown shook his head.

"Now this here story," said Wingle; "I read her forty-three times come next round-up, and blamed if I sabe her yet. Now, take it where the perfesser—a slim gent with large round eye-glasses behind which twinkled a couple of deep-set studyus eyes—so the book says; now, take it where he talks about them Hopi graves over there in the valley—"

"This here valley?" queried Sundown, immediately interested.

"Sure! Well, I can sabe all that. I seen 'em."

"Seen 'em?"

"Sure! Why Arizona's got more leavin's of history and dead Injuns and such, right on top of the ground, than any other State in the Union. Why, right over there in the canon of the Concho there's a hull ruined Injun village—stones piled up in little circles, and what was huts and caves and the leavin's of a old irrigatin' ditch and busted ollas, and bones and

Henry Hubert Knibbs

arrow-heads and picture-writin' on the rocks—bears and eagles and mounting-lions and hosses—scratched right on the rocks. Them cliffs there is covered with it."

"Them?" queried Sundown, pointing toward the canon, "Do they charge anything to see it?"

"Well, seein' they been dead about a thousand years, I reckon not."

"A thousand years! Huh! I ain't scared of no Injuns a thousand years old. How far is it to them picture-things?"

"'Bout three mile. You can take a hoss and mosey over if you like. Figure on gettin' back 'round noon."

"Any snakes over there?"

"Comf'table thick. You might get a pretty good mess of 'em, if you was to take your time. I never bother to look for 'em."

Sundown gazed at his length of nether limb and sighed.

"Snakes won't bother you none," said Wingle, reassuringly. "They get tired, same as anybody, and they'd have to climb too fur to see if you was to home."

Sundown rose and saddled a horse. He mounted and rode slowly toward the rim of the distant canon. At the canon's brink, he dismounted and led his horse down the trail, stopping frequently to gaze in wonderment at the painted cliffs and masses of red rock strewn along the slopes. High up on the perpendicular face of the canon walls he saw many caves and wondered how they came to be there. "Makes a fella feel like sayin' his prayers," he muttered. "Wisht I knowed one."

He drifted on down the trail, which wound around huge fragments of rock riven from the cliffs in prehistoric days. He was awed by the immensity of the chasm and talked continuously to his horse which shuffled along behind paying careful attention to the footing. Arrived at the stream the horse drank. Sundown mounted and rode along the narrow level paralleling the river course. The canon widened, and before he realized it he was in a narrow valley carpeted with bunch-grass and dotted with solitary cypress and infrequent clumps of pine. He paused to inspect a small mound of rock which was partially surrounded by a wall of neatly laid stone. Within the semicircular wall was a hole in the ground—the entrance to a cave. Farther along he came upon the ruins of a walled square, unmistakably of human construction. He became interested, and, tying his horse to a scrub-cedar, began to dig among the loose stones covering the interior of the square. He discovered a fragment of painted pottery—the segment of an olla, smooth, dark red, and decorated with a design in black. He rubbed the earth from the fragment and polished it on his overalls. He unearthed a larger fragment and found that it matched the other piece. He was happy. He forgot his surroundings, and scratched and dug in the ruin until he accumulated quite a little pile of shards, oddly marked and colored. Eventually he gathered up his spoils and tied them in his handkerchief.

Leaving his horse, he meandered down the valley until he came to another and larger cave. "Wonder what's down there?" he soliloquized. "Mebby one of them Injuns. Been there a thousand years waitin' for somethin' to turn up. 'Nough to make a fella tired, waitin' that long." He wanted to explore the cave, but he was afraid. Moreover, the interior was dark. He pondered. Finally his natural fondness for mild adventure overcame his fear. "Got some matches!" he exclaimed, joyfully. "Wonder if it's deep? Guess I could put me legs in first, and if nothin' bites me legs, why, I could follow 'em down to bottom." He put his head in the hole. "Hey!" he hallooed, "are you in there?" He rose to his feet. "Nothin' doin'. Well, here goes. I sure want to see what's down there."

In his excitement he overlooked the possibility of disturbing a torpid rattler. He slid feet first into the cave, found that he could all but stand upright, and struck a match.

The ancient Hopis buried their dead in a sitting posture on a woven grass mat, with an olla, and frequently a bone dagger, beside them. In the clean, dry air of the uplands of Arizona the process of decay is slow. Sundown, unaware of this, hardly anticipated that which confronted him as the match flamed blue and flared up, lighting the interior of the cave with instant brilliance. About six feet from where he crouched was the dried and shriveled figure of a Hopi chief, propped against the wall of the cave. Beside the figure stood the painted olla untarnished by age. The dead Indian's head was bowed upon his breast, and his skeleton arms, parchment-skinned and rigid, were crossed upon his knees.

Sundown scrambled for the circle of daylight above him. "Gee Gosh!" he panted, as he got to his feet outside the cave. "It was him!" He clambered over the circle of stones and backed away, eyeing the entrance as though he expected to see the Hopi emerge at any moment. He crouched behind a boulder, his pulses racing. He was keyed to a high tension of expectancy. In fact, he was in a decidedly receptive mood for that which immediately happened. He noticed that his horse, a hundred yards or so up the valley, was circling the cedar and pulling back on the reins. He wondered what was the matter with him. The horse was usually a well-behaved animal. The explanation came rapidly. Sundown saw the horse back and tear loose from the cedar; saw him whirl and charge down the valley snorting. "Guess he seen one, too!"

said Sundown making no effort to check the frightened animal. Almost immediately came the long-drawn bell of a dog following a hot scent. Sundown turned from watching his vanishing steed and saw a huge timber-wolf leap from a thicket. Behind the wolf came Chance, neck outstretched, and flanks working at top speed. The wolf dodged a boulder, flashing around it with no apparent loss of ground. Chance rose over the boulder as though borne on the wind. The wolf turned and snapped at him. Sundown decided instantly that the sepulcher of the dead Hopi was preferable to the proximity of the live wolf, and he made for the cave.

The wolf circled the wall of stones and also made for the cave. Sundown had arrived a little ahead of him. The top of Sundown's head appeared for an instant; then vanished. The wolf backed snarling against the wall as Chance leaped in. When Sundown's head again appeared, the whirling mass of writhing fur and kicking legs had taken more definite shape. Chance had fastened on the wolf's shoulder. The wolf was slashing effectively at the dog's side. Presently they lay down facing each other. Chance licked a long gash in his foreleg. The wolf snapped as he lay and a red slaver dripped from his fangs. Not twelve feet away, Sundown gazed upon the scene with fear-wide eyes. "Go to it, Chance!" he quavered, and his encouragement was all but the dog's undoing, for he lost the wolf's gaze for an instant, barely turning in time to meet the vicious charge. Sundown groaned as the wolf, with a slashing stroke, ripped the dog's neck from ear to shoulder. The stones in the enclosure were spattered with red as they whirled, each trying to reach the throat of the other. Suddenly Chance leaped up and over the wolf, lunging for his neck as he descended. The wolf rolled from under and backed toward the cave. "Hey!" yelled Sundown. "You can't come in here!"

Chance, weakened from loss of blood, lay watching the wolf

as it crouched tensely. Again the great gray shadow lunged and a bright streak sprung up on the dog's side. "Gee Gosh!" whined Sundown; "he can't stand much more of that!" Undoubtedly Chance knew it, for he straight-way gathered himself and leaped in, diving low for the wolf's fore leg. As the wolf turned his shoulder, Chance again sprang over him and, descending, caught him just behind the ear, and held. The wolf writhed and snarled. Chance gripped in and in, with each savage shake of his head biting deeper. In a mighty effort to free himself the wolf surged backward, dragging Chance around the enclosure. Sundown, rising from the cave's mouth, crouched before it. "You got him! You got him!" he cried. "Once more, now!"

The body of the wolf quivered and sagged, then stiffened as if for a last effort. Chance held. They were both lying on the stones now. Chance with fore feet braced against the wolf's chest. Presently the dog gave a final shake, drew back, and lay panting. From head to flanks he was soaked with blood. The wolf was dead.

Sundown stood up. "Good boy, Chance!" he said. The great, gaunt body of the dog raised itself on trembling legs, the pride of the conqueror lighting for a moment his dimming eyes. "It's me, Chance!" said Sundown, stroking the dog's head. Chance wagged his tail and reaching up his torn and bleeding muzzle licked Sundown's hand. Then slowly he sank to the ground, breathed heavily, and rolled to his side. Sundown knelt over him and unaccustomed tears ran down his lean cheeks and dripped on the clotted fur. "You was some fighter, Chance, ole pal! Gee Gosh! He's nothin' except cuts and slashes all over. Gee Gosh!" He drew the dog's head to his lap and sat crooning weird, broken words and stroking the torn ears. Suddenly he stopped and put his hand over the dog's heart. Then he leaped to his feet and, dumping the fragments of pottery from his bandanna, tore it in strips and began bandaging the wounds. The gash on Chance's neck still bled. Sundown drew his knife and cut the sleeve from his shirt. He ripped it open and bound the dog's neck. Realizing that Chance was not dead, he became valiant. "We sure put up the great scrap, didn't we, pal? We licked him! But if he'd 'a' licked you . . ." And Sundown gazed at the still form of the wolf and shuddered, not knowing that the wolf would have fled at sight of him had he been able to get away from Chance.

Two hours later, Eleanor Loring, riding along the canon stream, met a lean giant, one sleeve of his shirt gone, his hat missing, and his hands splotched with blood. His eyes were wild, his face white and set. He carried a great, shaggy dog in his arms.

"Are you hurt?" she asked, swinging from her pony and coming to him.

"Me? No, lady. But me pal here is hurt bad. Jest breathin'. Killed a wolf back there. Mebby I can save him."

"Why, it's Chance—of the Concho!"

"Yes, lady. What is left of him."

"Do you work for the Concho? Won't you take my horse?"

"I'm assistant cook at the camp. No, thanks, lady. Ridin' might joggle him and start him to bleedin'. I can carry him so he'll be easier-like."

"But how did it happen?"

"I dunno. Chance chased the wolf and they went to it where I was explorin' one of them caves. I guess I better be goin'."

Henry Hubert Knibbs

The girl reined her horse around and rode down the valley trail, pausing occasionally to watch the tall figure climbing the canon with that shapeless burden in his arms. "I wonder if any other man on the Concho would have done that?" she asked herself. And Sundown, despite his more or less terrifying appearance, won her estimation for kindness at once.

Slowly he climbed the canon trail, resting at each level. The dog hung a limp, dead weight in his arms. Midway up the trail Sundown rested again, and gazed down into the valley. He imagined he could discern the place of the fight. "That there wolf," he soliloquized, "he was some fighter, too. Mebby he didn't like to get licked any more than Chance, here. Wonder what they was fightin' about? I dunno. But, Gee Gosh, she was one dandy scrap!"

At the top of the canon wall he again rested. He expected to be discharged for being late, but solaced himself with the thought that if he could save Chance, it was worth the risk.

The riders had returned to the chuck-wagon when Sundown arrived lugging the inert body of the wolf-dog. They gathered around and asked brief questions. Sundown, busy washing the dog's wounds, answered as well as he could. His account of the fight did not suffer for lack of embellishment, and while he did not absolutely state that he had taken a hand in the fight, his story implied it.

"Don't see nothin' on you to show you been in a scrap," remarked a young puncher.

"That's because you can't see in deep enough," retorted Sundown. "If I wasn't in every jump of that fight, me heart was."

"Better shoot him and put him out of his sufferin'," suggested the puncher.

Sundown rose from beside the dog. Shoot Chance? Not so long as he could keep between the dog and the cowboy's gun. The puncher, half in jest, reached for his holster. Sundown's overwrought nerves gave way. He dropped to his knees and lifted his long arms imploringly. "Don't! Don't!" he wailed. "He ain't dead! Don't shoot my pal!"

Bud Shoop, who had kept silent, shouldered the puncher aside. "Cut it out, Sinker," he growled. "Can't you sabe that Sundown means it?"

Later in the evening, and fortified with a hearty meal. Sundown gave a revised version of the fight, wherein his participation was modified, though the story lost nothing in re-telling. And, indeed, his own achievement, of lugging Chance up the canon trail, awakened a kind of respect among the easy-going cowboys. To carry an eighty-pound dog up that trail took sand! Again Sundown had unconsciously won their respect. Nothing was said about his late return. And his horse had found its way back to the camp.

Sometime in the night, Bud Shoop was awakened by the man next him.

"What's goin' on?" queried Shoop, rising on his elbow.

"Ask me again," said the puncher. "Listen!"

From the vicinity of the wagon came the gurgle of water and then a distinctly canine sneeze.

"Dinged if he ain't fussin' with that dog again!" grumbled Shoop. "The dam' fool!" Which, as it is the spirit which giveth life to the letter, was not altogether uncomplimentary.

Henry Hubert Knibbs

CHAPTER XII

A GIFT

Warned by John Corliss of Loring's evident intent to graze his sheep on the west side of the Concho River, the cattle-men held a quiet meeting at the ranch of the Concho and voted unanimously to round up a month earlier than usual. The market was at a fair level. Beef was in demand. Moreover, the round-up would, by the mere physical presence of the riders and the cattle, check for the time being any such move as Loring contemplated, as the camps would be at the ford. Meanwhile the cattle-men again petitioned the Ranger at Antelope to stir up the service at Washington in regard to grazing allotments.

The round-up began. The Concho outfit moved camp to the ford and Sundown had his first introduction to real work. From morning till night and far into the night the fires were going. Groups of belated riders swung in and made for the chuck-wagons. Sundown, following a strenuous eighteen hours of uninterrupted toil, solemnly borrowed a piece of "tarp" from his outfit on which he lettered the legend:—

"CAFE DE CONCHO—MEELS AT ALL
HOURS—PRIVIT TABELS FOR LADYS"

He hung the tarp in a conspicuous place and retired to rest. The following morning his efforts were applauded with much picturesque expletive, and even criticism was evoked by a lean puncher who insisted "that the tall guy might be a good cook all right, but he sure didn't know how to spell 'calf.'" Naturally the puncher's erudition leaned toward cattle and the range.

At all times conspicuous, for he topped by a head and shoulders the tallest rider on the range. Sundown became doubly conspicuous as the story of his experience with the hold-ups and his rescue of Chance became known. If he strutted, it was pardonable, for he strutted among men difficult to wrest approval from, and he had won their approval.

At Hi Wingle's suggestion, he "packed a gun"—a formidable .45 lent him by that gracious individual, for it grieved the solid Wingle's soul to see so notable a character go unarmed. Sundown, like many a wiser man, was not indifferent to the effect of clothing and equipment. Obliged frequently to relate his midnight adventure with the robbers, he became a past-master in the art of dramatic expression. "If I'd 'a' had me gun with me," he was wont to say, slapping the holster significantly, "the deal might 'a' turned out different. I reckon it's luck I didn't." Which may have been true enough, for Sundown would undoubtedly have been afraid to use the weapon and Fadeaway might have misunderstood his bungling.

In his spare time he built a lean-to of odds and ends, and beneath it Chance drowsed away the long, sunny hours while Sundown was rustling firewood or holding hot argument with an obstreperous dutch-oven. And Chance became the pet and the pride of the outfit. Riders from distant ranches would stray over to the lean-to and look at him, commenting on his size and elaborating on the fact that it usually took two of the best dogs ever whelped to pull down a timber-wolf.

Even Fadeaway, now riding for the Blue, became enthusiastic and boasted of his former friendship with Chance. When he essayed the intimacy of patting the dog's head, some of the onlookers doubted him, for Chance received these overtures with a deep-throated growl.

"He won't let nobody touch him but that Sundown gent," cautioned a bystander.

"Guess he's loco since he got chewed up," said Fadeaway, retreating.

Chance licked his wounds and recovered slowly. He would lie in the sun, watching with unwinking gaze the camp and the cluster of men about it until the form of Sundown loomed through the mass. Then he would beat the ground with his tail and whine expectantly. As he became stronger, he ventured to stretch his wound-stiffened muscles in short pilgrimages to the camp, where the men welcomed him with hearty and profane zest. Was he not the slayer of their enemy's sheep and the killer of the timber-wolf? Eventually he was presented with a broad collar studded with brass spikes, and engraved upon it was the sanguinary and somewhat ambiguous legend: "Chance—The Killer of the Concho."

John Corliss, visiting the round-up, rode over to Sundown's tepee, as it was called. The assistant cook was greasing Chance's wounds.

"How is he getting along?" asked Corliss.

"Fine, boss, fine! This here is some little ole red-cross ward, believe me! He's gettin' over bein' lame and he eats regular."

"Here, Chance!" called Corliss.

The dog rose stiffly and stalked to his master, smelt of him and wagged his tail, then stood with lowered head as though pondering some serious dog-logic.

"He's kind of queer," explained Sundown, "but he's a whole pile better than he was a spell ago. Had to bring him water and feed him like a baby cuttin' teeth—though I never seen one doin' that. He wouldn't let nobody touch him 'ceptin' me."

"Is he able to travel?"

"Oh, some."

"Think he could make it to the Concho?"

Sundown hesitated. "Mebby. Yes, I reckon he could. He can run all right, only I guess he kind of likes hangin' around me." And Sundown glanced sideways at Corliss.

"He seems all right. I guess I'll take him back with me. I don't like the idea of his running loose here."

"He ain't bitin' nobody," assured Sundown.

Corliss glanced shrewdly at the other's lean, questioning face. "Guess you won't miss him much. How are you making it?"

"Me? Fine! Reckon I'll take out me papers for a full-chested range cook afore long. You see the L.D. outfit says that I could have a job with them after the round-up. It kind of leaked out about them pies. 'Course they was joshin', mebby. I dunno."

"The L.D. boys are all right," said Corliss. "If you want to make a change—"

"See here, boss! I done some ramblin' in my time. Guess because I was lookin' for somethin' new and excitin'. Well, I reckon they's plenty new and excitin' right to home on the Concho. Any time I get tired of fallin' off hosses, and gettin' beat up, and mixin' up in dog and wolf fights, why, I can go to bustin' broncos to keep me from goin' to sleep. Then Chance there, he needs lookin' after."

Corliss seemingly ignored the gentle hint. He mounted and called to the dog. Chance made no movement to follow him. Corliss frowned. "Here, Chance!" he commanded, slapping his thigh with his gauntleted hand. The dog followed at the horse's heels as Corliss rode across the hard-packed circle around the camp. Sundown's throat tightened. His pal was gone.

He puttered about, straightening the blankets. "Gee Gosh! but this here shack looks empty! Never knowed sick folks could be so much comp'ny. And Chance is folks, all right. Talk about blue blood! Huh! I reckon a thoroughbred dog is prouder than common folks, like me. Some king, he was! Layin' there lookin' out at them punchers and his eyes sad-like and proud, and turnin' his head slow, watchin' 'em like they was workin' for him. They's somethin' about class that gets a fella, even in a dog. And most folks knows it, but won't let on."

He took Chance's drinking-basin—a bread-pan appropriated from the outfit—and the frayed saddle-blanket that had been the dog's bed, and carried them to the cottonwoods edging the river. There he hid the things. He returned to the lean-to and threw himself on his blankets. He felt as though he had just buried a friend. A cowboy strolled up and squatted in front of the lean-to. He gazed at the interior, nodded to Sundown, and rolled a cigarette. He smoked for a while, glanced up at the sky, peered round the camp, and shrugged his shoulders.

Sundown nodded. "You said it all, Joe. He's gone."

The cowboy blew rings of smoke, watching them spread and dissolve in the evening air. "Had a hoss onct," he began slowly,—"ornery, glass-eyed, she-colt that got mixed up in a bob-wire fence. Seein' as she was like to make the buzzards happy 'most any day, I took to nussin' her. Me, Joe Scott, eh? And a laugh comin'. Well, the boys joshed—mebby you hearn some of 'em call me Doc. That's why. The boys joshed and went around like they was in a horsepital, quiet and steppin' catty. I could write a book out of them joshin's and sell her, if I could write her with a brandin'-iron or a rope. Anyhow, the colt she gets well and I turns her out on the range, which ought to be the end of the story, but it ain't. She come nickerin' after me like I was her man, hangin' around when I showed up at the ranch jest like I was a millionaire and she wantin' to get married. Couldn't get shet of her. So one day I ropes her and says to myself I'll make a trick hoss of her and sell her. The fust trick she done wasn't the one I reckoned to learn her. She lifted me one in the jeans and I like to lost all the teeth in my head. 'You're welcome, lady,' says I, 'for this here 'fectionate token of thanks for my nussin' and gettin' joshed to fare-ye-well. Bein' set on learnin' her, I shortened the rope and let her kick a few holes in the climate. When she got tired of that, I begins workin' on her head, easy-like and talkin' kind. Fust thing I knowed she takes a san'wich out of my shirt, the meat part bein' a piece of my hide. Then I got riled. I lit into her with the boots, and we

Henry Hubert Knibbs

had it. When I got tired of exercisin' my feet, she comes to me rubbin' her nose ag'in' me and kind of nickerin' and lovin' up tremendous, bein' a she-hoss. 'Now,' says I, 'I'm goin' to do the courtin', sister.' And I sot out to learn her to shake hands. She got most as good as a state senator at it: purfessional-like, but not real glad to see you. Jest put on. Then I learns her to nod yes. That was hard. Then I gets her so she would lay down and stay till I told her to get up. 'Course it takes time and I didn't have the time reg'lar. I feeds her every time, though. Then she took to sleepin' ag'in' the bunk-house every night, seein' as she run loose jest like a dog. When somebody'd get up in the mornin', there she would be with her eyes lookin' in the winder, shinin', and her ears lookin' in, too. You see she was waitin' for her beau to come out, which was me. She took to followin' me on the range when I rid out, and she got fat and sizable. The boys give up joshin' and got kind of interested. But that ain't what I'm gettin' at. Come one day, about two year after I'd been monkeyin' with learnin' her her lessons, when I thinks to break her to ride. I got shet of the idea of sellin' her and was goin' to keep her myself. The boys was lookin' for to see me get piled, always figurin' a pet hoss was worse to break than a bronc. She did some fussin', but she never bucked—never pitched a move. Thinks I, I sure got a winner. Next day she was gone. Never seen her after that. Trailed all over the range, but she sure vamoosed. And nobody never seen her after that. She sure made a dent in my feelin's."

Sundown sat up blinking. "I reckon that's the difference between a hoss and a dog," he said, slowly. "Now, a hoss and me ain't what you'd call a nacheral combination. And a hoss gets away and don't come back. But a dog comes back every time, if he can. 'Most any hoss will stay where the feedin' is good, but a dog won't. He wants to be where his boss is."

"And that there Chance is with the boss," said the cowboy,

gesturing toward the north. "Seen him foller him down the trail."

Sundown nodded. The cowboy departed, swaggering away in the dusk.

Just before Sundown was called to take his turn with the night-shift, a lean, brown shape tore through the camp, upsetting a pot of frijoles and otherwise disturbing the peace and order of the culinary department.

"Coyote!" shouted Wingle, vainly reaching for the gun that he had given to Sundown.

"Coyote nothin'!" said a puncher, laughing. "It's the Killer come back hot-foot to find his pardner."

Chance bounded into the lean-to: it was empty. He sniffed at the place where his bed had once been, found Sundown's tracks and followed them toward the river. Sundown was on his knees pawing over something that looked very much like a torn and frayed saddle-blanket. Chance volleyed into him, biting playfully at his sleeve, and whining.

Sundown jumped to his feet. He stood speechless. Then a slow grin crept to his face. "Gee Gosh!" he said, softly. "Gee Gosh! It's you!"

Chance lay down panting. He had come far and fast. Sundown gathered up the blanket and pan, rose and marched to the shack. "I was airin' 'em out against your comin' back," he explained, untruthfully. The fact was that he could not bear to see the empty bed in the lean-to and had hidden it in the bushes.

The dog watched him spread the blanket, but would not lie

Henry Hubert Knibbs

down. Instead he followed Sundown to the camp and found a place under the chuck-wagon, where he watched his lean companion work over the fires until midnight. If Sundown disappeared for a minute in search of something. Chance was up and at his heels. Hi Wingle expressed himself profanely in regard to the return of the dog, adding with unction, "There's a pair of 'em; a pair of 'em." Which ambiguity seemed to satisfy him immensely.

When Sundown finally returned to the lean-to, he was too happy to sleep. He built a small fire, rolled a cigarette and sat gazing into the flames. Chance sat beside him, proud, dignified, contented. Sundown became drowsy and slept, his head fallen forward and his lean arms crossed upon his knees. Chance waited patiently for him to waken. Finally the dog nuzzled Sundown's arm with little jerks of impatience. "What's bitin' you now?" mumbled Sundown. "We're here, ain't we?" Nevertheless he slipped his arm around the dog's muscular shoulders and talked to him. "How'd you get away? The boss'll raise peelin's over this, Chance. It ain't like to set good with him." He noticed that Chance frequently scratched at his collar as though it irritated him. Finally he slipped his fingers under the collar. "Suthin' got ketched in here," he said, unbuckling the strap. Tied inside the collar was a folded piece of paper. Sundown was about to throw it away when he reconsidered and unfolded it. In the flickering light of the fire he spread the paper and read laboriously:—

"Chance followed me to the Concho because I made him come. He showed that he didn't want to stay. I let him go. If he gets back to you, keep him. He is yours.

"JOHN CORLISS."

Sundown folded the note and carefully tucked it in his pocket. He rose and slapped his chest grandiloquently.

"Chance, ole pal," he said with a brave gesture, "you're mine! Got the dockyments to show. What do you think?"

Chance, with mouth open and lolling tongue, seemed to be laughing.

Sundown reached out his long arm as one who greets a friend.

The dog extended his muscular fore leg and solemnly placed his paw in Sundown's hand. No document was required to substantiate his allegiance to his new master, nor his new master's title to ownership. Despite genealogy, each was in his way a thoroughbred.

CHAPTER XIII

SUNDOWN, VAQUERO

The strenuous days of the round-up were over. Bands of riders departed for their distant ranches leaving a few of their number to ride line and incidentally to keep a vigilant eye On the sheep-camps.

David Loring, realizing that he had been checkmated in the first move of the game in which cattle and sheep were the pawns and cowboys and herders the castles, knights, and, stretching the metaphor a bit, bishops, tacitly admitted defeat and employed a diagonal to draw the cattle-men's forces elsewhere. He determined to locate on the abandoned water-hole ranch, homestead it, and, by so doing, cut off the supply of water necessary to the cattle on the west side of the Concho River. This would be entering the enemy's territory with a vengeance, yet there was no law prohibiting his homesteading the ranch, the title of which had reverted to the Government. Too shrewd to risk legal entanglement by placing one of his employees on the homestead, he decided to have his daughter file application, and nothing forbade her employing whom she chose to do the necessary work to prove up. The plan appealed to the girl for various reasons, one of which was that she might, by her presence, avert the long-threatened war between the two factions.

Sundown and, indirectly, Fadeaway precipitated the impending trouble. Fadeaway, riding for the Blue, was left with a companion to ride line on the mesas. Sundown, although very much unlike Othello, found that his occupation was gone. Assistant cooks were a drug on the range. He was equipped with a better horse, a rope, quirt, slicker, and instructions to cover daily a strip of territory between the Concho and the sheep-camps. He became in fact an itinerant patrol, his mere physical presence on the line being all that was required of him.

It was the Senora Loring who drove to the Concho one morning and was welcomed by Corliss to whom she gave the little sack of gold. She told him all that he wished to know in regard to his brother Will, pleading for him with motherly gentleness. Corliss assured her that he felt no anger toward his brother, but rather solicitude, and made her happy by his generous attitude toward the wrongdoer. He had already heard that his brother had driven to Antelope and taken the train for the West. His great regret was that Will had not written to him or come to him directly, instead of leaving to the good Senora the task of explanation. "Never figured that repenting by proxy was the best plan," he told the Senora. "But he couldn't have chosen a better proxy." At which she smiled, and in departing blessed him in her sincere and simple manner, assuring him in turn that should the sheep and cattle ever come to an understanding—the Spanish for which embraced the larger aspect of the problem—there was nothing she desired or prayed for more than the friendship and presence of Corliss at the Loring hacienda. Corliss drew his own inference from this, which was a pleasant one. He felt that he had a friend at court, yet explained humorously that sheep and cattle were not by nature fitted to occupy the same territory. He was alive to sentiment, but more keen than ever to maintain his position unalterably so far as business was concerned. The Senora liked him none the less for this. To her he was a man who stood straight, on both feet, and faced the sun. Her daughter Nell . . . Ah, the big Juan Corliss has such a fine way with him . . . what a husband for any woman! In the mean time . . . only thoughts, hopes were possible . . . yet . . . manana . . . manana . . . there was always to-morrow that would be a brighter day.

To say that Sundown was proud of his unaccustomed regalia from the crown of his lofty Stetson to the soles of his high-heeled riding-boots, would be putting it mildly. To say that he was especially useful in his new calling as vaquero would not be to put it so mildly. Under the more or less profane tutelage of his companions, he learned to throw a rope after a fashion, taking the laughing sallies of his comrades good-naturedly. He persevered. He was forever stealing upon some maternal and unsuspicious cow and launching his rope at her with a wild shout—possibly as an anticipatory expression of fear in case his rope should fall true. More than once he had been yanked bodily from the saddle and had arisen to find himself minus rope, cow, and pony, for no self-respecting cow-horse could watch Sundown's unprecedented evolutions and not depart thitherward, feeling ashamed and grieved to think that he had ever lived to be a horse. And Sundown, despite his length of limb, seemed unbreakable. "He's the most durable rider on the range," remarked Hi Wingle, incident to one of his late assistant's meteoric departures from the saddle. "He wears good."

One morning as Sundown was jogging along, engaged chiefly in watching his shadow bob up and down across the wavering bunch-grass, he saw that which appeared to be the back of a cow just over a rise. He walked his horse to the rise and for some fantastic reason decided to rope the cow. He swung his rope. It fell true—in fact, too true, for it encircled the animal's neck and looped tight just where the neck joins the shoulders. He took a turn of the rope around the saddle horn. At last he had mastered the knack of the thing! Why, it was as easy as rolling pie-crust! He was about to wonder what he was going to do next, when the cow—which happened to be a large and active steer—humped itself and departed for realms unknown.

With the perversity of inanimate objects the rope flipped in a loop around Sundown's foot. The horse bucked, just once, and Sundown was launched on a new and promising career. The ground shot beneath him. He clutched wildly at the bunch-grass, secured some, and took it along with him. Chance, who always accompanied Sundown, raced alongside, enjoying the novelty of the thing. He barked and then shot ahead, nipping at the steer's heels, and this did not add to his master's prospects of ultimate survival. Sundown shouted for help when he could, which was not often. Startled prairie-dogs disappeared in their holes as the mad trio shot past. The steer, becoming warmed up to his work, paid little attention to direction and much to speed. That a band of sheep were grazing ahead made no difference to the charging steer. He plunged into the band. Sundown dimly saw a sea of sheep surge around him and break in storm-tossed waves of wool on either side. He heard some one shout. Then he fainted.

When he again beheld the sun, a girl was kneeling beside him, a girl with dark, troubled eyes. She offered him wine from a wicker jug. He drank and felt better.

"Are you hurt badly?" she asked.

"Am—I—all here?" queried Sundown.

"I guess so. You seem to be."

"Was anybody else killed in the wreck?"

Henry Hubert Knibbs

The girl smiled. "You're feeling better. Let me help you to sit up."

Sundown for the moment felt disinclined to move. He was in fact pretty thoroughly used up. "Say, did he win?" he queried finally.

"Who?"

"Me dog, Chance. I got the start at first, but he kind of got ahead for a spell."

"I don't know. Chance is right behind you. He's out of breath."

"Huh! Reckon I'm out more'n that. He's in luck this trip."

"How did it happen?"

"That's what I'm wonderin', lady. And say, would you be so kind as to tell me which way is north?"

Despite her solicitude for the recumbent Sundown, Eleanor Loring laughed. "You are in one of the sheep-camps. I'm Eleanor Loring."

"Sheep-camp? Gee Gosh! Did you stop me?"

"Yes. I was just riding into camp when you—er—arrived. I headed the steer back and Fernando cut the rope."

"Thanks, miss. And Fernando is wise to his business, all right."

"Can you sit up now?" she asked.

"Ow! I guess I can. That part of me wasn't expectin' to be moved sudden-like. How'd I get under these trees?"

"Fernando carried you."

"Well, little old Fernando is some carrier. Where is he? I wouldn't mind shakin' hands with that gent."

"He's out after the sheep. The steer stampeded them."

"Well, miss, speakin' from me heart—that there steer was no lady. I thought she was till I roped him. I was mistook serious."

"He might have killed you. Let me help you up."

Sundown had been endeavoring to get to his feet. Finally he rose and leaned against a tree. Fortunately for him his course had been over a stretch of yielding bunch-grass, and not, as might have been the case, over the ragged tufa. As it was his shirt hung from his back in shreds, and he felt that his overalls were not all that their name implied. The numbness of his abrasions and bruises was wearing off. The pain quickened his senses. He realized that his hat was missing, that one spur was gone and the other was half-way up his leg. He was not pleased with his appearance, and determined to "make a slope" as gracefully and as quickly as circumstances would permit.

Chance, gnawing at a burr that had stuck between his toes, saw his master rise. He leaped toward Sundown and stood waiting for more fun.

"Chance seems all right now," said the girl, patting the dog's head.

"John Corliss give him to me, miss. He's my dog now. Yes, he's active all right, 'specially chasin' steers."

"I remember you. You're the man that carried Chance up the canon trail that day when he was hurt."

"Yes, miss. He ain't forgettin' either."

The girl studied Sundown's lean face as he gazed across the mesas, wondering how he was going to make his exit without calling undue attention to his dearth of raiment. She had heard that this man, this queer, ungainly outlander, had been companion to Will Corliss. She had also heard that Sundown had been injured when the robbery occurred. Pensively she drew her empty gauntlet through her fingers.

"Do you know who took the money—that night?" she asked suddenly, and Sundown straightened and gazed at her.

He blinked and coughed. "Bein' no hand to lie to a lady, I do," he said, simply. "But I can't tell, even if you did save me life from that there steer."

She bit her lips, and nodded. "I didn't really mean to ask. I was curious to know. Won't you take my horse? You can send him back to-morrow."

"And you beat it home afoot? Say, lady, I mebby been a Bo onct, but I ain't hurt that bad. If I can't find me trail back to where I started from, it won't be because it ain't there. Thanks, jest the same."

Sundown essayed a step, halted and groaned. He felt of himself gingerly. He did not seem to be injured in any special place, as he ached equally all over. "I'll be goin', lady. I say thanks for savin' me life."

The girl smiled and nodded. "Will you please tell Mr. Corliss that I should like to see him, to-morrow, at Fernando's camp? I think he'll understand."

"Sure, miss! I'll tell him. That Fernando man looks to be havin' some trouble with them sheep."

The girl glanced toward the mesa. Fernando and his assistant were herding the sheep closer, and despite their activity were really getting the frightened animals bunched well. When she turned again Sundown had disappeared.

Sundown's arrival in camp, on foot, was not altogether unexpected. One of the men had seen a riderless horse grazing on the mesa, and had ridden out and caught it. Circumstantial evidence—rider and rope missing—confirmed Hi Wingle's remark that "that there walkin' clothes-pin has probably roped somethin' at last." And the "walking clothes-pin's" condition when he appeared seemed to substantiate the cook's theory.

"Lose your rope?" queried Wingle as Sundown limped up.

"Uhuh. And that ain't all. You ain't got a pair of pants that ain't working have you?"

Wingle smiled. "Pants? Think this here's a Jew clothin'-store?"

"Nope. But if she was a horsepital now—"

"Been visitin'?"

"Uhuh. I jest run over to see some friends of mine in a sheep-camp."

"Did, eh? And mebby you can tell me what you run over?"

"'Most everything out there," said Sundown, pointing to the mesa. "Say, you ain't got any of that plaster like they put on a guy's head when he gets hit with a brick?"

"Nope. But I got salt."

"And pepper," concluded Sundown with some sarcasm. "Mebby I do look like a barbecue."

"Straight, Sun, salt and water is mighty healin'. You better ride over to the Concho and get fixed up."

"Reckon that ain't no dream, Hi. Got to see the boss, anyhow."

"Well, 'anyhow' is correc'. And, say, you want to see him first and tell him it's you. Your hoss is tied over there. Sinker fetched him in."

"Hoss? Oh, yes, hoss! My hoss! Uhuh!"

With this somewhat ambiguous string of ejaculations Sundown limped toward the pony. He turned when halfway there and called to Wingle. "The cattle business is fine, Hi, fine, but between you and me I reckon I'll invest in sheep. A fella is like to live longer."

Wingle stared gravely at the tall and tattered figure. He stared gravely, but inwardly he shook with laughter. "Say, Sun!" he managed to exclaim finally, "that there Nell Loring is a right fine gal, ain't she?"

"You bet!"

"And Jack ain't the worst . . ." Wingle spat and chewed ruminatively. "No, he ain't the worst," he asserted again.

"I dunno what that's got to do with gettin' drug sixteen mile," said Sundown. "But, anyhow, you're right."

CHAPTER XIV

ON THE TRAIL TO THE BLUE

In the shade of the forest that edged the mesa, and just back of Fernando's camp, a Ranger trail cuts through a patch of quaking-asp and meanders through the heavy-timbered land toward the Blue range, a spruce-clad ridge of southern hills. Close to the trail two saddle horses were tied.

Fadeaway, riding toward his home ranch on the "Blue," reined up, eyed the horses, and grinned. One of them was Chinook, the other Eleanor Loring's black-and-white pinto, Challenge. The cowboy bent in his saddle and peered through the aspens toward the sheep-camp. He saw Corliss and Nell Loring standing close together, evidently discussing something of more than usual import, for at that moment John Corliss had raised his broad Stetson as though bidding farewell to the girl, but she had caught his arm as he turned and was clinging to him. Her attitude was that of one supplicating, coaxing, imploring. Fadeaway, with a vicious twist to his mouth, spat. "The cattle business and the sheep business looks like they was goin' into partnership," he muttered. "Leave it to a woman to fool a man every time. And him pertendin' to be all for the long-horns!" He saw the girl turn from Corliss, bury her face in her arms, and lean against the tree beneath which they were standing. Fadeaway grinned. "Women are all crooked, when they want to be," he remarked,—"or any I ever knowed. If they can't work a guy by talkin' and lovin', then they take to cryin'."

Just then Corliss stepped to the girl and put his hand on her shoulder. Again she turned to him. He took her hands and held them while he talked. Fadeaway could see her lips move, evidently in reply. He could not hear what was being said, as his horse was restless, fretting and stamping. The saddle creaked. Fadeaway jerked the horse up, and in the momentary silence he caught the word "love."

"Makes me sick!" he said, spurring forward. "'Love,' eh? Well, mebby my little idea of puttin' Billy Corliss in wrong didn't work, but I'll hand Jack a jolt that'll make him think of somethin' else besides love, one of these fine mornin's!" And the cowboy rode on, out of tune with the peace and beauty of his surroundings, his whole being centered upon making trouble for a man who he knew in his heart wished him no ill, and in fact had all but forgotten him so far as considering him either as an enemy or a friend.

Just as he was about to swing out to the open of the mesa near the edge of the canon, he came upon a Mexican boy asleep beneath the low branches of a spruce. Fadeaway glanced across the mesa and, as he had expected, saw a band of sheep grazing in the sunshine. His trail ran directly toward the sheep. Beyond lay the canon. He would not ride around a herd of sheep that blocked his trail, not if he knew it! As he drew nearer the sheep they bunched, forcing those ahead to move on. Fadeaway glanced back at the sleeping boy, then set spur to his horse and waved his sombrero. The sheep broke into a trot. He rode back and forth behind them forcing them toward the canon. He beat upon his rolled slicker with his quirt. The sound frenzied the sheep and they leaped forward. Lambs, trailing behind, called dolefully to the plunging ewes that trampled each other in their terror. Again the cowboy glanced back. No one was in sight. He wondered, for an instant, what had become of Fernando, for he knew it was Fernando's herd. He shortened rein and spurred his pony, making him rear. The sheep plunged ahead, those in front swerving as they came to the canon's brink. The crowding mass behind forced them on. Fadeaway reined up. A great gray wave rolled over the cliff and disappeared into the soundless chasm. A thousand feet below lay the mangled carcasses of some five hundred sheep and lambs. A scattered few of the band had turned and were trotting aimlessly along the edge of the mesa. They separated as the rider swept up. One terror-stricken lamb, bleating piteously, hesitated on the very edge of the chasm. Fadeaway swung his hat and laughed as the little creature reared and leaped out into space. There had been but little noise—an occasional frightened bleat, a drumming of hoofs on the mesa, and they were swept from sight.

Fadeaway reined around and took a direct line for the nearest timber. Halfway across the open he saw the Mexican boy running toward him. He leaned forward in the saddle and hung his spurs in his pony's sides. A quick beat of hoofs and he was within the shadow of the forest. The next thing was to avoid pursuit. He changed his course and rode toward the heart of the forest. He would take an old and untraveled bridle-trail to the Blue. He was riding in a rocky hollow when he thought he heard the creak of saddle-leather. He glanced back. No one was following him. Farther on he stopped. He was certain that he had again heard the sound. As he topped the rise he saw Corliss riding toward him. The rancher had evidently swung from the Concho trail and was making his way directly toward the unused trail which Fadeaway rode. The cowboy became doubly alert. He shifted a little in the saddle, sitting straight, his right hand resting easily on his hip. Corliss drew rein and they faced each other. There was something about the rancher's grim, silent attitude that warned Fadeaway.

Yet he grinned and waved a greeting. "How!" he said, as though he were meeting an old friend.

Corliss nodded briefly. He sat gazing at Fadeaway with an unreadable expression.

"Got the lock-jaw?" queried Fadeaway, his pretended heartiness vanishing.

Corliss allowed himself to smile, a very little. "You better ride back with me," he said, quietly.

Fadeaway laughed. "I'm takin' orders from the Blue, these days," he said. "Mebby you forgot."

"No, I haven't."

"And I'm headed for the Blue," continued the cowboy. "Goin' my way?"

"You're on the wrong trail," asserted Corliss. "You've been riding the wrong trail ever since you left the Concho."

"Uhuh. Well, I been keepin' clear of the sheep camps, at that."

"Don't know about that," said Corliss, easily.

Fadeaway was too shrewd to have recourse to his gun. He knew that Corliss was the quicker man, and he realized that, even should he get the better of a six-gun argument, the ultimate result would be outlawry and perhaps death. He wanted to get away from that steady, heart-searching gaze that held him.

"Sheep business is lookin' up," he said, with an attempt at jocularity.

"We'll ride back and have a talk with Loring," said Corliss. "Some one put a band of his sheep into the canon, not two hours ago. Maybe you know something about it."

"Me? What you dreaming anyhow?"

"I'm not. It looks like your work."

"So you're tryin' to hang somethin' onto me, eh? Well, you want to call around early—you're late."

"No, I'm the first one on the job. Did you stampede Loring's sheep?"

"Did I stampede the love-makin'?" sneered Fadeaway.

Corliss shortened rein and drew close to the cowboy.

"Just explain that," he said.

"Oh, I don' know. You the boss of creation?"

Corliss's lips hardened. He let his quirt slip butt-first through his hand and grasped the lash. Fadeaway's hand slipped to his holster. Before he could pull his gun, Corliss swung the quirt. The blow caught Fadeaway just below the brim of his hat. He wavered and grabbed at the saddle-horn. As Corliss again swung his quirt, the cowboy jerked out his gun and brought it down on the rancher's head. Corliss dropped from the saddle. Fadeaway rode around and covered him. Corliss's hat lay a few feet from where he had fallen. Beneath his head a dark ooze spread a hand's-breadth on the trail. The cowboy dismounted and bent over him. "He's sportin' a dam' good hat," he said, "or that would 'a' fixed *him*. Guess he'll be good for a spell." Then he reached for his stirrup, mounted, and loped up the trail.

Old Fernando, having excused himself on some pretext when Corliss rode into the camp that morning, returned to find Corliss gone and Nell Loring strangely grave and white. She nodded as he spoke to her and pointed toward the mesa. "Carlos—is out—looking for the sheep," she said, her lips trembling. "He says some one stampeded them—run them into the canon."

Fernando called upon his saints and cursed himself for his negligence in leaving his son with the sheep. Nell Loring spoke to him quietly, assuring him that she understood why he had absented himself. "It's my fault, Fernando, not yours. The patron will want to know why you were away. You will tell him that John Corliss came to your camp; that you thought I wanted to talk with him alone. Then he will know that it was my fault. I'll tell him when I get back to the rancho."

Fernando straightened his wizened frame. "Si! As the Senorita says, I shall do. But first I go to look. Perhaps the patron shall not know that the vaquero Corlees was here this morning. It is that I ask the Senorita to say nothing to the patron until I look. Is it that you will do this?"

"What can you do?" she asked.

"It is yet to know. Adios, Senorita. You will remember the old Fernando, perhaps?"

"But you're coming back! Oh! it was terrible!" she cried. "I rode to the canon and looked down."

Fernando meanwhile had been thinking rapidly. With quaint dignity he excused himself as he departed to catch up one of the burros, which he saddled and rode out to where his son was standing near the canon. The boy shrank from him as he accosted him. Fernando's deep-set eyes blazed forth the anger that his lips imprisoned. He sent the boy back to the camp. Then he picked up the tracks of a horseman on the mesa, followed them to the canon's brink, glanced down, shrugged his shoulders, and again took up the horseman's trail toward the forest. With the true instinct of the outlander, he reasoned that the horseman had headed for the old trail to the Blue, as the tracks led diagonally toward the south. Finally he realized that he could never overtake the rider by following the tracks, so he dismounted and tied his burro. He struck toward the canon. A mile above him there was a ford. He would wait there and see who came. He made his perilous way down a notch in the cliff, dropped slowly to the level of the stream, and followed it to the ford. He searched for tracks in the sun-baked mud. With a sigh of satisfaction, perhaps of anticipation, he stepped to a clump of cotton-woods down the stream and backed within them. Scarcely had he crossed himself and drawn his gun from its weather-blackened holster, when he heard the click of shod hoofs on the trail. He stiffened and his eyes gleamed as though he anticipated some pleasant prospect. The creases at the corners of his eyes deepened as he recognized in the rider the vaquero who had set the Concho dog upon his sheep some months before. He had a score to settle with that vaquero for having shot at him. He had another and larger score to settle with him for—no, he would not think of his beloved sheep mangled and dead at the bottom of the canon. That would anger him and make his hand unsteady.

Fadeaway rode his horse into the ford and sat looking

downstream as the horse drank. Just as he drew rein, the old herder imitated with perfect intonation the quavering bleat of a lamb calling to its mother. Fadeaway jerked straight in the saddle. A ball of smoke puffed from the cottonwoods. The cowboy doubled up and slid headforemost into the stream. The horse, startled by the lunge of its rider, leaped to the bank and raced up the trail. A diminishing echo ran along the canon walls and rolled away to distant, faint muttering. Old Fernando had paid his debt of vengeance.

Leisurely he broke a twig from the cottonwoods, tore a strip from his bandanna, and cleaned his gun. Then he retraced his steps to the burro, mounted, and rode directly to his camp. After he had eaten he told his son to pack their few belongings. Then he again mounted the burro and rode toward the hacienda to face the fury of the patron.

He had for a moment left the flock in charge of his son. He had returned to find all but a few of the sheep gone. He had tracked them to the canon brink. Ah! could the patron have seen them, lying mangled upon the rocks! It had been a long hard climb to the bottom of the canon, else he should have reported sooner. Some one had driven the sheep into the chasm. As to the man who did it, he knew nothing. There were tracks of a horse—that was all. He had come to report and receive his dismissal. Never again should he see the Senora Loring. He had been the patron's faithful servant for many years. He was disgraced, and would be dismissed for negligence.

So he soliloquized as he rode, yet he was not altogether unhappy. He had avenged insult and the killing of his beloved sheep with one little crook of his finger; a thing that his patron, brave as he was, would not dare do. He would return to New Mexico. It was well!

CHAPTER XV

THEY KILLED THE BOSS!

Sundown, much to his dismay, was lost. With a sack of salt tied across his saddle, he had ridden out that morning to fill one of the salt-logs near a spring where the cattle came to drink. He had found the log, filled it, and had turned to retrace his journey when a flock of wild turkeys strung out across his course. His horse, from which the riders of the Concho had aforetime shot turkeys, broke into a kind of reminiscent lope, which quickened as the turkeys wheeled and ran swiftly through the timberland. Sundown clung to the saddle-horn as the pony took fallen logs at top speed. The turkeys made for a rim of a narrow canon and from it sailed off into space, leaving Chance a disconsolate spectator and Sundown sitting his horse and thanking the Arizona stars that his steed was not equipped with wings. It was then that he realized that the Concho ranch might be in any one of the four directions he chose to take. He wheeled the horse, slackened rein, and allowed that sagacious but apparently disinterested animal to pick its leisurely way through the forest. Chance trotted sullenly behind. He could have told his master something about hunting turkeys had he been able to speak, and, judging from the dog's dejected stride and expression, speech would have been a relief to his feelings.

The horse, nipping at scant shoots of bunch-grass and the blue-flowered patches of wild peas, gravitated toward the old trail to the Blue and, once upon it, turned toward home. Chance, refreshing his memory of the old trail, ran ahead, pausing at this fallen log and that fungus-spotted stump to investigate squirrel-holes with much sniffing and circling of the immediate territory. Sundown imagined that Chance was leading the way toward home, though in reality the dog was merely killing time, so to speak, while the pony plodded deliberately down the homeward trail.

Dawdling along in the barred sunshine, at peace with himself and the pleasant solitudes, Sundown relaxed and fell to dreaming of Andalusian castles builded in far forests of the south, and of some Spanish Penelope—possibly not unlike the Senorita Loring—who waited his coming with patient tears and rare fidelity. "Them there true-be-doors," he muttered, "like Billy used to say, sure had the glad job—singin' and wrastlin' out po'try galore! A singin'-man sure gets the ladies. Now if I was to take on a little weight—mebby . . ." His weird soliloquy was broken by a sharp and excited bark. Chance was standing in the trail, and beyond him there was something . . .

Sundown, anticipating more turkeys, slid from his horse without delay. He stalked stealthily toward the quivering dog. Then, dropping the reins, he ran to Corliss, knelt beside him, and lifted his head. He called to him. He ripped the rancher's shirt open and felt over his heart. "They killed me boss! They killed me boss!" he wailed, rising and striding back and forth in impotent excitement and grief. He did not know where to look for water. He did not know what to do. A sudden fury at his helplessness overcame him, and he mounted and rode down the trail at a wild gallop. Fortunately he was headed in the right direction.

Henry Hubert Knibbs

Wingle, Bud Shoop, and several of the men were holding a heated conference with old man Loring when Sundown dashed into the Concho. Trembling with rage and fear he leaped from his horse.

"They killed the boss!" he cried hoarsely. "Up there—in the woods."

"Killed who? Where? Slow down and talk easy! Who's killed?" volleyed the group.

"Me boss! Up there on the trail with his head bashed in! Chance and me found him layin' on the trail."

The men swung to their saddles. "Better come along, Loring," said Shoop, riding close to the old sheep-man. "Looks like they was more 'n one side to this deal. And you, too, Sun."

The riders, led by the gesticulating and excited Sundown, swung out to the road and crossed to the forest. Shoop and Hi Wingle spurred ahead while the others questioned Sundown, following easily. When they arrived at the scene of the fight, Corliss was sitting propped against a tree with Shoop and Wangle on either side of him. Corliss stared stupidly at the men.

"Who done it?" asked Wingle.

"Fadeaway," murmured the rancher.

Loring, in the rear of the group, laughed ironically.

Shoop's gun jumped from its holster and covered the sheep-man. "If one of your lousy herders done this, he'll graze clost to hell to-night with the rest of your dam' sheep!" he cried.

"Easy, Bud!" cautioned Wingle. "The boss ain't passed over yet. Bill, you help Sinker here get the boss back home. The rest of you boys hit the trail for the Blue. Fadeaway is like to be up in that country."

"Ante up, Loring!" said Shoop, mounting his horse. "I'll see your hand if it takes every chip in the stack."

"Here, too!" chorused the riders. "We're all in on this."

They trailed along in single file until they came to the ford. They reined up sharply. One of them dismounted and dragged the body of Fadeaway to the bank. They grouped around gazing at the hole in Fadeaway's shirt.

Shoop turned the body over. "Got it from in front," he said, which was obvious to their experienced eyes.

"And it took a fast gun to get him," asserted Loring.

The men were silent, each visualizing his own theory of the fight on the trail and the killing of Fadeaway.

"Jack was layin' a long way from here," said Wingle.

"When you found him," commented Loring.

"Only one hoss crossed the ford this morning," announced Shoop, wading across the stream.

"And Fade got it from in front," commented a puncher. "His tracks is headed for the Blue."

Again the men were silent. Shoop rolled a cigarette. The splutter of the sulphur-match, as it burned from blue to yellow, startled them. They relaxed, cursing off their nervous tension in monosyllables.

"Well, Fade's played his stack, and lost. Jack was sure in the game, but how far—I dunno. Reckon that's got anything to do with stampedin' your sheep?" asked Wingle, turning to Loring.

Loring's deep-set eyes flashed. "Fernando reported that a Concho rider done the job. He didn't say who done it."

"Didn't, eh? And did Fernando say anything about doin' a job himself?" asked Shoop.

"If you're tryin' to hang this onto any of my herders, you're ridin' on the wrong side of the river. I reckon you won't have to look far for the gun that got *him*." And Loring gestured toward the body.

Hi Wingle stooped and pulled Fadeaway's gun from its holster. He spun the cylinder, swung it out, and invited general inspection. "Fade never had a chance," he said, lowering the gun. "They's six pills in her yet. You got to show me he wasn't plugged from behind a rock or them bushes." And Wingle pointed toward the cottonwoods.

One of the men rode down the canon, searching for tracks. Chance, following, circled the bushes, and suddenly set off toward the north.

Sundown, who had been watching him, dismounted his horse. "Chance, there, mebby he's found somethin'."

"Well, he's your dog. Go ahead if you like. Mebby Chance struck a scent."

"Coyote or lion," said Wingle. "They ain't no trail down

them rocks."

Sundown, following Chance, disappeared in the canon. The men covered Fadeaway's body with a slicker and weighted it with stones. Then they sent a puncher to Antelope to notify the sheriff.

As they rode into the Concho, they saw that Corliss's horse was in the corral. Their first anger had cooled, yet they gazed sullenly at Loring. They were dissatisfied with his interpretation of the killing and not a little puzzled.

"Where's Fernando?" queried Shoop aggressively.

Loring put the question aside with a wave of his hand. "Jest a minute afore I go. You're tryin' to hang this onto me or mine. You're wrong. You're forgettin' they's five hundred of my sheep at the bottom of the Concho Canon, I guess. They didn't get there by themselves. Fadeaway's got his, which was comin' to him this long time. That's nothin' to me. What I want to see is Jack Corliss's gun."

Bud Shoop stepped into the ranch-house and presently returned with the Coitus. "Here she is. Take a look."

The old sheep-man swung out the cylinder and pointed with a gnarled and horny finger. The men closed in and gazed in silence. One of the shells was empty.

Loring handed the gun to Shoop. "I'll ask Jack," said the foreman. When he returned to the group he was unusually grave. "Says he plugged a coyote this mornin'."

Loring's seamed and weathered face was expressionless. "Well, he did a good job, if I do say it," he remarked, as though to himself.

Henry Hubert Knibbs

"Which?" queried Shoop.

"I don't say," replied Loring. "I'm lettin' the evidence do the talkin'."

"Well, you'll hear her holler before we get through!" asserted the irrepressible Bud. "Fade, mebby, wa'n't no lady's man, but he had sand. He was a puncher from the ground up, and we ain't forgettin' that!"

"And I ain't forgettin' them five hundred sheep." Loring reined around. "And you're goin' to hear from me right soon. I reckon they's law in this country."

"Let her come!" retorted Shoop. "We'll all be here!"

CHAPTER XVI

SUNDOWN ADVENTURES

By dint of perilous scrambling Sundown managed to keep within sight of Chance, who had picked up Fernando's tracks leading from the cottonwoods. The dog leaped over rocks and trotted along the levels, sniffing until he came to the rift in the canon wall down which the herder had toiled on his grewsome errand. Chance climbed the sharp ascent with clawing reaches of his powerful forelegs and quick thrusts of his muscular haunches. Sundown followed as best he could. He was keyed to the strenuous task by that spurious by-product of anticipation frequently termed a "hunch."

When the dog at last reached the edge of the timber and dashed into Fernando's deserted camp, Sundown was puzzled until he happened to recall the incidents leading to Fadeaway's discharge from the Concho. He reclined beneath a tree familiar to him as a former basis for recuperation. He felt of himself reminiscently while watching Chance nose about the camp. Presently the dog came and, squatting on his haunches, faced his master with the query, "What next?" scintillating in his glowing eyes.

"I dunno," replied Sundown. "You see, pardner, this here's Fernando's camp all right. Now, I ain't got nothin' ag'in' that

Henry Hubert Knibbs

little ole Fernando man, 'specially as it was him cut the rope that was snakin' me to glory onct. I ain't got nothin' ag'in' him, or nobody. Mebby Fade did set after them sheep. Mebby Fernando knows it and sets after him. Mebby he squats in them cotton-woods by the ford and 'Pom!' goes somethin' and pore Fadeaway sure makes his name good. Never did like him, but I ain't got nothin' ag'in' him now. You see, Chance, he's quit bein' mean, now. And say, gettin' killed ain't no dream. I been there three, four times myself— all but the singin'. Two wrecks, one shootin', and one can o' beans that was sick. It sure ain't no fun. Wonder if gettin' killed that way will square Fade with the Big Boss over there? I reckon not. 'T ain't what a fella gets done to him that counts. It's what he does to the other guy, good or bad. Now, take them martyrs what my pal Billy used to talk about. They was always standin' 'round gettin' burned and punctured with arrers, and lengthened out and shortened up when they ought to been takin' boxin' lessons or sords or somethin'. Huh! I never took much stock in them. If it's what a fella gets *done* to him, it's easy money I'll be takin' tickets at the gate instead of crawlin' under the canvas—and mebby tryin' to sneak you in, too—eh, Chance?"

To all of which the great wolf-dog listened with exemplary patience. He would have preferred action, but not unlike many human beings who strive to appear profound under a broadside of philosophical eloquence, applauding each bursting shrapnel of platitudes by mentally wagging their tails, Chance wagged his tail, impressed more by the detonation than the substance. And Chance was quite a superior dog, as dogs go.

When Sundown finally arrived at the Concho, he was met by Bud Shoop, who questioned him. Sundown gave a detailed account of his recent exploration.

"You say they was no burros at the camp—no tarp, or grub, or nothin'?"

"Nope. Nothin' but a dead fire," replied Sundown.

"Any sheep?"

"Mebby four or five. Didn't count 'em."

"Huh! Wonder where the rest of the greaser's herd is grazin'?"

"I dunno. I rode straight acrost to here."

"Looks mighty queer to me," commented the foreman. "I take it that Fernando's lit out."

"Will they pinch the boss?" queried Sundown.

"I don' know. Anyhow, they can't prove it on him. Even if Jack did—and I don't mind sayin' it to you—plug Fade, he did it to keep from gettin' plugged hisself. Do you reckon I'd let any fella chloroform me with the butt of a .45 and not turn loose? I tell you, if Jack had been a-goin' to get Fade *right*, you'd 'a' found 'em closter together. And that ain't all. If Jack had wanted to get Fade, you can bet he wouldn't got walloped on the head first. The gun that got Fade weren't packed by a puncher."

"Will they be any more shootin'?" queried Sundown.

"Gettin' cold feet, Sun?"

"Nope. But say, it ain't no fun to get shot up. It don't feel good and it's like to make a guy cross. A guy can't make pie or eat pie all shot up, nohow."

"Pie? You sure are loco. What you tryin' to rope now?"

"Nothin'. But onct I was in the repair shop with two docs explorin' me works with them there shiny little corkscrews, lookin' for a bullit that Clammie-the-dip let into me system— me bein' mistook for another friend of his by mistake. After the docs dug up the bullit they says, 'Anything you want to say?'—expectin' me to pass over, I reckon. 'There is,' says I. 'I want to say that I ain't et nothin' sense the day before Clammie done me dirt. An' if I'm goin' to hit the slide I jest as soon hit it full of pie as empty.' And them docs commenced to laugh. 'Let him have it,' says one. 'But don't you reckon ice-cream would be less apt to—er—hasten— the—er—' jest like that. 'Pussuble you're correct' says the other.'" Sundown scratched his ear. "And I et the ice-cream, feelin' kind o' sad-like seein' it wasn't pie. You see, Bud, gettin' shot up is kind of disconvenient."

"Well, you're the limit!" exclaimed Shoop. "Say, the boss wants to make a few talks to you to-morrow. Told me to tell you when you come back. You better go feed up. As I recollec' Hi's wrastlin' out some pie-dough right now."

"Well, I ain't takin' no chances, Bud."

"You tell that to Hi and see what he says."

"Nope. 'T ain't necessary. You see when them docs seen, about a week after, that I was comin' strong instead of goin', they says, 'Me man, if you'd 'a' had pie in your stummick when you was shot, you wouldn't be here to-day. You'd be planted—or somethin' similar. The fac' that your stummick was empty evidentially saved your life.' And," concluded Sundown, "they's no use temptin' Providence now."

Shortly after breakfast next morning Corliss sent for

Sundown. The rancher sat propped up in a wide armchair. He was pale, but his eyes were clear and steady.

"Bud told me about yesterday," he began, anticipating Sundown's leisurely and erratic recital. "I understand you found me on the trail and went for help."

"Yes. I thought you was needin' some about then."

"How did you come to find me?"

"Got lost. Hoss he took me there."

"Did you see any one on the trail?"

"Nope."

"Hear any shooting?"

"Nope. But I seen some turkeys."

"Well, I expect the sheriff will be here tomorrow. He'll want to talk to you. Answer him straight. Don't try to help me in any way. Just tell him what you know—not what you think."

"I sure will, boss. Wish Chance could talk. He could tell."

Corliss smiled faintly. "Yes, I suppose he could. You followed him to Fernando's camp?"

"Uhuh."

"All right. Now, I've had a talk with Bud about something that has been bothering me. I think I can trust you. I want you to ride to Antelope to-morrow morning and give a letter from me to the lawyer there, Kennedy. He'll tell you what to do after that. I don't feel like talking much, but I'll say this: You remember the water-hole ranch. Well, I want you to file application to homestead it. Kennedy will tell you what to do. Don't ask any questions, but do as he says. You'll have to go to Usher by train and he'll go with you. You won't lose anything by it."

"Me? Homestead? Huh! And have cows and pigs and things? I don't jest get you, boss, but what you say goes. Why, I'd homestead a ranch in hell and take chances on findin' water if you said it. Say, boss,"—and Sundown leaned toward Corliss confidentially and lowered his voice,—"I ain't what you'd call a nervy man, but say, I got somethin' jest as good. I—I—" and Sundown staggered around feeling for the word he wanted.

"I know. We'll look it up in the dictionary some day when we're in town. Here's ten dollars for your trip. If you need more, Kennedy will give it to you."

Sundown departed, thrilled with the thought that his employer had placed so much confidence in him. He wanted to write a poem, but circumstances forbade his signaling to his muse. On his way to the bunk-house he hesitated and retraced his steps to the ranch office. Corliss told him to come in. He approached his employer deferentially as though about to ask a favor.

"Say, boss," he began, "they's two things just hit me to onct. Can I take Chance with me?"

"If you like. Part of your trip will be on the train."

"I can fix that. Then I was thinkin': No! my hoss is lame. I got to ride a strange hoss, which I'm gettin' kind o' used to. But if you'll keep your eye on my hoss while I'm gone, it'll ease me mind considerable. You see he's been with me reg'lar and ain't learned no bad tricks. If the boys know I'm gone and get to learnin' him about buckin' and bitin' the arm offen a guy and kickin' a guy's head off and rollin' on him, and rarin' up and stompin' him, like some, they's no tellin' what might happen when I get back."

Corliss laughed outright. "That's so. But I guess the boys will be busy enough without monkeying with your cayuse. If you put that homestead deal through, you can have any horse on the range except Chinook. You'll need a team, anyway, when you go to ranching."

"Thanks, boss, but I'm gettin' kind of used to Pill."

"Pill? You mean Phil—Phil Sheridan. That's your horse's name."

"Mebby. I did try callin' him 'Phil.' It went all right when he was standin' quiet. But when he got to goin' I was lucky if I could holler just 'Whoa, Pill!' The 'h' got jarred loose every time. 'Course, bein' a puncher now,"—and Sundown threw out his chest,—"it's different. Anyhow, Pill is his name because there ain't anything a doc ever give a fella that can stir up your insides worse 'n he can when he takes a spell. Your head hurtin' much?"

"No. But it will be if you don't get out of here." And Corliss laughed and waved his hand toward the door.

CHAPTER XVII

THE STRANGER

Sundown, maintaining a mysterious and unusual silence, prepared to carry out his employer's plans. His preparations were not extensive. First, he polished his silver spurs. Then he borrowed a coat from one of the boys, brushed his Stetson, and with the business instinct of a Hebrew offered Hi Wingle nine dollars for a pair of Texas wing chaps. The cook, whose active riding-days were over, had no use for the chaps and would have gladly given them to Sundown. The latter's offer of nine dollars, however, interested Wingle. He decided to have a bit of fun with the tall one. He cared nothing for the money, but wondered why Sundown had offered nine dollars instead of ten.

"What you been eatin'?" he queried as Sundown made his bid. "Goin' courtin'?"

"Nope," replied the lean one. "Goin' east."

"Huh! Expect to ride all the way in them chaps?"

"Nope! But I need 'em. Heard you tell Bud you paid ten dollars for 'em 'way back fifteen years. Guess they's a dollar's worth worn off of 'em by now."

"Well, you sure do some close figurin'. I sure paid ten for 'em. Got 'em from a Chola puncher what was hard up. Mebby you ain't figurin' that they's about twenty bucks' worth of hand-worked silver conchas on 'em which ain't wore off any."

Sundown took this as Wingle's final word. The amused Hi noted the other's disappointment and determined to enhance the value of the chaps by making them difficult to obtain, then give them to his assistant. Wingle liked Sundown in a rough-shod way, though Sundown was a bit too serious-minded to appreciate the fact.

The cook assumed the air of one gravely concerned about his friend's mental balance. "Somethin' sure crawled into your roost, Sun, but if you're goin' crazy I suppose a pair of chaps won't make no difference either way. Anyhow, you ain't crazy in your legs—just your head."

"Thanks, Hi. It's accommodatin' of you to put me wise to myself. I know I ain't so durned smart as some."

"Say, you old fool, can't you take a fall to it that I'm joshin'? You sure are the melancholiest stretch of bones and hide I ever seen. Somehow you always make a fella come down to cases every time, with that sad-lookin' mug of yourn. You sure would 'a' made a good undertaker. I'll get them chaps."

And Wingle, fat, bald, and deliberate, chuckled as he dug among his belongings and brought forth the coveted riding apparel. "Them chaps has set on some good hosses, if I do say it," he remarked. "Take 'em and keep your nine bucks for life insurance. You'll need it."

Sundown grinned like a boy. "Nope. A bargain's a bargain. Here's the money. Mebby you could buy a fust-class cook-book with it and learn somethin'."

"Learn somethin'! Why, you long-geared, double-jointed, glass-eyed, hay-topped, star-smellin' st-st-steeple, you! Get out o' this afore I break my neck tryin' to see your face! Set down so I can look you in the eye!" And Wingle waved his stout arms and glowered in mock anger.

Sundown laid the money on the table. "Keep the change," he said mildly with a twinkle in his eye.

He picked up the chaps and stalked from the bunk-house. Chance, who had been an interested spectator of this lively exchange of compliment and merchandise, followed his master to the stable where Sundown at once put on the chaps and strutted for the dog's benefit, and his own. By degrees he was assuming the characteristics of a genuine cow-puncher. He would show the folks in Antelope what a rider for the Concho looked like.

The following morning, much earlier than necessary, he mounted and rode to the bunk-house, where Corliss gave him the letter and told him to leave the horse at the stables in Antelope until he returned from Usher.

Sundown, stiffened by the importance of his mission, rode straight up, looking neither to the right nor to the left until the Concho was far behind him. Then he slouched in the saddle, gazing with a pleased expression first at one leather-clad leg and then the other. For a time the wide, free glory of the Arizona morning mesas was forgotten. The shadow of his pony walked beside him as the low eastern sun burned across the golden levels. Long silhouettes of fantastic buttes spread across the plain. The sky was cloudless and the crisp thin air foretold a hot noon. The gaunt rider's face beamed with an inner light—the light of romance. What more could a man ask than a good horse, a faithful and intelligent dog, a mission of trust, and sixty undisturbed miles of wondrous upland o'er which to journey, fancy-free and clad in cowboy garb? Nothing more—except—and Sundown realized with a slight sensation of emptiness that he had forgotten to eat breakfast. He had plenty to eat in his saddle-bags, but he put the temptation to refresh himself aside as unworthy, for the nonce, of his higher self. Naturally the pent-up flood of verse that had been oppressing him of late surged up and filled his mind with vague and poignant fancies. His love for animals, despite his headlong experiences on the Concho, was unimpaired, so to speak. He patted the neck of the rangy roan which he bestrode, and settled himself to the serious task of expressing his inner-most being in verse. He dipped deep into the Pierian springs, and poesy broke forth. But not, however, until he had "cinched up," as he mentally termed it, the saddle of his Pegasus of the mesas.

Sundown paused and called the attention of his horse to the last line.

He hesitated, harking back for his climax. "Jing!" he exclaimed, "it's the durndest thing to put a finish on a piece of po'try! You get to goin' and she goes fine. Then you commence to feel that you're comin' to the end and nacherally you asks yourself what's the end goin' to be like. Fust thing you're stompin' around in your head upsettin' all that you writ tryin' to rope somethin' to put on the tail-end of the parade that'll show up strong. Kind o' like ropin' a steer. No tellin' where that pome is goin' to land you."

Sundown was more than pleased with himself. He again recited the verse as he plodded along, fixing it in his memory for the future edification of his compatriots of the Concho.

"The best thing I ever writ!" he assured himself. "Fust thing I

Henry Hubert Knibbs

know they'll be puttin' me in one of them doxologies for keeps. 'Sundown Slim, The Poet of the Mesas!' Sounds good to me. Reckon that's why I never seen a woman that I wanted to get married to. Writin' po'try kind of detracted me mind from love. Guess I could love a woman if she wouldn't laugh at me for bein' so dog-goned lengthy. She would have to be a small one, though, so as she'd be kind o' scared o' me bein' so big. Then mebby we could get along pretty good. 'Course, I wouldn't like her to be scared all the time, but jest kind o' respectable-like to me. Them's the best kind. Mebby I'll ketch one some day. Now there goes that Chance after a rabbit ag'in. He's a long piece off—jest can hardly see him except somethin' movin'. Well, if he comes back as quick as he went, he'll be here soon." And Sundown jogged along, spur-chains jingling a fairy tune to his oral soliloquies.

Aside from forgetting to have breakfast that morning, he had made a pretty fair beginning. He was well on his way, had composed a roan-colored lyric of the ranges, discoursed on the subject of love, and had set his spirit free to meander in the realms of imagination. Yet his spirit swept back to him with a rush of wings and a question. Why not get married? And "Gee! Gosh!" he ejaculated, startled by the abruptness of the thought. "Now I like hosses and dogs and folks, but livin' with hosses and dogs ain't like livin' with folks. If hosses and dogs take to you, they think you're the whole thing. But wimmen is different. If they take to you—why, they think they're the whole thing jest because they landed you. I dunno! Jest bein' good to folks ain't everything, either. But bein' good to hosses and dogs is. Funny. I dunno, though. You either got to understand 'em and be rough to 'em, or be good to 'em and then they understand you. Guess they ain't no regular guide-book on how to git along with wimmen. Well, I never come West for me health. I brung it with me, but I ain't goin' to take chances by fallin' in love. Writin' po'try is wearin' enough."

For a while he rode silently, enjoying his utter freedom. But followers of Romance must ever be minute-men, armed and equipped to answer her call with instant readiness and grace. Lacking, perhaps, the grace, nevertheless Sundown was loyal to his sovereign mistress, in proof of which he again sat straight in the saddle, stirred to speech by hidden voices. "Now, take it like I was wearin' a hard-boiled hat and a collar and buttin shoes, like the rest of them sports. Why, that wouldn't ketch the eye of some likely-lookin' lady wantin' to get married. Nix! When I hit town it's me for the big smoke and me picture on the front page, standin' with me faithful dog and a lot of them fat little babies without any clothes on, but wings, flyin' around the edge of me picture and down by me boots and up around me hat—and in big letters she'll say: 'Romance of A Cowboy. Western Cattle King in Search for his Long-lost Sweetheart. Sundown, once one of our Leading Hoboes, now a Wealthy Rancher, visits the Metrokolis on Mysterious Errand.' Huh! I guess mebby that wouldn't ketch a good one, mebby with money."

But the proverbial fly must appear in the equally proverbial amber. "'Bout as clost as them papers ever come to it," he soliloquized. "Anyhow, if she was the wrong one, and not me long-lost affiniky, and was to get stuck on me shape and these here chaps and spurs, reckon I could tell her that the papers made the big mistake, and that me Mexican wife does the cookin' with a bread-knife in her boot-leg, and that I never had no Mormon ideas, nohow. That ought to sound kind o' home-like, and let her down easy and gentle. I sure don't want to get sent down for breakin' the wimmen's hearts, so I got to be durned careful."

So immersed was he in his imaginings that he did not at once realize that his horse had stopped and was leisurely grazing at the edge of the trail. Chance, who had been running ahead, swung back in a wide circle and barked impatiently.

Sundown awakened to himself. "Here, you red hoss, this ain't no pie-contest. We got to hit the water-hole afore dark." Once more in motion, he reverted to his old theme, but with finality in his tone. "I guess mebby I can't tell them reporters somethin' about me hotel out here on the desert! 'The only prevailable road-house between Antelope and the Concho, run by the retired cattle-king, Sundown Slim.' Sounds good to me. Mebby I could work up a trade by advertisin' to some of them Eastern folks that eats nothin' tougher for breakfast than them quakin'-oats and buns and coffee. Get along, you red hoss."

About six o'clock that evening Sundown arrived at the deserted ranch. He unsaddled and led the horse to water. Then he picketed him for the night. Returning, he prepared a meal and ate heartily. Just as the light faded from the dusty windows, Chance, who was curled in a corner, rose and growled. Sundown strode to the door. The dog followed, sniffing along the crack. Presently Sundown heard the shuffling tread of a horse plodding through the sand. He swung open the door and stood peering into the dusk. He saw a horseman dismount and enter the gateway. Chance again bristled and growled. Sundown restrained him.

"Hello, there! That you, Jack?"

"Nope. It's me—Sundown from the Concho."

"Concho, eh? Was headed that way myself. Saw the dog. Thought mebby it was Jack's dog."

"Goin' to stop?" queried Sundown as the other advanced, leading his horse.

"Guess I'll have to. Don't fancy riding at night. Getting too old." And the short, genial-faced stranger laughed heartily.

"Well, they's plenty room. Had your supper?"

"No, but I got some chuck along with me. Got a match?"

Sundown produced matches. The other rolled a cigarette and studied Sundown's face covertly in the glow of the match. In the flare Sundown beheld a thick-set, rather short-necked man, smooth-shaven, and of a ruddy countenance. He also noticed that the stranger wore a coat, and at once surmised that he was neither cowboy nor herder.

"Guess I'll stake out the hoss," said the man. "See you later."

Chance, who had stood with head lowered and neck out-stretched, whined and leaped up at Sundown, standing with paws on his master's chest and vainly endeavoring to tell him something. The dog's eyes were eloquent and intense.

Sundown patted him. "It's all right, Chance. That guy's all right. Guess I know a good face when I see one. What's the matter, anyway?"

Chance dropped to his feet and stalked to his corner. He settled himself with a lugubrious sigh, as though unwillingly relinquishing his responsibilities in the matter.

When the stranger returned, Sundown had a fire going. "Feels good," commented the man, rubbing his hands and surveying the room in the glow that flared up as he lifted the stove-lid. "On your way in?"

"Me? Nope. I'm goin' to Antelope."

"So? Is Jack Corliss hurt bad?"

"He was kind o' shook up for a couple of days. Guess he's

gettin' along all right now. Reckon you heard what some-body done to Fadeaway."

The stranger nodded. "They got him, all right. Knew Fade pretty well myself. Guess I'll eat.—That coffee of yours was good, all right," he said as he finished eating. He reached for the coffee-pot and tipped it. "She's plumb empty."

"I'll fill her," volunteered Sundown, obligingly.

As he disappeared in the darkness, the stranger stepped to the rear door of the room and opened it. Then he closed the door and stooping laid his saddle and blankets against it. "He can't make a break that way," he said to himself. As Sundown came in, the man noticed that the front door creaked shrilly when opened or closed and seemed pleased with the fact. "Too bad about Fadeaway," he said, helping himself to more coffee. "Wonder who got him?"

"I dunno. I found me boss with his head busted the same day they got Fade."

"Been riding for the Concho long?"

"That ain't no joke, if you're meanin' feet and inches."

The other laughed. His eyes twinkled in the ruddy glow of the stove. Suddenly he straightened his shoulders and appeared to be listening. "It's the hosses," he said finally. "Some coyote's fussin' around bothering 'em. It's a long way from home as the song goes. Lend me your gun and I'll go see if I can plug one of 'em and stop their yipping."

Sundown presented his gun to the stranger, who slid it between trousers and shirt at the waist-band. "Don't hear 'em now," he announced finally. "Well, guess I'll roll in."

Strangely enough, he had apparently forgotten to return the gun. Sundown, undecided whether to ask for it or not, finally spread his blankets and called Chance to him. The dog curled at his master's feet. Save for the diminishing crackle of dry brush in the stove, the room was still. Evidently the ruddy-faced individual was asleep. Vaguely troubled by the stranger's failure to return his gun, Sundown drifted to sleep, not for an instant suspecting that he was virtually the prisoner of the sheriff of Apache County, who had at Loring's instigation determined to arrest the erstwhile tramp for the murder of Fadeaway. The sheriff had his own theory as to the killing and his theory did not for a moment include Sundown as a possible suspect, but he had a good, though unadvertised, reason for holding him. Accustomed to dealing with frontier folk, he argued that Sundown's imprisonment would eventually bring to light evidence leading to the identity of the murderer. It was a game of bluff, and at such a game he played a master hand.

The stranger seemed unusually affable in the morning. He made the fire, and, before Sundown had finished eating, had the two ponies saddled and ready for the road. Sundown thought him a little too agreeable. He was even more perplexed when the man said that he had changed his mind and would ride to Antelope with him. "Thought you said you was goin' to the Concho?"

"Well, seeing you say Jack can't ride yet, guess I'll wait."

"He can talk, all right," asserted Sundown.

The other paid no apparent attention to this remark but rode along pointing out landmarks and discoursing largely upon the weather, the feed, and price of hay and grain and a hundred topics associated with ranch-life. Sundown, forgetful of his pose as a vaquero of long standing (unintentional), assumed

Henry Hubert Knibbs

rather the attitude of one absorbing information on such topics than disseminating it. Nor did he understand the stranger's genial invitation to have supper with him at Antelope that night, as they rode into the town. He knew, however, that he was creating a sensation, which he attributed to his Mexican spurs and chaps. People stared at him as he stalked down the street and turned to stare again. His companion seemed very well known in Antelope. Nearly every one spoke to him or waved a greeting. Yet there was something peculiar in their attitudes. There was an aloofness about them that was puzzling.

"He sure looks like the bad man from Coyote Gulch," remarked one who stood in front of "The Last Chance" saloon.

"He ain't heeled," asserted the speaker's companion.

"Heeled! Do you reckon Jim's plumb loco? Jim took care of that."

All of which was music to Sundown. He was making an impression, yet he was not altogether happy. He did not object to being classed as a bad man so long as he knew at heart that he was anything but that. Still, he was rather proud of his instant notoriety.

They stopped in front of a square, one-story building. Sundown's companion unlocked the door. "Come on in," he said. "We'll have a smoke and talk things over."

"But I was to see Mr. Kennedy the lawyer," asserted Sundown.

"So? Well, it ain't quite time to see him yet."

Sundown's back became cold and he stared at the stranger with eyes that began to see the drift of things. "You ain't a cop, be you?" he asked timorously.

"They call it 'sheriff' here."

"Well, I call it kind o' warm and I'm goin' outside."

"I wouldn't. One of my deputies is sitting just across the street. He's a mighty good shot. Can beat me hands down. Suppose you drop back in your chair and tell me what you know about the shooting of Fadeaway."

"Me? You ain't joshin', be you?"

"Never more serious in my life! I'm interested in this case."

"Well, I ain't!" was Sundown's prompt remark. "And I got to go. I'm goin' on privut business for me boss and confiden-shell. Me and Chance."

"That's all right, my friend. But I have some private and confidential business that can't wait."

"But I ain't done nothin'," whined Sundown, lapsing into his old attitude toward the law.

"Maybe not. Mr. Loring telephoned me that Fadeaway had been shot and that a man answering your description—a tramp, he said—seemed to know something about it. You never was a puncher. You don't get on or off a cayuse like one. From what I learn you were a Hobo when Jack Corliss gave you a job. That's none of my business. I arrest you as a suspicious character, and I guess I'll have to keep you here till I find out more about Fadeaway's case. Have a cigar?"

"Huh! Say, don't you ever get mad?" queried Sundown, impressed by the other's most genial attitude.

The sheriff laughed. "Doesn't pay in my business. Now, you just ease up and tell me what you know. It will save time. Did you ever have trouble with Fadeaway?"

"Not on your life! I give him all the room he wanted."

"Did you know Fernando—one of Loring's herders?"

"I seen him onct. He saved me life from bein' killed by a steer. Did he say I done it?" parried Sundown.

The sheriff's opinion of Sundown's acumen was disturbed. Evidently this queer individual posing as a cowboy was not such a fool, after all.

"No. Have you seen him lately?"

"Nope. Chance and me was over to his camp, but he was gone. We kind o' tracked back there from the place where we found Fadeaway."

"That so?"

"Uhuh. It was like this." And Sundown gave a detailed account of his explorations.

When he had finished, the sheriff made a note on the edge of a newspaper. Then he turned to Sundown. "You're either the deepest hand I've tackled yet, or you're just a plain fool. You don't act like a killer."

"Killer! Say, mister, I wouldn't kill a bug that was bitin' me 'less'n he wouldn't let go. Why, ask Chance there!"

"I wish that dog could talk," said the sheriff, smiling. "Did you know that old Fernando had left the country—crossed the line into New Mexico?"

"What? Him?"

"Yes. I know about where he is."

"Guess his boss fired him for lettin' all the sheep get killed. Guess he had to go somewhere."

The sheriff nodded. "So you were going to take a little trip yourself, were you?"

"For me boss. You ask him. He can tell you."

"I reckon when he finds out where you are he'll come in."

"And you're goin' to pinch me?"

"You're pinched."

"Well, I'm dum clost to gettin' mad. You look here! Do you think I'd be ridin' to Antelope if I done anything like shoot a man? Do you think I'd hand you me gun without sayin' a word? And if you think I didn't shoot Fadeaway, what in hell you pinchin' me for? Ain't a guy got a right to live?"

"Yes. Fadeaway had a right to live."

"Well, I sure never wanted to see him cross over. That's the way with you cops. If a fella is a Bo, he gets pinched, anyhow. If he quits bein' a Bo and goes to workin' at somethin', then he gets pinched for havin' been a Bo onct. I been livin' honest and peaceful-like and straight—and I get pinched. Do you wonder a Bo gets tired of tryin' to brace up?"

"Can't say that I do. Got to leave you now. I'll fix you up comfortable in here." And the sheriff unlocked the door leading to the one-room jail. "I'll talk it over with you in the morning. The wife and kid will sure be surprised to see me back, so I'll mosey down home before somebody scares her to death telling her I'm back in town. So-long."

Sundown sat on the narrow bed and gazed at the four walls of the room. "Wife and kid!" he muttered. "Well, I reckon he's got a right to have 'em. Gee Gosh! Wonder if he'll feed Chance!"

CHAPTER XVIII

THE SHERIFF AND OTHERS

Chance, disconsolate, wandered about Antelope, returning at last to lie before the door of the sheriff's office. The sheriff, having reestablished himself, for the nonce, in the bosom of his family, strolled out to the street. He called to Chance, who dashed toward him, then stopped with neck bristling.

The sheriff's companion laughed. "I was going to feed him," explained the sheriff.

"I know what I'd feed him," growled his companion.

"What for? He's faithful to his boss—and that's something."

The other grunted and they passed up the street. Groups of men waylaid them asking questions. As they drifted from one group to another, the friend remarked that his companion seemed to be saying little. The stout sheriff smiled. He was listening.

Chance, aware that something was wrong, fretted around the door of Sundown's temporary habitation. Finally he threw himself down, nose on outstretched paws, and gazed at the lights and the men across the way. Later, when the town had

Henry Hubert Knibbs

become dark and silent, the dog rose, shook himself, and padded down the highway taking the trail for the Concho. He knew that his master's disappearance had not been voluntary. He also knew that his own appearance alone at the Concho would be evidence that something had gone wrong.

Once well outside the town, Chance settled to a long, steady stride that ate into the miles. At the water-hole he leaped the closed gate and drank. Again upon the road he swung along across the starlit mesas, taking the hills at a trot and pausing on each rise to rest and sniff the midnight air. Then down the slopes he raced, and out across the levels, the great bunching muscles of his flanks and shoulders working tirelessly. As dawn shimmered across the ford he trotted down the mud-bank and waded into the stream, where he stood shoulder-deep and lapped the cool water.

Corliss, early afoot, found him curled at the front door of the ranch-house. Chance braced himself on his fore legs and yawned. Then stretching he rose and, frisking about Corliss, tried to make himself understood. Corliss glanced toward the corral, half expecting to see Sundown's horse. Then he stepped to the men's quarters. He greeted Wingle, asking him if Sundown had returned.

"No. Thought he went east."

"Chance came back, alone."

And Corliss and the cook eyed each other simultaneously and nodded.

"Loring," said Wingle.

"Guess you're right, Hi."

"Sheriff must 'a' been out of town and got back just in time to meet up with Sundown," suggested Wingle. And he seized a scoop and dug into the flour barrel.

An hour later the buckboard stood at the ranch gate. Bud Shoop, crooning a range-ditty that has not as yet disgraced an anthology, stood flicking the rear wheel with his whip:—

"Oh, that biscuit-shooter on the Santa Fe,
—Hot coffee, ham-and-eggs, huckleberry pies,—
Got every lonely puncher that went down that way
With her yella-bird hair and them big blue eyes . . .

"For a two-bit feed and a two-bit smile . . ."

The song was interrupted by the appearance of Corliss, who swung to the seat and took the reins.

"I'll jog 'em for a while," he said as Shoop climbed beside him. "Go ahead, Bud. Don't mind me."

Shoop laughed and gestured over his shoulder. "Chance, there, is sleepin' with both fists this lovely mornin'. Wonder how Sun is makin' it?"

"We'll find out," said Corliss, shaking his head.

"Believe us! For we're goin' to town! Say, ain't you kind of offerin' Jim Banks a chance to get you easy?"

"If he wants to. If he locked Sundown up, he made the wrong move."

"It's easy!" said Shoop, gesturing toward the Loring rancho as they passed. "Goin' to bush at the water-hole to-night?"

"No. We'll go through."

Shoop whistled. "Suits me! And I reckon the team is good for it."

He glanced sideways at Corliss, who sat with eyes fixed straight ahead. The cattle-man's face was expressionless. He was thinking hard and fast, but chose to mask it.

Suddenly Shoop, who had watched him some little time, burst into song. "Suits me!" he reiterated, more or less ambiguously, by the way, for he had just concluded another ornate stanza of the "Biscuit-shooter" lyric.

"It's a real song," remarked Corliss.

"Well, now!" exclaimed Shoop. And thereafter he also became silent, knowing from experience that when Corliss had anything worth while to say, he would say it.

About noon they reached the water-hole where Corliss spent some time examining the fences and inspecting the outbuildings.

"She's in right good shape yet," commented Shoop.

"The title has reverted to the State. It's queer Loring hasn't tried to file on it."

"Mebby he's used his homestead right a'ready," suggested Shoop. "But Nell Loring could file."

They climbed back into the buckboard. Again Shoop began a stanza of his ditty. He seemed well pleased about something. Possibly he realized that his employer's attitude had changed; that he had at last awakened to the obvious necessity for doing something. As Corliss put the team to a brisk trot the foreman's song ran high. Action was his element. Inactivity tended to make him more or less cynical, and ate into his tobacco money.

Suddenly Corliss turned to him. "Bud, I'm going to homestead that ranch."

"Whoop!" cried the foreman. "First shot at the buck!"

"I'm going to put Sundown on it, for himself. He's steady and wouldn't hurt a fly."

Shoop became silent. He, in turn, stared straight ahead.

"What do you think of it?" queried Corliss.

"Nothin'. 'Cept I wouldn't mind havin' a little ole homestead myself."

Corliss laughed. "You're not cut out for it, Bud. You mean you'd like the chance to make the water-hole a base for operations against Loring. And the place isn't worth seed, Bud."

"But that water is goin' to be worth somethin'—and right soon. Loring can't graze over this side the Concho, if he can't get to water."

"That's it. If I put you on that ranch, you'd stand off Loring's outfit to the finish, I guess."

"I sure would."

"That's why I want Sundown to take it up. He'd let his worst enemy water sheep or cattle there. He won't fight, but he's loyal enough to my interests to sue Loring for trespass, if necessary."

"See you and raise you one, Jack. They'll bluff Sun clean off his hind feet. He won't stick."

"I'll chance it, Bud. And, besides, I need you right where you are."

"I'm sure happy!" exclaimed the irrepressible Bud, grinning.

Corliss laughed, then shook his head. "I'll tell you one thing," he said, facing his foreman. "I've been 'tending too many irons and some of 'em are getting cold. I don't want trouble with any one. I've held off from Loring because—oh—because I had a good reason to say nothing. Billy's out of it again. The coast is clear, and I'm going to give old man Loring the fight of his life."

The whoop which Shoop let out startled the team into a lunging gallop. "Go it, if you want to!" said Corliss as the buckboard swung around a turn and took the incline toward Antelope. "I'm in a hurry myself."

Nevertheless, he saved the team as they struck the level and held them to a trot. "Wise old head," was Shoop's inward comment. And then aloud: "Say, Jack, I ain't sayin' I'm glad to see you get beat up, but that bing on the head sure got you started right. The boys was commencin' to wonder how long you'd stand it without gettin' your back up. She's up. I smell smoke."

At Antelope, Shoop put up the horses. Later he joined his employer and they had supper at the hotel. Then they strolled out and down the street toward the sheriff's home. When they knocked at the door it was opened by a plump, dark-eyed woman who greeted them heartily.

"Come right in, boys. Jim's tendin' the baby." And she took their hats.

They stepped to the adjoining room where Sheriff Jim sat on the floor, his coat off, while his youngest deputy, clad only in an abbreviated essential garnished with a safety-pin, sat opposite, gravely tearing up the evening paper and handing the pieces to his proud father, who stuffed the pieces in his pants pocket and cheerfully asked for more.

"Election?" queried Shoop.

"And all coming Jim's way," commented Corliss.

The baby paused in his balloting and solemnly surveyed the dusty strangers. Then he pulled a piece of paper from his father's pocket and offered it to Shoop. "Wants me to vote, the little cuss! Well, here goes." And, albeit unfamiliar with plump aborigines at close range, the foreman entered into the spirit of the game and cast his vote for the present incumbent, deputizing the "yearlin'" to handle the matter. The yearling however, evidently thought it was time for a recount. He gravitated to the perspiring candidate and, standing on his hands and feet,—an attitude which seemingly caused him no inconvenience,—reached in the ballot-box and pulling therefrom a handful of votes he cast them ceiling-ward with a shrill laugh, followed by an unintelligible spluttering as he sat down suddenly and began to pick up the scattered pieces of paper.

"You're elected," announced Shoop.

And the by-play was understood by the three men, yet each maintained his unchanged expression of countenance.

Henry Hubert Knibbs

"You see how I'm fixed, boys," said the sheriff. "Got to stick by my constituent or he'll howl."

"We're in no hurry, Jim. Just drove into town to look around a little."

"I'll take him now," said Mrs. Jim, as she came from the kitchen drying her hands on her apron.

The elector, however, was of a different mind. He greeted his mother with a howl and a series of windmill revolutions of his arms and legs as she caught him up.

"Got mighty free knee-action," remarked Shoop. "Mebby when he's bedded down for the night you can come over to the 'Palace.'"

"I'll be right with you." And the sheriff slipped into his coat. "How you feeling, Jack?"

"Pretty good. That's a great boy of yours."

"Sure got your brand," added Shoop. "Built close to the ground like his dad."

Sheriff Banks accepted these hardy compliments with an embarrassed grin and followed his guests to the doorway.

"Good-night!" called Mrs. Jim from the obscurity of the bedroom.

"Good-night, ma'am!" from Shoop.

"Good-night!" said Corliss. "Take good care of that yearling."

"Well, now, John, as if I wouldn't!"

"Molly would come out," apologized Jim, "only the kid is—is grazin'. How's the feed holdin' out on the Concho?" which question following in natural sequence was not, however, put accidentally.

"Fair," said Corliss. "We looked for you up that way."

"I was over on the Reservation. I sent Tom up there to see after things," and the sheriff gestured toward the distant Concho. "Sent him up to-night. Let's go over to the office."

Corliss shook his head. "Don't want to see him, just now. Besides, I want to say a few things private."

"All right. There was a buyer from Kansas City dropped in to town to-day. Didn't see him, did you?"

"Cattle?"

"Uhuh."

"No. We just got in."

They turned and walked up the street, nodding to an occasional lounger, laughing and talking easily, yet each knew that their banter was a meandering current leading to something deeper which would be sounded before they separated.

Sheriff Banks suddenly stopped and slapped his thigh. "By Gum! I clean forgot to ask if you had chuck. You see that kid of mine—"

"Sure! But we put the 'Palace' two feeds to the bad," asserted Shoop.

They drifted to the hotel doorway and paused at the counter where each gravely selected a cigar. Then they clumped upstairs to Corliss's room. Jim Banks straddled a chair and faced his friends.

Shoop, excusing himself with humorous politeness, punched the pillows together and lay back on the bed which creaked and rustled beneath his weight. "These here corn-husk mattresses is apologizin'," he said, twisting around and leaning on his elbow.

"Well, Jack," said the smiling sheriff, "shoot the piece."

"Or the justice of the peace—don't matter," murmured Shoop.

Corliss, leaning forward, gazed at the end of his cigar. Then he raised his eyes. "Jim," he said quietly, "I want Sundown."

"So do I."

Corliss smiled. "You've got him, all right. What's your idea?"

"Well, if anybody else besides you asked me, Jack, they'd be wasting time. Sundown is your man. I don't know anything about him except he was a Hobo before he hit the Concho. But I happen to know that he was pretty close to the place where Fadeaway got his, the same day and about the same time. I've listened to all the talk around town and it hasn't all been friendly to you. You can guess that part of it."

"If you want me—" began Corliss.

"No." And the sheriff's gesture of negation spread a film of cigar-ash on the floor. "It's the other man I want."

"Sundown?" asked Shoop, sitting up suddenly.

"You go to sleep, Bud," laughed the sheriff. "You can't catch me that easy."

Shoop relaxed with the grin of a school-boy.

"I'll go bail," offered Corliss.

"No. That would spoil my plan. See here, Jack, I know you and Bud won't talk. Loring telephoned me to look out for Sundown. I did. Now, Loring knows who shot Fadeaway, or I miss my guess. Nellie Loring knows, too. So do you, but you can't prove it. It was like Fade to put Loring's sheep into the canon, but we can't prove even that, now. I'm pretty sure your scrap with Fade didn't have anything to do with his getting shot. You ain't that kind."

"Well, here's my side of it, Jim. Fadeaway had it in for me for firing him. He happened to see me talking to Nellie Loring at Fernando's camp. Later we met up on the old Blue Trail. He said one or two things that I didn't like. I let him have it with the butt of my quirt. He jerked out his gun and hit me a clip on the head. That's all I remember till the boys came along."

"You didn't ride as far as the upper ford, that day?"

"No. I told Fadeaway I wanted him to come back with me and talk to Loring. I was pretty sure he put the sheep into the canon."

"Well, Jack, knowing you since you were a boy, that's good enough for me."

"But how about Sundown?"

"He stays. How long do you think I'll hold Sundown before Nell Loring drives into Antelope to tell me she can like as not prove he didn't kill Fade?"

"But if you know that, why do you hold him?"

"To cinch up my ideas, tight. Holding him will make talk. Folks always like to show off what they know about such things. It's natural in 'em."

"New Mex. is a comf'table-sized State," commented Shoop from the bed.

"And he was raised there," said the sheriff. "He's got friends over the line and so have I. Sent 'em over last week."

"Thought Sun was raised back East?" said Shoop, again sitting up.

Corliss smiled. "Better give it up, Bud."

"Oh, *very* well!" said Shoop, mimicking a *grande dame* who had once stopped at Antelope in search for local color. "Anyhow, you got to set a Mexican to catch a Mexican when he's hidin' out with Mexicans." With this bit of advice, Shoop again relapsed to silence.

"Going back to the Concho to-morrow?" queried Banks.

"No. Got a little business in town."

"I heard Loring was due here to-morrow." The sheriff stated this casually, yet with intent. "I was talking with Art Kennedy 'bout two hours ago—"

"Kennedy the land-shark?" queried Shoop.

"The same. He said something about expecting Loring."

Bud Shoop had never aspired to the distinction of being called a diplomat, but he had an active and an aggressive mind. With the instinct for seizing the main chance by its time-honored forelock, he rose swiftly. "By Gravy, Jack! I gone and left them things in the buckboard!"

"Oh, they'll be all right," said Corliss easily. Then he caught his foreman's eye and read its meaning. His nod to Shoop was all but imperceptible.

"I dunno, Jack. I'd hate to lose them notes."

"Notes?" And the sheriff grinned. "Writing a song or starting a bank, Bud?"

"Song. I was composin' it to Jack, drivin' in." And the genial Bud grabbed his hat and swept out of the room.

Long before he returned, Sheriff Jim had departed puzzling over the foreman's sudden exit until he came opposite "The Last Chance" saloon. There he had an instant glimpse of Bud and the one known as Kennedy leaning against the bar and conversing with much gusto. Then the swing-door dropped into place. The sheriff smiled and putting two and two together found that they made four, as is usually the case. He had wanted to let Corliss know that Loring was coming to Antelope and to let him know casually, and glean from the knowledge anything that might be of value. Sheriff Banks knew a great deal more about the affairs of the distant ranchers than he was ordinarily given credit for. He had long wondered why Corliss had not taken up the water-hole homestead.

Corliss was in bed when Shoop swaggered in. The foreman

did a few steps of a jig, flung his hat in the corner, and proceeded to undress.

"Did you see Kennedy?" yawned Corliss.

"Bet your whiskers I did! Got the descriptions in my pocket. You owe me the price of seven drinks, Jack, to say nothin' of what I took myself. Caught him at 'The Last Chance' and let on I was the pore lonely cowboy with a sufferin' thirst. Filled him up with 'Look-out-I'm-Comin'' and landed him at his shack, where he dug up them ole water-hole descriptions, me helpin' promiscus. He kind o' bucked when I ast him for them papers. Said he only had one copy that he was holdin' for another party. And I didn't have to strain my guesser any, to guess who. I told him to saw off and get busy quick or I'd have him pinched for playin' favorites. Guess he seen I meant business, for he come acrost. She toots for Antelope six-forty tomorrow mornin'. This is where I make the grand play as a homesteader, seein' pore Sundown's eatin' on the county. Kind o' had a hunch that way."

"We'll have to nail it quick. If you file you'll have to quit on the Concho."

"Well, then, I quit. Sinker is right in line for my bunk. Me for the big hammer and the little ole sign what says: 'Private property! Keep off! All trespassers will be executed!' And underneath, kind o' sassy-like, 'Bud Shoop, proprietor.'"

CHAPTER XIX

THE ESCAPE

About midnight Corliss and his foreman were awakened by a cry of "Fire!" They scrambled from bed and pawed around in the dark for their clothes.

"Spontinuous conibustication," said Shoop, with a yawn. "A Jew clothin'-store and a insurance-policy. Wonder who's ablaze?"

"I can see from here," said Corliss at the window. "Keep on dressing, Bud, it's the sheriff's office!"

"Sundown!" Shoop exclaimed, dancing about inelegantly with one foot halfway down his pants-leg.

They tramped down the stairs and ran across to the blazing building. A group of half-dressed citizens were passing buckets and dashing their final and ineffectual contents against the spouting flames.

"He's sure done on both sides if he's in there," remarked Shoop. He ran around to the back of the jail and called loudly on Sundown. Jumping, he caught the high wooden bars of the window and peered into the rear room. A rivulet of flame crept along the door that led from the jail to the office. The room seemed to be empty. Shoop dropped to the ground and strolled around to the front. "Tryin' to save the buildin' or the prisoner?" he asked of a sweating bucket-passer.

The man paused for a second, slopping water on his boots and gazing about excitedly. "Hey, boys!" he shouted. "Get an axe and chop open the back! The long gent is roastin' to death in there!"

"And I reckon that'll keep 'em busy while Sun fans it," soliloquized Shoop. "Hello, Jack!" And he beckoned to Corliss. "He ain't in there," he whispered, "But how he got out, gets me!"

"We might as well go back to bed," said Corliss. "They'll get him, anyway. There's one of Jim's deputies on a cayuse now."

"Where do you reckon he'll head for?"

"Don't know, Bud. If he heads for the water-hole, they'll get him in no time."

"Think he set her on fire?"

"Maybe he dropped a cigarette. I don't think he'd risk it, on purpose."

Shoop glanced at his watch, tilting it toward the light of the flames. "It's just one. Hello! There comes the agent. Reckon he thought the station was afire."

"Guess not. He's lighting up. Must be a special going to stop."

"He's sure set the red. Say, I'm goin' over to see. Wait a minute."

Shoop followed the agent into the station. Presently the foreman reappeared and beckoned to Corliss. "Listen, Jack! Reddy says he's got some runnin' orders for the Flyer and she's got to stop to get 'em. That means we can eat breakfast in Usher, 'stead of here. No tellin' who'll be on the six-forty headed for the same place, tomorrow mornin'.'"

Corliss pondered. His plan of homesteading the water-hole ranch had been upset by the arrest of Sundown. Still, that was no reason for giving up the plan. From Shoop's talk with Kennedy, the lawyer, it was evident that Loring had his eye on the deserted ranch.

Far down the track he saw a glimmering dot of fire and heard the faint muffled whistle of the Flyer. "All right, Bud. I'll get the tickets. Get our coats. We can just make it."

When they stepped from the Flyer at Usher, the faint light of dawn was edging the eastern hills. A baggage-truck rumbled past and they heard some one shout, "Get out o' that!" In the dim light they saw a figure crawl from beneath the baggage-car and dash across the station platform to be swallowed up in the shadowy gloom of a side street.

"I only had seven drinks," said Shoop, gazing after the disappearing figure. "But if Sundown ain't a pair of twins, that was him."

"Hold on, Bud!" And Corliss laid his hand on Shoop's arm. "Don't take after him. That's the way to stampede him. We go easy till it's light. He'll see us."

They sauntered up the street and stopped opposite an

"all-night" eating-house.

"We won't advertise the Concho, this trip," said Corliss, as they entered.

Shoop, with his legs curled around the counter stool, sipped his coffee and soliloquized. "Wise old head! Never was a hotel built that was too good for Jack when he's travelin'. And he don't do his thinkin' with his feet, either."

The waiter, who had retired to the semi-seclusion of the kitchen, dozed in a chair tilted back against the wall. He was awakened by a voice at the rear door. Shoop straightened up and grinned at Corliss. The waiter vocalized his attitude with the brief assertion that there was "nothin' doin'."

"It's him!" said Shoop.

"I got the price," came from the unseen.

"Then you beat it around to the front," suggested the waiter.

Shoop called for another cup of coffee. As the waiter brought it, Sundown, hatless, begrimed, and showing the effects of an unupholstered journey, appeared in the doorway. Shoop turned and stood up.

"Well, if it ain't me old pal Buddy!" exclaimed Sundown. "What you doin' in this here burg?"

"Why, hello, Hawkins! Where'd you fall from? How's things over to Homer?"

Sundown took the hint and fabricated a heart-rending tale of an all-night ride on "a cayuse that had been tryin' to get rid of him ever since he started and had finally piled him as the

Flyer tooted for Usher."

"You do look kind o' shook-up. Better eat."

"I sure got room," said Sundown. "Fetch me a basket of doughnuts and a pail of coffee. That there Fly—cayuse sure left me, but he didn't take me appetite."

After the third cup of coffee and the seventh doughnut, Sundown asserted that he felt better. They sauntered out to the street.

"How in blazes did you get loose?" queried Shoop, surveying the unkempt adventurer with frank amazement.

"Blazes is correct. I clumb out of the window."

"Set her on fire?"

"Not with mellishus extent, as the judge says. Mebby it was a cigarette. I dunno. First thing I know I was dreamin' I smelt smoke and the dream sure come true. If them bars had been a leetle closter together, I reckon I would be tunin' a harp, right now."

"How did you happen to jump our train—and get off here?" asked Corliss.

"It was sure lucky," said Sundown, grinning. "I run 'round back of the station and snook up and crawled under the platform in front. I could see everybody hoppin' 'round and I figured I was safer on the job, expectin' they'd be lookin' for me to beat it out of town. Then you fellas come up and stood talkin' right over me head. Bud he says somethin' about eatin' breakfast in Usher, and bein' hungry and likin' good comp'ny, I waits till the train pulls up and crawls under the baggage. And here I be."

"We'll have to get you a hat and a coat. We'll stop at the next barber-shop. You wash up and get shaved. We'll wait. Then we'll head for the court-house."

"Me ranch?" And Sundown beamed through his grime. "Makes me feel like writin' a pome! Now, mebby—"

"Haven't time, now. Got to scare up two more witnesses to go on your paper. There's a place, just opening up."

They crossed the street. Next to the barbershop was a saloon.

Sundown eyed the sign pensively. "I ain't a drinkin' man— regular," he said, "but there are times . . ."

"There are times," echoed Corliss, and the three filed between the swing-doors and disappeared.

An hour later three men, evidently cow-men from their gait and bearing, passed along the main street of Usher and entered the court-house, where they were met by two citizens. The five men were admitted to the inner sanctum of the hall of justice, from which they presently emerged, laughing and joking. The tallest of them seemed to be receiving the humorous congratulations of his companions. He shook hands all around and remarked half-apologetically: "I ain't a drinkin' man, reg'lar . . . but there are times . . ."

The five men drifted easily toward the swing-doors. Presently they emerged. Shoop nudged his employer. David Loring and his daughter had just crossed the street. The old sheep-man glanced at the group in front of the saloon and blinked hard. Of the West, he read at a glance the situation. Sundown, Corliss, and Shoop raised their hats as Eleanor

Loring bowed.

"Beat him by a neck!" said Shoop. "Guess we better fan it, eh, Jack?"

"There's no hurry," said Corliss easily. Nevertheless, he realized that Sundown's presence in Usher was quite apt to be followed by a wire from the sheriff of Antelope which would complicate matters, to say the least. He shook hands with the two townsmen and assured them that the hospitality of the Concho was theirs when they chose to honor it. Then he turned to Bud Shoop. "Get the fastest saddle-horse in town and ride out to the South road and wait for us. I'm going to send Sundown over to Murphy's. Pat knows me pretty well. From there he can take the Apache road to the Concho. We can outfit him and get him settled at the water-hole ranch before any one finds out where he is."

"But Jim'll get him again," said Shoop.

"I expect him to. That'll be all right."

"Well, you got me. Thought I knowed somethin' about your style, but I don't even know your name."

"Let's move on. You go ahead and get the cayuse. I want to talk to Sundown."

Then Corliss explained his plan. He told Sundown to keep the water-hole fenced and so keep the sheep-men from using it. This would virtually control several thousand acres of range around the water-hole ranch. He told Sundown that he expected him to homestead the ranch for himself—do the necessary work to secure a title, and then at his option either continue as a rancher or sell the holding to the Concho. "I'll start you with some stock—a few head, and a horse or two.

All you have to do is to 'tend to business and forget that I have ever spoken to you about homesteading the place. You'll have to play it alone after you get started."

"Suits me, boss. I ain't what you'd call a farmer, but me and Chance can scratch around and act like we was. But the smooth gent as pinched me—ain't he goin' to come again?"

"Sure as you're wearing spurs! But you just take it easy and you'll come out all right. Loring put Jim Banks after you. Jim is all right and he's business. Loring wants the water-hole ranch. So do I. Now, if Loring tells the sheriff he saw you in Usher, and later at the water-hole, Jim will begin to think that Loring is keeping pretty close trail on you. When Jim finds out you've filed on the water-hole,—and he already knows that Loring wants it,—he'll begin to figure that Loring had you jailed to keep you out of his way. And you can take it from me, Jim Banks is the squarest man in Apache County. He'll give you a chance to make good. If we can keep you out of sight till he hears from over the line, I think you'll be safe after that. If we can't, why, you still have your title to the water-hole ranch and that holds it against trespassers."

"Well, you're sure some shark on the long think! Say, I been scared stiff so long I'm just commencin' to feel me legs again. The sun is shinin' and the birds are sawin' wood. I get you, boss! The old guy that owns the wool had me pinched. Well, I ain't got nothin' ag'in' him, but that don't say I ain't workin' for you. Say, if he comes botherin' around me farm, do I shoot?"

"No. You just keep right on. Pay no attention to him."

"Just sick Chance on him, eh?"

"He'd get Chance. I'm going to run some cattle over that way soon. Then you'll have company. You needn't be scared."

"Cattle is some comp'ny at that. Say, have I got to ride that there bronc Bud jest went down the street on?"

"As soon as we get out of town."

"Which wouldn't be long if we had hosses like him, eh?"

"I'll give you a note to Murphy. He'll send your horse back to Usher and let you take a fresh horse when you start for the Concho. Take it easy, and don't talk."

"All right, boss. But I was thinkin'—"

"What?"

"Well, it's men like me and you that puts things through. It takes a man with sand to go around this country gettin' pinched and thrun and burnt up and bein' arrested every time he goes to spit. Folks'll be sayin' that there Sundown gent is a brave man—me! Never shot nobody and dependin' on his nerve, every time. They's nothin' like havin' a bad repetation."

"Nothing like it," assented Corliss, smiling. "Well, here's your road. Keep straight on till you cross the river. Then take the right fork and stick to it, and you'll ride right into Murphy's. He'll fix you up, all right."

"Did you think in this note to tell him to give me a hoss that only travels one way to onct?" queried Sundown.

Corliss laughed. "Yes, I told him. Don't forget you're a citizen and a homesteader. We're depending on you."

"You bet! And I'll be there with the bells!"

Shoop and Corliss watched Sundown top a distant rise and disappear in a cloud of dust. Then they walked back to the station. As they waited for the local, Shoop rolled a cigarette. "Jest statin' it mild and gentle," he said, yawning, "the last couple of weeks has been kind of a busy day. Guess the fun's all over. Sundown's got a flyin' start; Loring's played his ace and lost, and you and me is plumb sober. If I'd knowed it was goin' to be as quiet as this, I'd 'a' brought my knittin' along."

"There are times . . ." said Corliss.

"And we got just five minutes," said Shoop. "Come on."

CHAPTER XX

THE WALKING MAN

Sundown's sense of the dramatic, his love for posing, with his linguistic ability to adopt the vernacular of the moment so impressed the temperamental Murphy that he disregarded a portion of his friend Corliss's note, and the morning following his lean guest's arrival at the ranch the jovial Irishman himself saddled and bridled the swiftest and most vicious horse in the corral; a glass-eyed pinto, bronc from the end of his switching tail to his pink-mottled muzzle. He was a horse with a record which he did not allow to become obsolete, although he had plenty of competition to contend with in the string of broncs that Murphy's riders variously bestrode. Moreover, the pinto, like dynamite, "went off" at the most unexpected intervals, as did many of his riders. Sundown, bidding farewell to his host, mounted and swung out of the yard at a lope. The pinto had ideas of his own. Should he buck in the yard, he would immediately be roped and turned into the corral again. Out on the mesas it would be different—and it was.

He paid no attention to a tumble-weed gyrating across the Apache road. Neither did he seem disturbed when a rattler burred in the bunch-grass. Even the startled leap of a rabbit that shot athwart his immediate course was greeted with nothing more than a snort and a toss of his swinging head. Such things were excuses for bad behavior, but he was of that type which furnishes its own excuse. He would lull his rider to a false security, and then . . .

The pinto loped over level and rise tirelessly. Sundown stood in his stirrups and gazed ahead. The wide mesas glowing in the sun, the sense of illimitable freedom, the keen, odorless air wrought him to a pitch of inspiration. He would, just over the next rise, draw rein and woo his muse. But the next rise and the next swept beneath the pinto's rhythmic hoofs. The poetry of motion swayed his soul. He was enjoying himself. At last, he reflected, he had mastered the art of sitting a horse. He had already mastered the art of mounting and of descending under various conditions and at seemingly impossible angles. As Hi Wingle had once remarked—Sundown was the most *durable* rider on the range. His length of limb had no apparent relation to his shortcomings as a vaquero.

Curiosity, as well as pride, may precede a fall. Sundown eventually reined up and breathed the pinto, which paced with lowered head as though dejected and altogether weary—which was merely a pose, if an object in motion can be said to pose. His rider, relaxing, slouched in the saddle and dreamed of a peaceful and domestic future as owner of a small herd of cattle, a few fenced acres of alfalfa and vegetables, a saddle-horse something like the pinto which he bestrode, with Chance as companion and audience—and perhaps a low-voiced senora to welcome him at night when he rode in with spur-chains jingling and the silver conchas on his chaps gleaming like stars in the setting sun. "But me chaps did their last gleam in that there fire," he reflected sadly. "But I got me big spurs yet." Which after-thought served in a measure to mitigate his melancholy. Like a true knight, he had slept spurred and belted for the chance encounter while held in durance vile at Antelope. "But me ranch!" he exclaimed. "Me! And mebby a tame cow and chickens and things,—eh, Chance!" But Chance, he immediately realized, was not with him. He would have a windmill and shade-trees and a border of roses along the roadway to the house—like the Loring rancho. But the senorita to be wooed and won—that was a different matter. "'T ain't no woman's country nohow—this here Arizona. She's fine! But she's a man's country every time! Only sech as me and Jack Corliss and Bud and them kind is fit to take the risks of makin' good in this here State. But we're makin' good, you calico-hoss! Listen:—

"Oh, there's sunshine on the Concho where the little owls are cryin',
And red across the 'dobe strings of chiles are a-dryin';
And if Arizona's heaven, tell me what's the use of dyin'?
Yes, it's good enough down here, just breathin' air;

"For the posies are a-bloomin' and the mockin'-birds are matin',
And somewhere in Arizona there's a Chola girl a-waitin'
For to cook them enchiladas while I do the irrigatin'
On me little desert homestead over there.

"While I'm ridin' slow and easy . . ."

"Whoa! Wonder what that is? Never seen one of them things before. 'T ain't a lizard, but he looks like his pa was a lizard. Mebby his ma was a toad. Kind of a Mormon, I guess."

He leaned forward and gravely inspected the horned toad that blinked at him from the edge of the grass. The pinto realized that his rider's attention was otherwise and thoroughly occupied. With that unforgettable drop of head and arch of spine the horse bucked. Sundown did an

Henry Hubert Knibbs

unpremeditated evolution that would have won him much applause and gold had he been connected with a circus. He landed in a clump of brush and watched his hat sail gently down. The pinto whirled and took the homeward road, snorting and bounding from side to side as the dust swirled behind him. Sundown scratched his head. "Lemme see. 'We was ridin', slow and easy . . .' Huh! Well, I ain't cussin' because I don' know how. Lemme see . . . I was facin' east when I started. Now I'm lit, and I'm facin' south. Me hat's there, and that there toad-lizard oughter be over there, if he ain't scared to death. Reckon I'll quit writin' po'try jest at present and finish gettin' acquainted with that there toad-lizard. Wonder how far I got to walk? Anyhow, I was gettin' tired of ridin'. By gum! me eats is tied to the saddle! It's mighty queer how a fella gets set back to beginnin' all over ag'in every onct in a while. Now, this mornin' I was settin' up ridin' a good hoss and thinkin' poetical. Now I'm settin' down restin'. The sun is shinin' yet, and them jiggers in the brush is chirpin' and the air is fine, but I ain't thinkin' poetical. I'd sure hate to have a real lady read what I'm thinkin', if it was in a book. 'Them that sets on the eggs of untruth,' as the parson says, 'sure hatches lies.' Jest yesterday I was tellin' in Usher how me bronc piled me when I'd been ridin' the baggage, which was kind of a hoss-lie. I must 'a' had it comin'."

He rose and stalked to the roadway. The horned toad, undisturbed, squatted in the grass and eyed him with bright, expressionless eyes.

"If I was like some," said Sundown, addressing the toad, "I'd pull me six-shooter, only I ain't got it now, and bling you to nothin'. Accordin' to law you're the injudicious cause preceding the act, which makes you guilty accordin' to the statues of this here commonwealth, and I seen lots of 'em on the same street, in Boston, scarin' hosses to death and makin' kids and nuss-girls cry. But I ain't goin' to shoot you. If I was to have the sayin' of it, I'd kind o' like to shoot that hoss, though. He broke as fine a pome in the middle as I ever writ, to say nothin' of hurtin' me personal feelin's. Well, so-long, leetle toad-lizard. Just tell them that you saw me—and they will know the rest—if anybody was to ask you, a empty saddle and a man a-foot in the desert is sure circumvential evidence ag'in the hoss. Wonder how far it is to the Concho?"

With many a backward glance, inspired by fond imaginings that the pinto *might* have stopped to graze, Sundown stalked down the road. Waif of chance and devotee of the goddess "Maybeso," he rose sublimely superior to the predicament in which he found himself. "The only reason I'm goin' east is because I ain't goin' west," he told himself, ignoring, with warm adherence to the glowing courses of the sun the frigid possibilities of the poles. Warmed by the exercise of plodding across the mesa trail in high-heeled boots, he swung out of his coat and slung it across his shoulder. Dust gathered in the wrinkles of his boots, and more than once he stopped to mop his sweating face with his bandanna. Rise after rise swept gently before him and within the hour he saw the misty outline of the blue hills to the south. Slowly his moving shadow shifted, bobbing in front of him as the sun slipped toward the western horizon. A little breeze sighed along the road and whirls of sand spun in tiny cones around the roots of the chaparral. He reached in his pocket, drew forth a silver dollar, and examined it. "Now if they weren't any folks on this here earth, I reckon silver and gold and precious jools wouldn't be worth any more than rocks and mud and gravel, eh? Why, even if they weren't no folks, water would be worth more to this here world than gold. Water makes things grow and—and keeps a fella from gettin' thirsty. And mud makes things grow, too, but I dunno what rocks are for. Just to sit on when you're tired, I reckon." The sibilant burring of a rattler in the brush set his neck and back tingling. "And what snakes was made for, gets me! They ain't good to eat, nohow. And they ain't friendly like some of the bugs and things. I'm thinkin' that that there snake what clumb the tree and got Mrs. Eve interested in the apple business would 'a' been a whole lot better for folks, if he'd 'a' stayed up that tree and died, instead o' runnin' around and raisin' young ones. Accordin' to my way of thinkin' a garden ain't a garden with a snake in it, nohow. Now, Mrs. Eve—if she'd had to take a hammer and nails and make a ladder to get to them apples, by the time she got the ladder done I reckon them apples wouldn't 'a' looked so good to her. That's what comes of havin' a snake handy. 'Course, bein' a woman, she jest nacherally couldn't wait for 'em to get ripe and fall off the tree. That would 'a' been too easy. It sure is funny how folks goes to all kinds o' trouble to get into it. Mebby she did get kind o' tired eatin' the same breakfast-food every mornin'. Lots o' folks do, and hankers to try a new one. But I never got tired of drinkin' water yet. Wisht I had a barrel with ice in it. Gee Gosh! Ice! Mebby a cup of water would be enough for a fella, but when he's dry he sure likes to see lots ahead even if he can't drink it all. Mebby it's jest knowin' it's there that kind o' eases up a fella's thirst. I dunno."

Romance, as romance was wont to do at intervals, lay in wait for the weary Sundown. Hunger and thirst and a burning sun may not be immediately conducive to poetry or romantic imaginings. But the 'dobe in the distance shaded by a clump of trees, the gleam of the drying chiles, the glow of flowers, offered an acceptable antithesis to the barren roadway and the empty mesas. Sundown quickened his pace. Eden, though circumscribed by a barb-wire fence enclosing scant territory, invited him to rest and refresh himself. And all unexpected the immemorial Eve stood in the doorway of the 'dobe, gazing down the road and doubtless wondering why this itinerant Adam, booted and spurred, chose to walk the dusty highway.

At the gate of the homestead Sundown paused and raised his broad sombrero. Anita, dusky and buxom daughter of Chico Miguel, "the little hombre with the little herd," as the cattlemen described him, nodded a bashful acknowledgment of the salute, and spoke sharply to the dog which had risen and was bristling toward the Strange wayfarer.

"Agua," said Sundown, opening the gate, "Mucha agua, Senorita," adding, with a humorous gesture of drinking, "I'm dry clean to me boots."

The Mexican girl, slow-eyed and smiling, gazed at this most wonderful man, of such upstanding height that his hat brushed the limbs of the shade-trees at the gateway. Anita was plump and not tall. As Sundown stalked up the path assuming an air of gallantry that was not wasted on the desert air, the girl stepped to the olla hanging in the shade and offered him the gourd. Sundown drank long and deep. Anita watched him with wondering eyes. Such a man she had never seen. Vaqueros? Ah, yes! many of them, but never such a man as this. This one smiled, yet his face had much of the sadness in it. He had perhaps walked many weary miles in the heat. Would he—with a gesture interpreting her speech—be pleased to rest awhile? Without hesitation, he would. As he sat on the doorstep gazing contentedly at the flowers bordering the path, Anita's mother appeared from some mysterious recess of the 'dobe and questioned Anita with quick low utterance. The girl's answer, interpretable to Sundown only by its intonation, was music to him. The Mexican woman, more than buxom, large-eyed and placid, turned to Sundown, who rose and again doffed his sombrero.

"I lost me horse—back there. I'm headed for the Concho— ma'am. Concho," he reiterated in a louder tone. "Sabe?"

The mother of Anita nodded. "You sick?" she asked.

"What? Me? Not on your life, lady! I'm the healthiest Ho—puncher in this here State. You sabe Concho?"

"Si! Zhack Corlees—'Juan,' we say. Si! You of him?"

"Yes, lady. I'm workin' for him. Lost me hoss."

Anita and her mother exchanged glances. Sundown felt that his status as a vaquero was in question. Would he let the beautiful Anita know that he had been ignominiously "piled" by that pinto horse? Not he. "Circumventions alters cases," he soliloquized, not altogether untruthfully. Then aloud, "Me hoss put his foot in a gopher-hole. Bruk his leg, and I had to shoot him, lady. Hated to part with him." And the inventive Sundown illustrated with telling gesture the imaginary accident.

Sympathy flowed freely from the gentle-hearted Senora and her daughter. "Si!" It was not of unusual happening that horses met with such accidents. It was getting late in the afternoon. Would the unfortunate caballero accept of their hospitality in the way of frijoles and some of the good coffee, perhaps? Sundown would, without question. He pressed a dollar into the palm of the reluctant Senora. He was not a tramp. Of that she might be assured. He had met with misfortune, that was all. And would the patron return soon? The patron would return with the setting of the sun. Meanwhile the vaquero of the Concho was to rest and perhaps enjoy his cigarette? And the "vaquero" loafed and smoked many cigarettes while the glowing eyes of Anita shone upon him with large sympathy. As yet Sundown had not especially noticed her, but returning from his third visit to the cooling olla, he caught her glance and read, or imagined he read, deep admiration, lacking words to utter.

From that moment he became a changed man. He shed his weariness as a tattered garment is thrown aside. He straightened his shoulders and held his head high. At last a woman had looked at him and had not smiled at his ungainly stature. Nay! But rather seemed impressed, awe-stricken, amazed. And his heart quickened to faster rhythm, driving the blood riotously through his imaginative mind. He grew eloquent, in gesture, if not in speech. He told of his wanderings, his arrival at the Concho, of Chance his great wolf-dog, his horse "Pill," and his good friends Bud Snoop and Hi Wangle. Sundown could have easily given Othello himself "cards and spades" in this chance game of hearts and won—moving metaphor!—in a canter. That the little Senorita with the large eyes did not understand more than a third of that which she heard made no difference to her. His ambiguity of utterance, backed by assurance and illumined by the divine fire of inspiration, awakened curiosity in the placid breast of this Desdemona of the mesas. It required no sophistication on her part to realize that this caballero was not as the vaqueros she had heretofore known. He made no boorish jests; his eyes were not as the eyes of many that had gazed at her in a way that had tinged her dusky cheeks with warm resentment. She felt that he was endeavoring to interest her, to please her rather than to woo. And more than that—he seemed intensely interested in his own brave eloquence. A child could have told that Sundown was single-hearted. And with the instinct of a child—albeit eighteen, and quite a woman in her way—Anita approved of this adventurer as she had never approved of men, or man, before. His great height, his long, sweeping arms, moving expansively as he illustrated this or that incident, his silver spurs, his loose-jointed "tout ensemble," so to speak, combined with an eloquent though puzzling manner of speech, fascinated her. Warmed to his work, and forgetful of his employer's caution in regard to certain plans having to do with the water-hole ranch, Sundown elaborated, drawing heavily on future possibilities, among which he towered in imagination monarch of rich mellow acres and placid herds. He intimated delicately that a rancher's life was lonely at best, and enriched the tender intimation with the assurance that he was more than fond of enchiladas, frijoles, carne-con-chile, tamales, adding as an afterthought that he was some-what of an expert himself in "wrastlin' out" pies and doughnuts and various other gastronomical delicacies.

A delicate frown touched the gentle Anita's smooth forehead when her mother interrupted Sundown with a steaming cup of coffee and a plate of frijoles, yet Anita realized, as she saw his ardent expression when the aroma of the coffee reached him, that this was a most sensible and fitting climax to his glowing discourse. Her frown vanished together with the coffee and beans.

Fortified by the strong black coffee and the nourishing frijoles, Sundown rose from his seat on the doorstep and betook himself to the back of the house where he labored with an axe until he had accumulated quite a pile of firewood. Then he rolled up his sleeves, washed his hands, and asked permission to prepare the evening meal. Although a little astonished, the Senora consented, and watched Sundown, at first with a smile of indulgence, then with awakening curiosity, and finally with frank and compli-mentary amazement as he deftly kneaded and rolled pie-crust and manufactured a pie that eventually had, for those immediately concerned, historical significance.

The "little hombre," Chico Miguel, returning to his 'dobe that evening, was greeted with a tide of explanatory utterances that swept him off his feet. He was introduced to Sundown, apprised of the strange guest's manifold accomplishments, and partook of the substantial evidence of his skill until of the erstwhile generous pie there was nothing left save tender reminiscence and replete satisfaction.

Later in the evening, when the Arizona stars glowed and shimmered on the shadowy adobe, when the wide mesas grew mysteriously beautiful in the soft radiance of the slow moon, Chico Miguel brought his guitar from the bedroom, tuned it, and struck a swaying cadence from its strings. Then Anita's voice, blending with the rhythm, made melody, and Sundown sat entranced. Mood, environment, temperament, lent romance to the simple song. Every singing string on the old guitar was silver—the singer's girlish voice a sunlit wave of gold.

The bleak and almost barren lives of these isolated folk became illumined with a reminiscent glow as the tinkling notes of the guitar hushed to faint echoes of fairy bells hung on the silver boughs of starlit trees. "Adios, linda Rosa," ran the song. Then silence, the summer night, the myriad stars.

Sundown, turning his head, gazed spellbound at the dark-eyed singing girl. In the dim light of the lamp she saw that his lean cheeks were wet with tears.

CHAPTER XXI

ON THE MESA

With the morning sun came a brave, cloudless day and a more jovial mood to Sundown as he explained the necessity for haste to the Concho. Chico Miguel would gladly furnish horse and saddle. Juan Corlees was of men the finest! Once upon a time, in fact, Chico Miguel had ridden range for the father of Senor Corlees, but that was in years long past, Ah, yes! Then there were no sheep in the country—nothing but cattle and vaqueros. Would the caballero accept the loan of horse and saddle? The horse could be returned at his convenience. And possibly—and here Chico Miguel paused to roll a cigarette, light it, and smoke awhile reflectively—and possibly the caballero would again make their humble home beautiful with his presence. Such pie as the Senor made was a not unworthy meal for the saints. Indeed, Chico Miguel himself had had many pleasant dreams following their feast of the evening before. Would Sundown condescend to grace their home with his presence again and soon? Sundown would, be Gosh! He sure did like music, especially them Spanish songs what made a fella kind of shivery and sad-like from his boots up. And that part of the country looked good to him. In fact he was willing to be thrun from—er—have his hoss step in a gopher-hole any day if the accident might terminate as pleasantly as had his late misfortune. He aspired to become a master of the art of cooking Mexican dishes. 'Course at reg'lar plain-cookin' and deserts he wasn't such a slouch, but when it come to spreadin' the chile, he wasn't, as yet, an expert.

Meanwhile he clung tenaciously to the few Spanish words he knew, added to which was "Linda Rosa"—"pretty rose,"—which he intended to use with telling effect when he made his adieux. After breakfast he rose and disappeared. When he again entered the house the keen Senora noticed that his shirt front swelled expansively just above his heart. She wondered if the tall one had helped himself to a few of her beloved chiles.

Presently Chico Miguel appeared with the pony. Sundown mounted, hesitated, and then nodded farewell to the Senora and the almost tearful Anita who stood in the doorway. Things were not as Sundown would have had them. He was long of arm and vigorous, but to cast a bouquet of hastily gathered and tied flowers from the gateway to the hand of the Senorita would require a longer arm and a surer aim than his. "Gee Gosh!" he exclaimed, dismounting hurriedly. "What's that on his hind foot?"

He referred to the horse. Chico Miguel, at the gate, hastened to examine the pony, but Sundown, realizing that the Senorita still stood beside her mother, must needs create further delay. He stepped to the pony and, assuming an air of experience, reached to take up the horse's foot and examine it. The horse, possibly realizing that its foot was sound, resented Sundown's solicitude. The upshot—used advisedly—of it was that Sundown found himself sitting in the road and Chico Miguel struggling with the pony.

With a scream Anita rushed to the gateway, wringing her hands as Sundown rose stiffly and felt of his shirt front. The

Henry Hubert Knibbs

flowers that he had picked for his adored, were now literally pressed to his bosom. He wondered if they "were mushed up much?" Yet he was not unhappy. His grand climax was at hand. Again he mounted the pony, turned to the Senorita, and, drawing the more or less mangled blossoms from his shirt, presented them to her with sweeping gallantry. Anita blushed and smiled. Sundown raised his hat. "Adios! Adios! Mucha adios! Senorita! For you sure are the lindaest little linda rosa of the whole bunch!" he said.

And with Anita standing in rapt admiration, Chico Miguel wondering if the kick of the horse had not unsettled the strange caballero's reason, and the Senora blandly aware that her daughter and the tall one had become adepts in interpreting the language of the eyes, Sundown rode away in a cloud of dust, triumphantly joyous, yet with a peculiar sensation in the region of his heart, where the horse had kicked him. When he realized that admiring eyes could not follow him forever, he checked the horse and rubbed his chest.

"It hurts, all right! but hoss-shoes is a sign of *luck*—and posies is a sign of *love*—and them two signs sure come together this mornin'. 'Oh, down in Arizona there's a—' No, I reckon I won't be temptin' Providence ag'in. This hoss might have some kind of a dislikin' for toad-lizards and po'try mixed, same as the other one. I can jest kind o' work the rest of that poem up inside and keep her on the ice till—er—till she's the right flavor. Wonder how they're makin' it at the Concho? Guess I'll stir along. Mebby they're waitin' for me to show up so's they can get busy. I dunno. It sure is wonderful what a lot is dependin' on me these here days. I'm gettin' to be kind of a center figure in this here country. Lemme see. Now I bruk jail—hopped the Limited, took out me homesteader papers, got thrun off a hoss, slumped right into love with that sure-enough Linda Rosa, and got kicked by another hoss. And they say I ain't a enterprisin' guy! Gee Gosh!"

Never so much at home as when alone, the mellifluous Sundown's imagination expanded, till it embraced the farthest outpost of his theme. He became the towering center of things terrestrial. The world revolved around but one individual that glorious morning, and he generously decided to let it revolve. He felt—being, for the first time in his weird career, very much in love—that Dame Fortune, so long indifferent to his modest aspirations, had at last recognized in him a true adventurer worthy of her grace. He was a remarkable man, physically. He considered himself a remarkable man mentally, and he was, in Arizona. "Why," he announced to his horse, "they's folks as says they ain't no romantics left in this here world! Huh! Some of them writin' folks oughter jest trail my smoke for a week, instead o' settin' in clubs and drinkin' high-balls and expectin' them high-balls to put 'em wise to real life! Huh! A fella's got to sweat it out himself. The kind of romantics that comes in a bottle ain't the real thing. Pickles is all right, but they ain't cucumbers, nohow. Wisht I had one—and some salt. The stories them guys write is like pickles, jest two kinds of flavor, sweet and sour. Now, when I write me life's history she'll be a cucumber sliced thin with a few of them little red chiles to kind o' give the right kick, and mebby a leetle onion representin' me sentiment, and salt to draw out the proper taste, and 'bout three drops o' vinegar standin' for hard luck, and the hull thing fixed tasty-like on a lettuce leaf, the crinkles representin' the mountings and valleys of this here world, and me name on the cover in red with gold edges. Gee Gosh!"

The creak of the saddle, the tinkle of his spurs, the springy stride of the horse furnished a truly pastoral accompaniment to Sundown's "romantics."

Henry Hubert Knibbs

As he rode down a draw, he came suddenly upon two coyotes playing like puppies in the sun. He reined up and watched them, and his heart warmed to their antics. "Now, 'most any fella ridin' range would nacherally pull his gun and bling at 'em. What for? Search me! They ain't botherin' nobody. Jest playin'. Guess 'most any animals like to play if they wasn't scared o' gettin' shot all the time. Funny how some folks got to kill everything they see runnin' wild. What's the use? Now, mebby them coyotes is a pa and ma thinkin' o' settin' up ranchin' and raisin' alfalfa and young ones. Or mebby he's just a-courtin' her and showin' how he can run and jump better than any other coyote she ever seen. I dunno. There they go. Guess they seen me. Say! but they are jest floatin' across the mesa—they ain't runnin'. Goin' easy, like their legs belonged to somebody else and they was jest keepin' up with 'em. So-long, folks! Here's hopin' you get settled on that coyote-ranch all right!"

Thus far on his journey Sundown had enjoyed the pleasing local flavor of the morning and his imaginings. The vinegar, which was to represent "hard luck," had not as yet been added to the salad.

As he ascended the gentle slope of the draw he heard a quick, blunt sound, as though some one had struck a drum and immediately muffled the reverberations with the hand. He was too deeply immersed in himself to pay much attention to this. Topping the rise, the fresh vista of rolling mesa, the far blue hills, and a white dot—the distant Concho—awakened him to a realization of his whereabouts. Again he heard that peculiar, dull sound. He lifted his horse to a lope and swept along, the dancing shadow at his side shortening as noon overtook him. He was about to dismount and partake of the luncheon the kindly Senora had prepared for him, when he changed his mind. "Lunch and hunch makes a rhyme," he announced. "And I got 'em both. Guess

I'll jog along and eat at the Concho. Mebby I'll get there in two, three hours."

As the white dot took on a familiar outline and the eastern wall of the canon of the Concho showed sharply against the sky, he saw a horseman, strangely doubled up in the saddle, riding across the mesa toward the ranch-house. Evidently he also was going to the Concho. Possibly it was Bud, or Hi Wingle, or Lone Johnny. Following an interval of attending strictly to the trail he raised his eyes. He pulled his horse up and sat blinking. Where there had been a horse and rider there was but the horse, standing with lowered head. He shaded his eyes with his palm and gazed again. There stood the horse. The man had disappeared. "Fell into one of them Injun graves," remarked Sundown. "Guess I'll go see."

It took much longer than he had anticipated to come up with the riderless horse. He recognized it as one of the Concho ponies. Almost beneath the animal lay a huddled something. Sundown's scalp tingled. Slowly he got from his horse and stalked across the intervening space. He led the pony from the tumbled shape on the ground. Then he knelt and raised the man's shoulders. Sinker, one of the Concho riders, groaned and tore at the shirt over his stomach. Then Sundown knew. He eased the cowboy back and called his name. Slowly the gray lids opened. "It's me, Sundown! Who done it?"

The cowboy tried to rise on his elbow. Sundown supported his head, questioning him, for he knew that Sinker had but little time left to speak. The wounded man writhed impotently, then quieted.

"God, Sun!" he moaned, "they got me. Tell Jack—Mexican—Loring—sheep at—waterhole. Tried to bluff—'em off—orders not to shoot. They got orders to shoot—all right. Tell

Jack—Guess I'm bleedin' inside—So-long—pardner."

The dying man writhed from Sundown's arms and rolled to his face, cursing and clutching at the grass in agony. Sundown stood over him, his hat off, his gaze lifted toward the cloudless sky, his face white with a new and strange emotion. He raised his long arms and clenched his hands. "God A'mighty," he whispered, rocking back and forth, "I got to tell You that sech things is *wrong*. And from what I seen sence I come to this country, You don't care. But some of us does care . . . and I reckon we got to do somethin' if You don't."

The cowboy raised himself on rigid arms, he lifted his head, and his eyes, filmed with the chill of death, grew clear for an instant. "'Sandro—the herder—got me," he gasped. His lips writhed back from his clenched teeth. A rush of blood choked him. He sank to the ground, quivered, and was still.

"'Sandro . . . the herder" . . . whispered Sundown. "Sinker was me friend. I reckon God's got to leave the finish of this to me."

CHAPTER XXII

WAIT!

To see a man's life go out and to stand by unable to help, unable to offer comfort or ease mortal agony, is a bitter experience. It brings the beholder close to the abyss of eternity, wherein the world shrinks to a speck of whirling dust and the sun is but a needle-point of light. Then it is that the fleshless face of the unconquerable One leans close and whispers, not to the insensate clay that mocks the living, but to the impotent soul that mourns the dead.

That Sundown should consider himself morally bound to become one of those who he knew would avenge the killing of the cowboy, and without recourse to law, was not altogether strange. The iron had entered his soul. Heretofore at loose ends with the world, the finding of Sinker, dying on the mesas, kindled within him righteous wrath against the circumstance rather than the individual slayer. His meandering thoughts and emotions became crystallized. His energies hardened to a set purpose. He was obsessed with a fanaticism akin to that of those who had burned witches and thanked their Maker for the opportunity.

In his simple way he wondered why he had not wept. He rode slowly to the Concho. Chance leaped circling about his

Henry Hubert Knibbs

horse. He greeted the dog with a word. When he dismounted, Chance cringed and crept to him. Without question this was his master, and yet there was something in Sundown's attitude that silenced the dog's joyous welcoming. Chance sat on his haunches, whined, and did his best by his own attitude to show that he was in sympathy with his master's strange mood.

John Corliss saw instantly that there was something wrong, and his hearty greeting lapsed into terse questioning. Sundown pointed toward the northern mesas.

"What's up?" he queried.

"Sinker—he's dead—over there."

"Sinker?" Corliss ran to the corral, calling to Wingle, who came from the bunk-house. The cook whisked off his apron, grabbed his hat, and followed Corliss. "Sinker's done for!" said Corliss. "Saddle up, Hi. Sun found him out there. Must have had trouble at the water-hole. I should have sent another man with him."

Wingle, with the taciturnity of the plainsman, jerked the cinchas tight and swung to the saddle. Sinker's death had come like a white-hot flash of lightning from the bulked clouds that had shadowed disaster impending—and in that shadow the three men rode silently toward the north. Again Corliss questioned Sundown. Tense with the stress of an emotion that all but sealed his lips, Sundown turned his white face to Corliss and whispered, "Wait!" The rancher felt that that one terse, whispered word implied more than he cared to imagine. There was something uncanny about the man. If the killing of Sinker could so change the timorous, kindly Sundown to this grim, unbending epitome of lean death and vengeance, what could he himself do to check the wild fury of his riders when they heard of their companion's passing from the sun?

Sinker's horse, grazing, lifted its head and nickered as they rode up. They dismounted and turned the body over. Wingle, kneeling, examined the cowboy's six-gun.

Corliss, in a burst of wrath, turned on Sundown. "Damn you, open your mouth. What do you know about this?"

Sundown bit his nails and glowered at Corliss. "God A'mighty sent me—" he began.

With a swift gesture Corliss interrupted. "You're working for the Concho. Was he dead when you found him?"

Sundown slowly raised his arm and pointed across the mesa.

Corliss fingered his belt and bit his lip impatiently.

"A herder—over there to my ranch—done it. Sinker told me—'fore he crossed over. Said it was 'Sandro. Said he had orders not to shoot. He tried to bluff 'em off, for they was bringin' sheep to the water-hole. He said to tell you."

Corliss and Wingle turned from looking at Sundown and gazed at each other. "If that's right—" And the rancher hesitated.

"I reckon it's right," said Wingle. And he stooped and together they lifted the body and laid it across the cowboy's horse.

Sundown watched them with burning eyes. "We'll ride back home," said Corliss, motioning to him.

"Home? Ain't you goin' to do nothin'?"

Corliss shook his head. Sundown slowly mounted and followed them to the Concho. He watched them as they carried Sinker to the bunkhouse.

When Corliss reappeared, Sundown strode up to him. "This here hoss belongs to that leetle Mexican on the Apache road, Chico Miguel—said you knowed him. I was goin' to take him back with my hoss. Now I reckon I can't. I kind o' liked it over there to his place. I guess I want my own hoss, Pill."

"I guess you better get something to eat and rest up. You're in bad shape, Sun."

Sundown shook his head. "I got somethin' to do—after that mebby I can rest up. Can I have me hoss?"

"Yes, if it'll do you any good. What are you going to do?"

"I got me homesteader papers. I'm goin' to me ranch."

"But you're not outfitted. There's no grub there. You better take it easy. You'll feel better to-morrow."

"I don't need no outfit. I reckon I'll saddle Pill."

Sundown turned the Mexican's pony into the corral and saddled his own horse which he led to the bunk-house. "I ain't got no gun," he said. "The sheriff gent's got mine. Mebby you'd be lendin' me one?"

Wingle stepped to the doorway and stood beside Corliss. "What does he want, Jack?"

"He's loco. Wants to borrow a gun." The rancher turned to

Sundown. "See here, Sun, there's no use thinking you've got to take a hand in this. Some of the boys'll get the Mexican sure! I can't stop them, but I don't want you to get in trouble."

"No. You come on in and eat," said Wingle. "You got a touch of sun, I guess."

Sundown mounted. "Ain't you goin' to do nothin'?" he asked again.

Corliss and Wingle glanced at each other. "No, not now."

"Then me and Chance is," said Sundown. "Come on, Chance."

Corliss and the cook watched the tall figure as it passed through the gateway and out to the mesa. "I'll go head him off, if you say the word, Jack."

Corliss made a negative gesture. "He'll come back when he gets hungry. It's a long ride to the water-hole. Sinker had sand to get as near home as he did. It's going to be straight hell from now on, Hi."

Wingle nodded. Through force of habit he reached for his apron to wipe his hand—his invariable preliminary before he shook hands with any one. His apron being off, he hesitated, then stepped to his employer. "It sure is," he said, "and I'm ridin' with you."

They shook hands. Moved by a mutual impulse they glanced at the long, rigid shape covered with a blanket. "When the boys come—" began Wingle.

"It will be out of our hands," concluded Corliss.

"If Sun—"

"I ought to ride out after him," said Corliss, nodding. "But I can't leave. And you can't."

Wingle stepped to the doorway and shaded his eyes. Far out on the mesa the diminishing figure of a horseman showed black against the glare of the sun. Wingle turned and, with a glance at the shrouded figure on the bunk-house floor, donned his apron and shuffled to the kitchen. Corliss tied his horse and strode to the office.

Hi Wingle puttered about the kitchen. There would be supper to get for fifteen hungry—No! fourteen, to-night. He paused, set down the pan that he held and opened the door of the chuck-room. With finger marking the count he totaled the number of chairs at the table. Fifteen. Then he stepped softly to the bunk-room, took Sinker's hat and stepped back to the table. He placed the hat on the dead cowboy's chair. Then he closed the door and turned to the preparation of the evening meal. "Jack'll report to Antelope and try and keep the boys quiet. I'm sure with Jack—only I was a puncher first afore I took to cookin'. And I'm a puncher yet—inside." Which was his singular and only spoken tribute to the memory of Sinker. He had reasoned that it was only right and fitting that the slayer of a cowman should be slain by a cowman—a code that held good in his time and would hold good now— especially when the boys saw the battered Stetson, every line of which was mutely eloquent of its owner's individuality.

Sundown drifted through the afternoon solitudes, his mind dulled by the monotony of the theme which obsessed him. It was evening when he reached the water-hole. Around the enclosure straggled a few stray sheep. He cautioned Chance against molesting them. Ordinarily he would have approached the ranch-house timidly, but he was beyond fear.

He rode to the gate, tied his horse, and stepped to the doorway. The door was open. He entered and struck a match. In the dusk he saw that the room was empty save for a tarpaulin and a pair of rawhide kyacks such as the herders use. Examining the kyacks he found that they contained flour, beans, salt, sugar, and coffee. Evidently the herders had intended making the deserted ranch-house their headquarters. He wondered vaguely where the Mexicans were. The thought that they might return did not worry him. He knew what he would do in that instance. He would find out which one was 'Sandro . . . and then . . .

The bleating of the stray sheep annoyed him. He told Chance to stay in the room. Then he stalked out and opened the gate. "Mebby they want water. I dunno. Them's Loring's sheep, all right, but they ain't to blame for—for Sinker." With the idea came a more reasonable mood. The sheep were not to blame for the killing of Sinker. The sheep belonged to Loring. The herders, also, practically belonged to Loring. They were only following his bidding when they protected the sheep. With such reasoning he finally concluded that Loring, not his herder, was responsible for the cowboy's death. He returned to the house, built a fire, and cooked an indifferent meal.

Sundown sat up suddenly. In the dim light of the moon flickering through the dusty panes he saw Chance standing close to the door with neck bristling and head lowered. Throwing back his blanket he rose and whispered to the dog. Chance came to him obediently. Sundown saw that the dog was trembling. He motioned him back and stepped to the door. His slumbers had served to restore him to himself in a measure. His old timidity became manifest as he hesitated, listening. In the absolute silence of the night he thought he heard a shuffling as of something being dragged across the enclosure. Tense with anticipating he knew not what, he listened. Again he heard that peculiar slithering sound. He

Henry Hubert Knibbs

opened the door an inch and peered out. In the pallid glow of the moon he beheld a shapeless object that seemed to be crawling toward him. Something in the helpless attitude of the object suggested Sinker as he had risen on his arm, endeavoring to tell of the disaster which had overtaken him. With a gesture of scorn at his own fear he swung open the door. Chance crept at his heels, whining. Then Sundown stepped out and stood gazing at the strange figure on the ground. Not until a groan of agony broke the utter silence did he realize that the night had brought to him a man, wounded and suffering terribly. "Who are you?" he questioned, stooping above the man. The other dragged himself to Sundown's feet and clawed at his knees. "'Sandro . . . It is— that I—die. You don' keel . . . You don' . . ."

Sundown dragged the herder to the house and into the bedroom. He got water, for which the herder called piteously. With his own blanket he made him as comfortable as he could. Then he built a fire that he might have light. The herder was shot through the thigh, and had all but bled to death dragging himself across the mesa from where he had fallen from his horse. Sundown tried to stop the bleeding with strips torn from his bandanna. Meanwhile the wounded man was imploring him not to kill him.

"I'm doin' me best to fix you up, Dago," said Sundown. "But you better go ahead and say them prayers—and you might put in a couple for Sinker what you shot. I reckon his slug cut the big vein and you got to go. Wisht I could do somethin' . . . to help . . . you stay . . . but mebby it's better that you cross over easy. Then the boys don't get you."

The Mexican seemed to understand. He nodded as he lay gazing at the lean figure illumined by the dancing light of the open stove. "Si. You good hombre, si," he gasped.

Sundown frowned. "Now, don't you take any idea like that along to glory with you. Sinker—what you shot—was me friend. I ought to kill you like a snake. But God A'mighty took the job off me hands. I reckon that makes me square with—with Sinker—and Him."

Again Sundown brought water to the herder. Gently he raised his head and held the cup to his lips. Chance stood in the middle of the room strangely subdued, yet he watched each movement of his master with alert eyes. The moonlight faded from the window and the fire died down. The air became chill as the faint light of dawn crept in to emphasize the ghastly picture—the barren, rough-boarded room, the rusted stove, the towering figure of Sundown, impassively waiting; and the shattered, shrunken figure of the Mexican, hopeless and helpless, as the morning mesas welcomed the golden glow of dawn and a new day.

The herder, despite his apparent torpor, was the first to hear the faint thud of hoofs in the loose sand of the roadway. He grew instantly alert, raising himself on his elbow and gazing with fear-wide eyes toward the south.

Sundown nodded. "It's the boys," he said, as though speaking to himself. "I was hopin' he could die easy. I dunno."

'Sandro raised his hands and implored Sundown to save him from the riders. Sundown stepped to the window. He saw the flash of spurs and bits as a group of the Concho boys swept down the road. One of them was leading a riderless horse. In a flash he realized that they had found the herder's horse and had tracked 'Sandro to the water-hole. He backed away from the window and reaching down took the Mexican's gun from its holster. "'T ain't what I figured on," he muttered. "They's me friends, but this is me ranch."

With a rush and a slither of hoofs in the loose sand the Concho riders, headed by Shoop, swung up to the gate and dismounted. Sundown stepped to the doorway, Chance beside him.

Shoop glanced quickly at the silent figure. Then his gaze drifted to the ground.

"'Mornin', Sun! Seen anybody 'round here this mornin'?"

"Mornin', fellas. Nope. Just me and Chance."

The men hesitated, eyeing Sundown suspiciously.

Corliss stepped toward the ranch-house.

"Guess we'll look in," he said, and stepped past Shoop.

Sundown had closed the door of the bedroom. He was at a loss to prevent the men entering the house, but once within the house he determined that they should not enter the bedroom.

He backed toward it and stood with one shoulder against the lintel. "Come right in. I ain't got to housekeepin' yet, but . . ."

He ceased speaking as he saw Corliss's gaze fixed on the kyacks. "Where did you get 'em?" queried the rancher.

The men crowded in and gazed curiously at the kyacks—then at Sundown.

Shoop strode forward. "The game's up, Sun. We want the Mexican."

"This is me ranch," said Sundown. "I got the papers—here.

You fellas is sure welcome—only they ain't goin' to be no shootin' or such-like. I ain't joshin' this time."

A voice broke the succeeding silence. "If the Mexican is in there, we want him—that's all."

Sundown's eyes became bright with a peculiar expression. Slowly—yet before any one could realize his intent—he reached down and drew the Mexican's gun. "You're me friends," he said quietly. "He's in there—dyin'. I reckon Sinker got him. He drug himself here last night and I took him in. This is me home—and if you fellas is *men*, you'll let him die easy and quiet."

"I'm from Missouri," said Shoop, with a hard laugh. "You got to show me that he's—like you say, or—"

Sundown leveled his gun at Shoop. "I ain't lyin' to you, Bud. Sinker was me friend. And I ain't lyin' when I says that the fust fella that tries to tech him crosses over afore he does."

Some one laughed. Corliss touched Shoop's arm and whispered to him. With a curse the foreman turned and the men clumped out to the yard.

"He's right," said Corliss. "We'll wait."

They stood around talking and commenting upon Sundown's defense of the Mexican.

"'Course we could 'a' got him," said Shoop, "but it don't set right with me to be stood up by a tenderfoot. Sundown's sure loco."

"I don't know, Bud. He's queer, all right, but this is his ranch. He's got a right to order us out."

Shoop was about to retort when Sundown came to the doorway. "I guess you can come in now," he said. "And you won't need no gun." The men shuffled awkwardly, and finally led by Corliss they filed into the room and one by one they stepped to the open door of the bedroom and gazed within. Then they filed out silently.

"I'll send over some grub," said Corliss as they mounted. Sundown nodded.

The band of riders moved slowly back toward the Concho. About halfway on their homeward journey they met Loring in a buckboard. The old sheep-man drove up and would have passed them without speaking had not Corliss reined across the road and halted him.

"One of your herders—'Sandro—is over at the water-hole," said Corliss. "If you're headed for Antelope, you might stop by and take him along."

Loring glared at the Concho riders, seemed about to speak, but instead clucked to his team. The riders reined out of his way and he swept past, gazing straight ahead, grim, silent, and utterly without fear. He understood the rancher's brief statement, and he already knew of the killing of Sinker. 'Sandro's assistant, becoming frightened, had left his wounded companion on the mesas, and had ridden to the Loring rancho with the story of the fight and its ending.

CHAPTER XXIII

THE PEACEMAKER

"But I ain't no dove—more like a stork, I guess," reflected Sundown as he stood in the doorway of his house. "And storks brings responsibilities in baskets, instead of olive branches. No wonder ole man Noah fired the dove right out ag'in—bringin' him olives what wa'n't pickled, instead of a bunch of grapes or somethin' you can eat! And that there dove never come back. I reckon he figured if he did, ole man Noah'd shoot him. Anyhow, if I ain't no dove of peace, I'm goin' to do the best I can. Everybody 'round here seems like they was tryin' to ride right into trouble wishful, 'stead of reinin' to one side an' givin' trouble a chance to get past. Gee Gosh! If I'd 'a' knowed what I know now—afore I hit this country—but I'm here. Anyhow, they's nothin' wrong with the country. It's the folks, like it 'most always is. Reckon I ought to keep on buildin' fence this mornin', but that there peace idea 's got to singin' in me head. I'll jest saddle up Pill and ride over and tell ole man Loring that I'm takin' care of his sheep charitable what's been hangin' around here since 'Sandro passed over. Mebby that'll kind o' start the talk. Then I can slip him a couple of ideas 'bout how neighbors ought to act. Huh! Me nussin' them sheep for two weeks and more, an' me just dyin' for a leetle taste o' mutton. Mebby his herders was scared to come for 'em, I dunno."

Henry Hubert Knibbs

Sundown was established at the water-hole. Corliss had sent a team to Antelope for provisions, implements, and fencing. Meanwhile, Sundown had been industrious, not alone because he felt the necessity for something to occupy his time, but that he wanted to forget the tragedy he had so recently witnessed. And he had dreams of a more companionable future which included Mexican dishes served hot, evenings of blissful indolence accompanied by melody, and a Senora who would sing "Linda Rosa, Adios!" which would be the "piece de resistance" of his pastoral menu.

The "tame cow," which he had so ardently longed for, now grazed soulfully in a temporary enclosure out on the mesa. Two young and sprightly black pigs prospected the confines of their littered hermitage. Four gaunt hens and a more or less dilapidated rooster stalked about the yard, no longer afraid of the watchful Chance, who had previously introduced himself to the rooster without the formality of Sundown's presence as mediator. Sundown was proud of his chickens. The cow, however, had been, at first, rather a disappointment to him. Milk had not heretofore been a conspicuous portion of Sundown's diet, nor was he versed in the art of obtaining it except over the counter in tins. With due formality and some trepidation he had placed a pail beneath "Gentle Annie" as he called her, and had waited patiently. So had Gentle Annie, munching a reflective cud, and Sundown, in a metaphorical sense, doing likewise. He had walked around the cow inspecting her with an anxious and critical eye. She seemed healthful and voluptuously contented. Yet no milk came. Bud Shoop, having at that moment arrived with the team, sized up the situation. When he had recovered enough poise to stand without assistance and had wiped the wild tears from his eyes, he instructed the amazed Sundown as to certain manipulations necessary to produce the desired result. "Huh! Folks says cows *give* milk. But I reckon that ain't right," Sundown had asserted. "You got to take it away from 'em." So he had taken what he could, which was not, at first, a great deal.

This momentous morning he had decided that his unsolicited mission was to induce or persuade Loring to arbitrate the question of grazing-rights. It was a strange idea, although not incompatible with Sundown's peculiar temperament. He felt justified in taking the initiative; especially in view of the fact that Loring's sheep had been trespassing on his property.

He saddled "Pill," and called to Chance. "See here, Chance, you and me's pals. No, you ain't comin' this trip. You stick around and keep your eye on me stock. What's mine is yourn exceptin' the rooster. Speakin' poetical, he belongs to them hens. If he ain't here when I get back, I can pretty nigh tell by the leavin's where he is. When I git back I look to find you hungry, sabe? And not sneakin' around lookin' at me edgeways with leetle feathers stickin' to your nose. I reckon you understand."

Chance followed his master to the road, and there the dog sat gazing at the bobbing figure of Sundown until it was but a speck in the morning sunshine. Then Chance fell to scratching his ear with his hind foot, rose and shook himself, and stalked indolently to the yard where he lay with his nose along his outstretched fore legs, watching the proscribed rooster with an eloquence of expression that illustrated the proverbial power of mind over matter.

Sundown kept Pill loping steadily. It was a long ride, but Sundown's mind was so preoccupied with the preparing of his proposed appeal to the sheep-man that the morning hours and the sunlit miles swept past unnoticed. The dark green of the acacias bordering the hacienda, the twinkling white of the speeding windmill, and the dull brown of the adobes became distinct and separate colors against the far edge of the eastern sky. He reined his pony to a walk. "When you're in a hurry to do somethin'," he informed his horse, "it ain't always good politics to let folks know it. So we'll ride up easy, like we had money to spend, and was jest lookin' over the show-case." And Pill was not averse to the suggestion.

Sundown dismounted, opened the gate, and swinging to the saddle, rode up to the ranch-house. Had he known that Anita, the daughter of Chico Miguel, was at that moment talking with the wife of one of Loring's herders; that she was describing him in glowing terms to her friend, and moreover, as he passed up the driveway, that Anita had turned swiftly, dropping the pitcher of milk which she had just brought from the cooling-room as she saw him, he might well have been excused from promulgating his mission of peace with any degree of coherence. Sublimely ignorant of her presence,— spiritualists and sentimentalists to the contrary in like instances,—he rode directly to the hacienda, asked for the patron, and was shown to the cool interior of the house by the mildly astonished Senora. Senor Loring would return presently. Would the gentleman refresh himself by resting until the Senor returned? Possibly she herself could receive the message—or the Senorita, who was in the garden?

"Thanks, lady. I reckon Pill is dry—wants a drink—agua— got a thirst. No, ma'am. I can wait. I mean me horse."

"Oh! Si! But Juan would attend to the horse and at once."

"Thanks, lady. And if Miss Loring ain't too busy, I reckon I'd like to see her a minute."

The Senora disappeared. Sundown could hear her call for Juan. Presently Nell Loring came to the room, checked an exclamation of surprise as she recognized him, and stepping forward, offered her hand. "You're from Mr. Corliss. I remember. . . . Is Chance all right now?"

"Yes, ma'am. He is enjoyin' fust-rate health. He eats reg'lar—and rabbits in between. But I ain't from the Concho, lady. I'm from me own ranch, down there at the water-hole. Me boss ain't got nothin' to do with me bein' here. It's me own idea. I come friendly and wishful to make a little talk to your pa."

Wondering what could have induced Sundown to call at her home, especially under the existing circumstances, Nell Loring made him welcome. After he had washed and strolled over to the stables to see to his horse. Sundown, returning, declined an invitation to come in, and sat on the veranda, smoking cigarettes and making mental note of the exterior details of the hacienda: its garden, shade-trees, corrals, and windmill. Should prosperity smile upon him, he would have a windmill, be Gosh! Not a white one—though white wasn't so bad—but something tasty; red, white and blue, mebby—a real American windmill, and in the front of the house a flagpole with the American flag. And he would keep the sign "American Hotel" above the gate. There was nothin' like bein' paterotic. Mexican ranches—some of 'em—was purty enough in a lazy kind of style, but he was goin' to let folks know that a white man was runnin' the water-hole ranch!

And all unknown to him, Anita stood in the doorway of one of the herder's 'dobes, more than ever impressed by the evident importance of her beau-ideal of chivalry, who took the kick of horses as a matter of course, and rose smilingly from such indignities to present flowers to her with eyes which spake of love and lips that expressed, as best they could, admiration. Anita was a bit disappointed and perhaps a bit pleased that he had not as yet seen her. As it was she could worship from a distance that lent security to her tender embarrassment. The tall one must, indeed, be a great

Henry Hubert Knibbs

caballero to be made welcome at the patron's home. Assuredly he was not as the other vaqueros who visited the patron. *He* sat upon the veranda and smoked in a lordly way, while they inevitably held forth in the less conspicuous latitude of the bunk-house and its environs. Anita was happy.

Sundown, elated by the righteousness of his mission as harbinger of peace, met Loring returning from one of the camps with gracious indifference to the other's gruff welcome.

They sat at the table and ate in silence for a while. With the refreshing coffee Sundown's embarrassment melted. His weird command of language, enhanced by the opportunity for exercise in a good cause, astonished and eventually interested his hearers. He did not approach his subject directly, but mounted the metaphorical steps of his rostrum leisurely. He discoursed on the opportunities afforded by the almost limitless free range. He hinted at the possibility of internecine strife eventually awakening the cupidity of "land-sharks" all over the country. If there was land worth killing folks for, there was land worth stealing. If the Concho Valley was once thrown open to homesteaders, then farewell free range and fat cattle and sheep. And the mention of sheep led him to remark that there was a small band at the water-hole, uncared-for save by himself. "And he was no sheep-man, but he sure hated to see any critters sufferin' for water, so he had allowed the sheep to drink at the water-hole." Then he paused, anticipating the obvious question to which he made answer: "Yes. The water-hole ranch is me ranch. I filed on her the same day that you and Miss Loring come to Usher. Incondescent to that I was in the calaboose at Antelope. Somebody tole the sheriff that I was a suspicious character. Mebby I am, judgin' from the outside, but inside I ain't. You can't always tell what the works is like by the case, I ain't got no hard feelin's for nobody, and I'm wishful that folks don't have no hard feelin's ag'in' me or anybody else."

Loring listened in silence. Finally he spoke. "I'll take care of my sheep. I'll send for 'em to-day. Looks like you're tryin' to play square, but you don't figure in this deal. Jack Corliss is at the bottom of it and he's using you. And he'll use you hard. What you goin' to do with the overflow from the water-hole?"

"I'm goin' to irrigate me ranch," said Sundown.

Loring nodded. "And cut off the water from everybody?"

"Not from me friends."

"Which means the Concho."

"Sure! Jack Corliss is me friend. But that ain't all. If you want to be me friend, I ain't kickin' even if you did tell the sheriff he ought to git acquainted with me closer. I'm goin' to speak right out. I reckon it's the best way. I got a proposition. If you'll quit sickin' them herders onto cowboys and if Jack'll quit settin' the punchers at your herders, I'll open up me spring and run her down to where they's water for everybody. If cows comes, they drink. If sheep comes, *they* drink. If folks comes, they drink, likewise. But no fightin'."

Sundown as arbiter of peace felt that he had, in truth, "spoken right out." He was not a little surprised at himself and a bit fearful. Yet he felt justified in his suggestion. Theoretically he had made a fair offer. Practically his offer was of no value. Sheep and cattle could not occupy the same range. Loring grumbled something and shoved back his chair. They rose and stepped to the veranda.

"If you can get Corliss to agree to what you say—and quit

Henry Hubert Knibbs

runnin' cattle on the water-hole side—I'll quit runnin' sheep there." And Loring waved his hand toward the north.

"But the Concho is on the west side—" began Sundown.

"And cattle are grazin' on the east side," said Loring.

Sundown scratched his head. "I reckon I got to see Jack," he said.

"And you'll waste time, at that," said Loring. "Look here! Are you ranchin' to hold down the water-hole for Corliss or to make a livin'?"

Sundown hesitated. He gazed across the yard to the distant mesa. Suddenly a figure crossed the pathway to the gate. He jerked up his head and stood with mouth open. It couldn't be—but, yes, it was Anita—Linda Rosa! Gee Gosh! He turned to Loring. "I been tellin' you the truth," he said simply. "'Course I got to see me boss, now. But it makes no difference what he says, after this. I'm ranchin' for meself, because I'm—er—thinkin' of gettin' married."

Without further explanation, Sundown stalked to the stable and got his horse. He came to the hacienda and made his adieux. Then he mounted and rode slowly down the roadway toward the gate.

Anita's curiosity had overcome her timidity. Quite accidentally she stood toying with a bud that she had picked from the flower-bordered roadway. She turned as Sundown jingled up and met him with a murmur of surprise and pleasure. He swung from his horse hat in hand and advanced, bowing. Anita flushed and gazed at the ground.

"'Mornin', Senorita! I sure am jest hoppin' glad to see you

ag'in. If I'd 'a' knowed you was here . . . But I come on business—important. Reckon you're visitin' friends, eh?"

"Si, Senor!"

"Do you come here reg'lar?"

"Only to see the good aunt sometimes."

"Uhuh. I kind of wish your aunt was hangin' out at the Concho, though. This here ain't a reg'lar stoppin'-place for me."

"You go away?" queried Anita.

"I reckon I got to after what I said up there to the house. Yes, I'm goin' back to feed me pigs and Chance and the hens. I set up housekeepin' since I seen you. Got a ranch of me own—that I was tellin' you about. You ought to see it! Some class! But it's mighty lonely, evenin's."

Anita sighed and glanced at Sundown. Then her gaze dwelt on the bud she held. "Si, Senor—it is lonely in the evenings," she said, and although she spoke in Spanish, Sundown did not misunderstand.

He grinned hugely. "You sure don't need to talk American to tell it," he said as one who had just made a portentous discovery. "It was worryin' me how we was goin' to get along—me short on the Spanish and you short on my talk. But I reckon we'll get along fine. Your pa in good health, and your ma?"

Anita nodded shyly.

Sundown was at a loss to continue this pleasant conversation.

He brightened, however, as a thought inspired him. "And the leetle hoss, is he doin' well?"

"That Sarko I do not like that he should keeck you!" flamed Anita, and Sundown's cup of happiness was full to overflowing.

Quite unconsciously he was leading his horse toward the gate and quite unconsciously Anita was walking beside him. Forgotten was the Loring ranch, the Concho, his own homestead. He was with his inamorata, the "Linda Rosa" of his dreams.

At the gateway he turned to her. "I'm comin' over to see your folks soon as I git things to runnin' on me ranch. Keeps a fella busy, but I'm sure comin'. I ain't got posies to growin' yet, but I'm goin' to have some—like them," and he indicated the bud which she held.

"You like it?" she queried. And with bashful gesture she gave him the rose, smiling as he immediately stuck it in the band of his sombrero.

Then he held out his hand. "Linda Rosa," he said gently, "I can't make the big talk in the Spanish lingo or I'd say how I was lovin' you and thinkin' of you reg'lar and deep. 'Course I got to put your pa and ma wise first. But some day I'm comin'—me and Chance—and tell you that I'm ready—that me ranch is doin' fine, and that I sure want you to come over and boss the outfit. I used to reckon that I didn't want no woman around bossin' things, but I changed me mind. Adios! Senorita!—for I sure got to feed them hens."

Sundown extended his hand. Anita laid her own plump brown hand in Sundown's hairy paw. For an instant he hesitated, moved by a most natural impulse to kiss her. Her girlish face, innocently sweet and trusting, her big brown eyes glowing with admiration and wonder, as she gazed up at him, offered temptation and excuse enough. It was not timidity nor lack of opportunity that caused Sundown to hesitate, but rather that innate respect for women which distinguishes the gentle man from the slovenly generalization "gentleman." "Adios! Linda Rosa!" he murmured, and stooping, kissed her brown fingers. Then he gestured with magnificence toward the flowers bordering the roadway. "And you sure are the lindaest little Linda Rosa of the bunch!"

And Anita's heart was filled with happiness as she watched her brave caballero ride away, so tall, so straight, and of such the gentle manner and the royal air!

It was inevitable that he should turn and wave to her, but it was not inevitable that she should have thrown him a pretty kiss with the grace of her pent-up emotion—but she did.

Henry Hubert Knibbs

CHAPTER XXIV

AN UNEXPECTED VISIT

It was late in the evening when Sundown returned to his ranch. Chance welcomed him with vocal and gymnastic abandon. Sundown hastened to his "tame cow" and milked her while the four hens peeped and clucked from their roost, evidently disturbed by the light of the lantern. Meanwhile Chance lay gravely watching his master until Gentle Annie had been relieved of the full and creamy quota of her donation to the maintenance of the household. Then the wolf-dog followed his master to the kitchen where they enjoyed, in separate dishes, Gentle Annie's warm contribution, together with broken bread and "a leetle salt to bring out the gamey flavor."

Solicitous of the welfare of his stock, as he termed them, he betook himself to the hen-house to feed the chickens. "Huh!" he exclaimed, raising the lantern and peering round, "there's one rooster missin'!" *The* rooster had in truth disappeared. He put down the lantern and turned to Chance. "Lemme look at your mouth. No, they ain't no signs on you. Hold on! Be Gosh, if they ain't some leetle red hairs stickin' to your chops. What's the answer?"

Chance whined and wagged his tail. "You don't look like you

was guilty. And that there rooster wasn't sportin' red hair the last time I seen him. Did you eat him fust and then swaller a rabbit to cover his tracks? I reckon not. You're some dog— but you ain't got boiler-room for a full-size Rhode Island Red and a rabbit and two quarts of bread-and-milk. It ain't reas'nable. I got to investigate."

The dog seemed to understand. He leaped up and trotted to the yard, turning his head and silently coaxing his master to follow him. Sundown, with a childish and most natural faith in Chance's intelligence, followed him to the fence, scrambled through and trailed him out on the mesa. In a little hollow Chance stopped and stood with crooked fore leg. Sundown stalked up. At his feet fluttered his red rooster and not far from it lay the body of a full-grown coyote. Chance ran to the coyote and diving in shook the inanimate shape and growled. "Huh! Showin' me what you done to him for stealin' our rooster, eh? Well, you sure are goin' to get suthin' extra for this! You caught him with the goods—looks like. And look here!"—and Sundown deposited the lantern on a knoll and sat down facing the dog. "What I'm goin' to give you that extra for ain't for killin' the coyote. That is your business when I ain't to home. You could 'a' finished off Jimmy"—and he gestured toward the rooster—"and the evidence would 'a' been in your favor, seein' as you was wise to show me the coyote. I got some candy put by for—for later, if she likes it, but we're goin' to bust open that box of candy and celebrate. Got to see if I can repair Jimmy fust, though, or else use the axe. I dunno."

Jimmy was a sad spectacle. His tail-feathers were about gone and one leg was maimed, yet he still showed the fighting spirit of his New England sires, for, as Sundown essayed to pick him up, he pecked and squawked energetically.

They returned to the house, where Sundown examined the

Henry Hubert Knibbs

bedraggled bird critically. "I ain't no doc, but I have been practiced on some meself. Looks like his left kicker was bruk. Guess it's the splints for him and nussin' by hand. Here, you! Let go that button! That ain't a bug! There! 'T ain't what you'd call a perfessional job, but if you jest quit runnin' around nights and take care of your health, mebby you'll come through. Don' know what them hens'll think, though. You sure ain't no Anner Dominus no more. If you was a lady hen, you could pertend you was wearin' evenin' dress like—low-neck and suspenders. But bein' a he, 't ain't the style. Wonder if you got your crow left? You ain't got a whole lot more to tell you from jest a hen."

With Jimmy installed in a box of straw in the kitchen, the pigs fed, and Gentle Annie grazing contentedly, Sundown felt able to relax. It had been a strenuous day for him. He drew a chair to the stove, and before he sat down he brought forth from beneath the bed a highly colored cardboard box on which was embossed a ribbon of blue sealed with a gold paster-seal. Chance watched him gravely. It was a ceremony. Sundown opened the box and picking out a chocolate held it up that Chance might realize fully that it was a ceremony. The dog's nose twitched and he licked his chops. "Tastes good a'ready, eh? Well, it's yourn." And he solemnly gave Chance the chocolate. "Gee Gosh! What'd you do with it? That ain't no way to eat candy! You want to chew her slow and kind o' hang on till she ain't there. Then you get your money's worth. Want another?"

Later Sundown essayed to smoke, but found the flavor of chocolate incompatible with the enjoyment of tobacco. Chance dozed by the fire, and Jimmy, with neck stretched above the edge of the box, watched Sundown with beady, blinking eyes.

Sundown slept late next morning. The lowing of Gentle

Annie as she mildly endeavored to make it known that milking-time was past, the muffled grunting of the two pigs as they rooted in the mud or poked flat flexible noses through the bars, the restless padding of Chance to and from the bedroom, merely harmonized in chorus with audible slumbers until one of the hens cackled. Then Jimmy, from his box near the stove, lifted his clarion shrill in reply to the hen. Sundown sat up, scratched his ear, and arose.

He was returning from a practice of five-finger exercise on Gentle Annie, busy with his thoughts and the balance of the pail, when a shout brought his gaze to the road. John Corliss and Bud Shoop waved him greeting, and dismounting led their horses to the yard.

"Saves me a ride," muttered Sundown. Then, "How, folks! Come right in!"

He noticed that the ponies seemed tired—that the cinchas were mud-spattered and that the riders seemed weary. He invited his guests to breakfast. After the meal the three foregathered outside the house.

"That was right good beef you fed us," remarked Shoop, slightly raising one eyebrow as Corliss glanced at him.

"The best in the country," cheerfully assented Sundown.

"How you making it, Sun?"

"Me? Oh, I'm wigglin' along. Come home last night and found Jimmy with his leg bruk. Everything else was all right."

"Jimmy?"

Henry Hubert Knibbs

"Uhuh. Me rooster."

"Coyote grab him?"

"Uhuh. And Chance fixed Mr. Coyote. I was to Loring's yesterday on business."

Shoop glanced at Corliss who had thus far remained silent.

"We had a little business to talk over," said the rancher. "You're located now. I'm going to run some cattle down this way next week. Some of mine and some of the Two-Bar-O." Corliss, who had been standing, stepped to the doorway and sat down. Shoop and Sundown followed him and lay outstretched on the warm earth. "Funny thing, Bud, about that Two-Bar-O steer we found cut up."

"Sure was," said Shoop.

"Did he get in a fence?" queried Sundown.

"No. He was killed for beef. We ran across him yesterday and did some looking around last night. Trailed over this way to have a talk."

"I'm right glad to see you. I wanted to speak a little piece meself after you get through."

"All right. Here's the story." And Corliss gazed across the mesa for a moment. "The South Spring's gone dry. The fork is so low that only a dozen head can drink at once. It's been a mighty dry year, and the river is about played out except in the canon, and the stock can't get to the water there. This is about the only natural supply outside the ranch. I want to put a couple of men in here and ditch to that hollow over there. It'll take about all your water, but we got to have it. I want you to put in a gas-engine and pump for us. Maybe we'll have to pipe to tanks before we get through. I'll give you fifty a month to run the engine."

"I'll sure keep that leetle ole gas-engine coughin' regular," said Sundown. "I was thinkin' of somethin' like that meself. You see I seen Loring yesterday. I told him that anybody that was wishful could water stock here so long as she held out—except there was to be no shootin' and killin', and the like. Ole man Loring says to tell you what I told him and see what you said. I reckon he'll take his sheep out of here if you folks'll take your cattle off the east side. I ain't playin' no favorites. You been my friend—you and Bud. You come and make me a proposition to pump water for you—and the fifty a month is for the water. That's business. Loring ain't said nothin' about buyin' water from me, so you get it. You see I was kind of figurin' somethin' like this when I first come to this here place—'way back when I met you that evenin'. Says I to meself, 'a fella couldn't even raise robins on this here farm, but from the looks of that water-hole he could raise water, and folks sure got to have water in this country.' I was thinkin' of irrigatin' and raisin' alfalfa and veg'tables, but fifty a month sounds good to me. Bein' a puncher meself, I ain't got no use for sheep, but I was willin' to give ole man Loring a chance. If the mesas is goin' dry on the east side, what's he goin' to do?"

"I don't know, Sun. He's got a card up his sleeve, and you want to stay right on the job. Bud here got a tip in Antelope that a bunch of Mexicans came in last week from Loring's old ranch in New Mexico. Some of 'em are herders and some of 'em are worse. I reckon he'll try to push his sheep across and take up around here. He'll try it at night. If he does and you get on to it before we do, just saddle Pill and fan it for the Concho."

Henry Hubert Knibbs

"Gee Gosh! But that means more fightin'!"

Shoop and Corliss said nothing. Sundown gazed at them questioningly.

Presently Corliss gestured toward the south. "They'll make it interesting for you. Loring's an old-timer and he won't quit. This thing won't be settled until something happens—and I reckon it's going to happen soon."

"Well, I'm sure sittin' on the dynamite," said Sundown lugubriously. "I reckoned to settle down and git m—me farm to goin' and keep out of trouble. Now it looks like I was the cat what fell out of a tree into a dog-fight by mistake. They was nothin' left of that cat."

Shoop laughed. "We'll see that you come out all right."

Sundown accepted this meager consolation with a grimace. Then his face beamed. "Say! What's the matter of me tellin' the sheriff that there's like to be doin's—and mebby he could come over and kind of scare 'em off."

"The idea is all right, Sun. But Jim is a married man. Most of his deputies are married. If it comes to a mix some of 'em 'd get it sure. Now there isn't a married man on the Concho— which makes a lot of difference. Sabe?"

"I reckon that's right," admitted Sundown, "Killin' a married man is like killin' the whole fambly."

"And you're a single man—so you're all right," said Shoop.

"Gee Gosh! Mebby that ought to make me feel good, but it don't. Supposin' a fella was goin' to get married?"

"Then—he'd—better wait," said Corliss, smiling at his foreman.

Corliss stood up and yawned. "Oh, say, Sun, where'd you get that beef?" he asked casually.

"The beef? Why, a Chola come along here day afore yesterday and say if I wanted some meat. I says yes. Then he rides off and purty soon he comes back with a hind-quarter on his saddle. I give him two dollars for it. It looked kind of funny, but I thought he was mebby campin' out there somewhere and peddlin' meat."

Shoop and Corliss glanced at each other. "They don't peddle meat that way in this country, Sun. What did the Mexican look like?"

"Kind of fat and greasy-like, and he was as cross-eyed as a rabbit watchin' two dogs to onct."

"That so? Let's have a look at that hind-quarter."

"Sure! Over there in the well-shed."

When Corliss returned, he nodded to Shoop. Then he turned to Sundown. "We found a Two-Bar-O steer killed right close to here yesterday. Looks queer. Well, we'll be fanning it. I'll send to Antelope and have them order the pump and some pipe. Got plenty of grub?"

"Plenty 'nough for a couple of weeks."

"All right. So-long. Keep your eye on things."

Henry Hubert Knibbs

CHAPTER XXV

VAMOSE, EH?

The intermittent popping of the gasoline engine, as it forced water to the big, unpainted tank near the water-hole, became at first monotonous and finally irritating. Sundown, clad in oil-spotted overalls that did not by many inches conceal his riding-boots and his Spanish spurs, puttered about the engine until he happened to glance at the distant tank. A silvery rill of water was pouring from the top of the tank. He shut off the engine, wiped his hands, and strode to the house.

He was gone a long time, so long in fact that Chance decided to investigate. The dog got up, stretched lazily, and padded to the doorway. He could hear Sundown muttering and shuffling about in the bedroom. Chance stalked in quietly and stood gazing at his master. Sundown had evidently been taking a bath,—not in the pail of water that stood near him, but obviously round and about it. At the moment he was engaged in tying a knot in the silk bandanna about his neck. Chance became animated. His master was going somewhere! Sundown turned his head, glancing at the dog with a preoccupied eye. The knot adjusted to his satisfaction, he knelt and drew a large box from beneath the bed. From the box he took an immaculate and exceedingly wide-brimmed Stetson with an exceedingly high crown. He dented the crown until the hat had that rakish appearance dear to the heart of the cowboy. Then he took the foot-square looking-glass from the wall and studied the effect at various and more or less unsatisfactory angles. Again he knelt—after depositing the hat on the bed—and emerged with a pair of gorgeous leather chaps that glittered with the polished silver of conchas from waist-band to heel. Next he drew on a pair of elaborate gauntlets embellished with hand-worked silk roses of crimson. Then he glanced at his boots. They were undoubtedly serviceable, but more or less muddy and stained. That wouldn't do at all! Striding to the kitchen he poked about and finally unearthed a box of stove-polish that he had purchased and laid away for future use against that happy time when stove-polish would be doubly appreciated. The metallic luster of his boots was not altogether satisfactory, but it would do. "This here bein' chief engineer of a popcorn machine ain't what it's said to be in the perspectus. Gets a fella lookin' greasy and feelin' greasy, but the pay kind of makes up for it. Me first month's wages blowed in for outside decoratin'—but I reckon the grub'll hold out for a spell."

Then he strode from the house and made his rounds, inspecting the pigs, shooing the chickens to their coop, and finally making a short pilgrimage to where Gentle Annie was grazing. After he had saddled "Pill," he returned to the house and reappeared with a piece of wrapping-paper on which he had printed:—

Help yourself to grub—but no fighting on thees premisus.

SUNDOWN, Propriter.

"It's all right trustin' folks," he remarked as he gazed proudly at the sign and still more proudly at the signature. "And I sure hate to put up anything that looks kind of religious, but

Henry Hubert Knibbs

these days I don't trust nobody but meself, and I sure have a hard time doin' that, knowin' how crooked I could be if I tried."

He gathered up the reins and mounted Pill. "Come on, Chance!" he called. "We don't need any rooster-police today. Jimmy's in there talkin' to his hens, and like as not cussin' because I shet him up. And he sure ought to be glad he ain't goin' on crutches."

He rode out to the mesa and, turning from the trail, took as direct a course as he could approximate for the home of Chico Miguel, and incidentally Anita. His mission would have been obvious to an utter stranger. He shone and glistened from head to heel—his face with the inner light of anticipation and his boots with the effulgence of hastily applied stove-polish.

He rode slowly, for he wished to collect himself, that his errand might have all the grace of a chance visit and yet not lack the most essential significance. He did not stop to reason that Anita's father and mother were anything but blind.

The day was exceptionally hot. The sun burned steadily on the ripening bunch-grass. His pony's feet swept aside bright flowers that tilted their faces eagerly like the faces of questioning children. He glanced at his watch. "Got to move along, Pill. Reckon we'll risk havin' somethin' to say when we get there—and not cook her up goin' along. It sure is hot. Huh! That there butte over there looks jest like a city athletic club with muscles all on its front of fellas wrastlin' and throwin' things at themselves. Wisht I had a big lookin'-glass so I could see meself comin'. Gee Gosh, but she's hot!"

He put the horse to a lope, and with the subdued rhythm of

the pony's feet came Euterpe with a song. Recitation of verse at a lope is apt to be punctuated according to the physical contour of the ground:—

"In the Pull—man *car* with turnin' *fans*,
The desert *looks* like a lovely p—*lace*.
But crossin' a*lone* on the *burn*in' sands,
She's hell, with a *grin* on her face."

"Got to slow up to get that right," he said, "or jest stop an' git off. But we ain't got time. 'Oh, down in Arizona there's a . . .' No. I reckon I won't. I want to sing, but I can't take no risks."

That "the Colonel's lady and Julie O'Grady are sisters under their skins," is not to be doubted. That Romeo and Sundown are brothers, with the odds slightly in favor of Sundown, is apparent to those who have been, are, or are willing to be, in love. "Will this plume, these trunks and hose, this bonnet please my fair Juliet?" sighs Romeo to his mirror. And "Will these here chaps and me bandanna and me new Stetson make a hit with me leetle Anita?" asks Sundown of the mesas.

That the little Anita was pleased, nay, overwhelmed by the arrival of her gorgeous caballero was more than apparent to the anxious Sundown. She came running to the gate and stood with clasped hands while he bowed for the seventh time and slowly dismounted, giving his leg an unnecessary shake that the full effect of spur and concha might not be lost. He felt the high importance of his visit, and Anita also surmised that something unusual was about to happen. He strode magnificently to the house and again doffed his Stetson to the astonished and smiling Senora. Evidently the strange vaquero had met with fortune. With experienced eye the mother of Anita swiftly estimated the monetary outlay necessary to possess such an equipment. It was well to be courted, of that she was reminiscently certain. Yet it was also well to be courted by one who bore the earmarks—so to speak—of prosperity. Sundown was made heartily welcome. After they had had dinner,—Chico Miguel would return at night as usual,—Sundown mentally besought his stars to aid him, lend him eloquence and the Senora understanding, and found excuse to follow the Senora to the kitchen where he offered to wipe the dishes. This she would not hear of, but being wise in her generation she dismissed Anita on a trivial errand and motioned her guest to a seat. What was said is a matter of interest only to those immediately concerned. Love is his own interpreter and labors willingly, yet in this instance his limitations must be excused by the result. The Senora and Sundown came to a perfect understanding. The cabellero was welcome to make the state of his heart known to Anita. As for her father, she—the Senora—would attend to him. And was Sundown fond of the tortillas? He was, be Gosh! It was well. They would have tortillas that evening. Chico Miguel was especially fond of the tortillas. They made him of the pleasant disposition and induced him to tune the big guitar.

The Senora would take her siesta. Possibly her guest would smoke and entertain Anita with news from the Concho and of the Patron Loring and of his own rancho. Anita was not of what you say the kind to do the much talking, but she had a heart. Of that the Senora had reason to be assured. Had not Anita gone, each day, to the gate and stood gazing down the road? Surely there was nothing to see save the mesas. Had she not begged to be allowed to visit the Loring hacienda not of so very long time past? And Anita had not been to the Loring hacienda for a year or more. Such things were significant. And the Senora gestured toward her own bosom, implying that she of a surety knew from which quarter the south wind blew.

All of which delighted the already joyous Sundown. He saw

before him a flower-bordered pathway to his happiness, and incidentally, as he gazed down the pathway toward the gate of Chico Miguel's homestead, he saw Anita standing pensively beneath the shade of an acacia, pulling a flower to pieces and casting quick glances at the house. "Good-night, Senora,—I mean—er—here's hopin' you have a good sleep. It sure is refreshin' this hot weather." The Senora nodded and disappeared in the bedroom. Sundown strode jingling down the pathway, a brave figure in his glittering chaps and tinkling spurs. Anita's eyes were hidden beneath her long black lashes. Perhaps she had anticipated something of that which followed—perhaps she anticipated even more. In any event, Sundown was not a disappointment. He asked her to sit beside him beneath the acacia. Then he took her hand and squeezed it. "Let's jest sit here and look out at them there mesas dancin' in the sun; and say, 'Nita, let's jest say nothin' for a spell. I'm so right down happy that suthin' hurts me throat."

When Chico Miguel returned in the dusk of evening, humming a song of the herd, he was not a little surprised to find that Anita was absent. He questioned the Senora, who smiled as she bustled about the table. "Tortillas," she said, and was gratified at the change in Chico Miguel's expression. Then she explained the presence of the broad new Stetson that lay on a chair, adding a gesture toward the gateway. "It is the tall one and our daughter—he of the grand manner and the sad countenance. It is possible that a new home will be thought of for Anita." There had been conversations that afternoon with the tall caballero and understandings. Chico Miguel was to wash himself and put on his black suit. It was an event—and there were tortillas.

Chico Miguel wondered why the hour of eating had been so long past. To which the Senora replied that he had just arrived, and, moreover, that she had already called to Anita

Henry Hubert Knibbs

this the third time, yet had had no response. Chico Miguel moved toward the doorway, but his wife laid her hand on his arm. "It is that you take the big guitar and play the 'Linda Rosa, Adios.' Then, to be sure, they will hear and the supper will not grow cold."

Grumblingly Chico Miguel took his guitar and struck the opening chords of the song. Presently up the pathway came two shadowy figures, close together and seemingly in no haste. As they entered the house, Sundown apologized for having delayed supper, stating that he had been so interested in discussing with Anita the "best breed of chickens to raise for eggs," that other things had for the nonce not occupied his attention. "And we're sure walkin' on music," he added. "Jest steppin' along on the notes of that there song. I reckon I got to get one of them leetle potato-bug mandolins and learn to tickle its neck. There's nothin' like music—exceptin'"— and he glanced at the blushing Anita—"exceptin' ranchin'."

It was late when Sundown finally departed, He grew anxious as he rode across the mesas, wondering if he had not taken advantage, as it were, of Gentle Annie's good nature, and whether or not the chickens were very hungry. Chance plodded beside him, a vague shadow in the starlight. The going was more or less rough and Pill dodged many gopher-holes, to the peril of his rider's equilibrium. Yet Sundown was glad that it was night. There was nothing to divert him from the golden dreams of the future. He felt that success, as he put it, "was hangin' around the door whinin' to be let in." He formulated a creed for himself and told the stars. "I believe in meself—you bet." Yet he was honest with his soul. "I know more about everything and less about anything than anybody—exceptin' po'try and cookin'. But gettin' along ain't jest what you know. It's more like what you do. They's fellas knows more than I could learn in four thousand eight hundred and seventy-six years, but that don't help 'em get along none. It's what you know inside what counts."

He lapsed into silence and slouched in the saddle. Presently he nodded, recovered, and nodded again. He would not wittingly have gone to sleep in the saddle, being as yet too unaccustomed to riding to relax to that extent. But sleep had something to say anent the matter. He dozed, clasping the saddle-horn instinctively. Pill plodded along patiently. The east grew gray, then rose-pink, then golden. The horse lifted its head and quickened pace. Sundown swayed and nodded.

His uneasy slumber was broken by an explosive bark from Chance. Sundown straightened and rubbed his eyes. Before him lay the ranch-house, glittering in the sun. Out on the mesa grazed a herd of sheep and past them another and another. Again he rubbed his eyes.

Then he distinguished several saddle-horses tied to the fence surrounding the water-hole and there were figures of men walking to and from his house, many of them. He set spur to Pill and loped up to the fence. A Mexican with a hard, lined face stepped up to him. "You vamose!" he said, pointing down the road.

Sundown stared at the men about the yard. Among them he recognized several of Loring's herders, armed and evidently equipped with horses, for they were booted and spurred. He pushed back his hat. "Vamose, eh? I'll be damned if I do."

CHAPTER XXVI

THE INVADERS

The Mexican whipped his gun out and covered Sundown, who wisely put up his hands. Two of the men crawled through the fence, secured Sundown's horse, and ordered him to dismount. Before both feet had touched the ground one of the Mexicans had snatched Sundown's gun from its holster. Chance leaped at the Mexican, but Sundown's "Here, Chance!" brought the dog growling to his master.

At that moment Loring stepped from the house, and shouldering aside the men strode up to Sundown. The sheep-man was about to speak when the tall one raised his arm and shook his fist in Loring's face.

"Fer two pins I'd jump you and stomp the gizzard out of you, you low-down, dried-up, whisker-faced, mutton-eatin' butcher, you! I goes to you and makes you a square offer and you come pussy-footin' in and steals me ranch when I ain't there! If Jack Corliss don't run you plumb off the edge afore to-morrow night, I'll sure see if there's any law—" and Sundown paused for lack of breath.

"Law? Mebby you think you got somethin' to say about this here water-hole, and mebby not," said Loring. "Don't get het up. I come to this country before you knew it was here. And for law—I reckon seein' you're wanted by the law that them papers of yourn is good for startin' a fire—and nothin' more. The *law* says that no man wanted by the law kin homestead. The water-hole is open to the fust man that wants it and I'm the fust. Now mebby you can think that over and cool off."

Sundown was taken aback. Though unversed in the intricacies of the law, he was sensible enough to realize that Loring was right. Yet he held tenaciously to his attitude of proprietor of the water-hole. It was his home—the only home that he had known in his variegated career. The fact that he was not guilty buoyed him up, however. He decided that discretion had its uses. As his first anger evaporated, he cast about for a plan whereby to notify Corliss of the invasion of the water-hole ranch. His glance wandered to Chance.

Then he raised his eyes. "Well, now the fireworks is burned down, what you goin' to do?"

Loring gestured toward the house. "That's my business. But you can turn in and cook grub for the men. That'll keep you from thinkin' too hard, and we're like to be busy."

"Then you're takin' me prisoner?" queried Sundown.

"That's correc'."

"How about the law of that?"

"This outfit's makin' its own laws these days," said Loring.

And so far as Loring was concerned that ended the argument. Not so, however, with Sundown. He said nothing. Had Loring known him better, that fact would have caused him to suspect his prisoner. With evident meekness the tall one entered the house and gazed with disconsolate eyes at the piled kyacks of provisions, the tarpaulins and sheepskins. His citadel of dreams had been rudely invaded, in truth. He was not so much angered by the possible effects of the invasion as by the fact. Gentle Annie was lowing plaintively. The chickens were scurrying about the yard, cackling hysterically as they dodged this and that herder. The two pigs, Sundown reflected consolingly, seemed happy enough. Loring, standing in the doorway, pointed to the stove. "Get busy," he said tersely. That was the last straw. Silently Sundown stalked to the stove, rolled up his sleeves, and went to work. If there were not a score of mighty sick herders that night, it would not be his fault. He had determined on a bloodless but effective victory, wherein soda and cream-of-tartar should be the victors.

Soda and cream-of-tartar in proper proportions is harmless. But double the proportion of cream-of-tartar and the result is internal riot. "And a leetle spice to kill the bitter of the taste ought to work all right," he soliloquized. Then he remembered Chance. Loring had left to oversee the establishment of an outlying camp. The Mexican who assisted Sundown seemed stupid and sullen. Sundown found excuse to enter his bedroom, where he hastily scrawled a note to Corliss. Later he tied the note to the inside of the dog's collar. The next thing was to get Chance started on the road to the Concho. He rolled down his sleeves and strolled to the doorway. A Mexican sat smoking and watching the road. Sundown stepped past him and began to tinker with the gas-engine. Chance stood watching him. Presently the gas-engine started with a cough and splutter. Sundown walked to the door and seemed about to enter when the Mexican called to him and pointed toward the distant tank. Water was pouring over its rim. "Gee Gosh!" exclaimed Sundown. "I got to shut her off." He ran to the engine and its sound ceased. Yet the water still poured from the rim of the tank. "Got to fix that!" he asserted, and started toward the tank. The Mexican followed him to the fence.

"You come back?" he queried significantly.

"Sure thing! I ain't got a hoss, have I?"

The Mexican nodded. Sundown crawled through the fence and strode slowly to the tank. He pretended to examine it first in view of the house and finally on the opposite side. As Chance sniffed along the bottom of the tank, Sundown spoke to him. The dog's ears pricked forward. Sundown's tone suggested action. "Here, Chance,—you fan it for the Concho—Jack—the boss. Beat it for all you're worth. The Concho! Sabe?" And he patted the dog's head and pointed toward the south.

Chance hesitated, leaping up and whining.

"That's all right, pardner. They ain't nothin' goin' to happen to me. You go!"

Chance trotted off a few yards and then turned his head inquiringly.

"That's right. Keep a-goin'. It's your stunt this time." And Sundown waved his arm.

The return of Sundown without the dog occasioned no suspicion on the Mexican's part. He most naturally thought, if he considered the fact at all, that the dog was hunting the mesas. Then Sundown entered the house and experimented with soda and cream-of-tartar as though he were concocting a high explosive with proportions of the ingredients calculated to produce the most satisfactory results. His plan,

Henry Hubert Knibbs

however, was nipped in the bud. That night the herders refused to eat the biscuits after tasting them.

Hi Wingle, coming from the bunk-house, wiped his hands on his apron, rolled a cigarette, and squatted in the shade. From within came the clatter of knives and forks and the rattle of dishes. The riders of the Concho were about through dinner. Wingle, gazing down the road, suddenly cast his cigarette away and rose. The road seemed empty save for a lean brown shape that raced toward the Concho with sweeping stride. "It's the dog. Wonder what's up now?"

Chance, his muzzle specked with froth and his tongue lolling, swung into the yard and trotted to Wingle. "Boss git piled ag'in?" queried the cook, patting Chance's head. "What you scratchin' about?"

The dog lay panting and occasionally pawing at his collar.

"What's the matter? Cockle-burr?" And Wingle ran his fingers under the collar. "So? Playin' mail-man, eh?"

He spread out the note and read it. Slowly he straightened up and slowly he walked to the bunk-house. "No. Guess I'll tell Jack first."

He strode to the office and laid the note on Corliss's desk. The rancher, busy running up totals on the pay-roll, glanced at the sweat-stained piece of paper. He read it and pushed it from him. "All right, Hi."

Wingle hesitated, then stepped out and over to the bunk-house. "Takes it mighty cool! Wonder what he's got up his sleeve. Somethin'—sure!"

Corliss studied the note. Then he reached for paper and

envelopes and wrote busily. One of the letters was to the sheriff in Antelope. It was brief.

I'm going to push a bunch of stock over to the water-hole range. My boys have instructions not to shoot. That's the best I can do for them and the other side.

JOHN CORLISS.

The other letter was to Nell Loring. Then he rose and buckled on his gun. At the bunk-house he gave the letters to Lone Johnny, who saddled and departed immediately.

Without making the contents of the note known, he told the men that they would join Bud Shoop and his outfit at the Knoll and push the herd north. Later he took Wingle aside and told him that he could stay and look after the rancho.

The indignant Hi rolled down his sleeves, spat, and glared at Corliss. "I quit," he snapped. "You can hire a new cook."

Despite his preoccupation Corliss smiled. "All right, Hi. Now that you're out of a job, you might saddle up and ride with us. We'll need some one to keep us good-natured, I reckon."

"Now you're whistlin'!" said Wingle. "Got a gun I can use? I give mine to Sundown."

"There's one over in the office on the desk. But we're going to push the herd over to the water-hole. We're not going there to fight."

"Huh! Goin' to be quiet, eh? Mebby I better take my knittin' along to pass the time."

And Wingle departed toward the office. Rejoining Corliss

Henry Hubert Knibbs

they rode with the men to the Knoll. Bud Shoop nodded gravely as his employer told him of Loring's occupation of the west bank of the river. Then the genial Bud rode over to the herd that was bunched in anticipation of just such a contingency as had developed. "It's a case of push 'em along easy—and all night," he told his men. "And if any of you boys is out of cartridges there's plenty in the wagon."

John Corliss rode with his men. He told them to cut out any stray Two-Bar-O stock they saw and turn them back. Toward evening they had the cattle in motion, drifting slowly toward the north. The sixteen riders, including Corliss and Wingle, spread out and pushed the herd across the afternoon mesas. The day was hot and there was no water between the Knoll and Sundown's ranch. Corliss intended to hold the cattle when within a mile of the water-hole by milling them until daylight. When they got the smell of water, he knew that he would not be able to hold them longer, nor did he wish to. He regretted the fact that Chance was running with him, for he knew that Loring's men, under the circumstances, would shoot the dog if they had opportunity.

Toward evening the outfit drew up in a draw and partook of a hearty supper. The cattle began to lag as they were urged forward, and Chance was called into requisition to keep after the stragglers. As the herd was not large,—in fact, numbered but five hundred,—it was possible to keep it moving steadily and well bunched, throughout the night.

Within a short mile of the water-hole the riders began to mill the herd.

Bud Shoop, riding up to Corliss, pointed toward the east. "Reckon we can't hold 'em much longer, Jack. They're crazy dry—and they smell water."

"All right, Bud. Hold 'em for fifteen minutes more. Then take four of the boys with you and fan it for the road. You can cache in that draw just north of the water-hole. About sunup the herd'll break for water. Loring's outfit will be plenty busy on this side, about then. If he's got any gunmen handy, they'll be camped at the ranch. Chances are that when the cattle stampede a band or two of sheep, he'll turn his men on us. That's your time to ride down and take possession of the ranch. Most likely you won't have to draw a gun."

Shoop reined close to Corliss and held out his hand. "Mebby not, Jack. But if we do—so-long."

Then the genial Bud loped to the outriders, picking them up one by one. The cattle, freed from the vigilance of the circling horsemen, sniffed the dawn, crowded to a wedge, and began to trot, then to run. Shoop and his four companions spurred ahead, swung to the road, and thundered past the ranch-house as a faint edge of light shot over the eastern horizon. They entered the mouth of the draw, swung around, and reined up.

"We're goin' to chip in when Jack opens the pot," said Shoop. "Just how strong we'll come in depends on how strong Jack opens her." Then with seeming irrelevance he remarked casually: "Sinker wasn't such a bad ole scout."

"Which Loring's goin' to find out right soon," said "Mebby-So," a lean Texan.

"Sinker's sure goin' to have company, I take it," remarked "Bull" Cassidy.

"Boss's orders is to take her without makin' any noise," said Shoop.

"Huh! *I'm* plumb disappointed," asserted Mebby-So. "I was figurin' on singin' hymns and accompanyin' meself on me—me cayuse. Listen! Somethin' 's broke loose!"

Thundering like an avalanche the herd swept down on the water-hole, ploughing through a band of sheep that were bedded down between them and the ranch. The herder's tent was torn to ribbons. Wingle, trailing behind the herd, dismounted, and, stooping, disarmed the bruised and battered Mexican who had struggled to his feet as he rode up.

From the water-hole came shouts, and Corliss saw several men come running from the house to seize their horses and ride out toward the cattle. The band of riders opened up and the distant popping of Winchesters told him that the herders were endeavoring to check the rush of the thirst-maddened steers. The carcasses of sheep, trampled to pulp, lay scattered over the mesa.

"It sure is hell!" remarked Wingle, riding up to Corliss.

"Hell is correct," said Corliss, spurring forward. "Now I reckon we'll ride over to the rancho and see if Loring wants any more of it."

Silently the rancher and his men rode toward the water-hole. As they drew near the line fence, the Mexican riders, swinging in a wide circle, spurred to head them off.

"Hold on!" shouted Corliss. "We'll pull up and wait for 'em."

"Suits me," said Wingle, loosening his gun from the holster.

The Mexicans, led by Loring, loped up and reined with a slither of hoofs and the snorting of excited ponies. Corliss held up his hand. Loring spurred forward and Corliss rode to meet him.

"Want any more of it?" queried Corliss.

"I'll take all you got," snarled Loring.

"All right. Just listen a minute." And Corliss reached in his saddle-pocket. "Here's a lease from the Government covering the ten sections adjoining the water-hole ranch, on the south and west. And here's a contract with the owner of the water-hole, signed and witnessed, for the use of the water for my stock. You're playing an old-fashioned game, Loring, that's out of date. Want to look over these papers?"

"To hell with your papers. I'm here and I'm goin' to stay."

"Well, we'll visit you regular," shouted a puncher.

"Better come over to the house and talk things over," said Corliss. "I don't want trouble with you—but my boys do."

Loring hesitated. One of his men, spurring up, whispered to him.

Wingle, keenly alert, restrained a cowboy who was edging forward. "Don't start nothin'," he said. "If she's goin' to start, she'll start herself."

Loring turned to Corliss. "I'd like to look at them papers," he said slowly.

"All right. We'll ride over to the house."

The two bands of riders swung toward the north, passed the tank, and trotted up to the ranch-gate. They dismounted and were met by Shoop and his companions. Loring blinked and muttered. He had been outgeneraled. One of the Concho riders laughed. Loring's hand slipped to his belt. "Don't," said Corliss easily. The tension relaxed, and the men began joking and laughing.

"Where's Sundown?" queried Corliss.

Loring gestured toward the house.

"I'll go," said Wingle. And he shouldered through the group of scowling herders and entered the house.

Sundown, with hands tied, was sitting on the edge of his bed. "They roped me," he said lugubriously, "in me own house. Bud he was goin' to untie me, but I says for the love of Mike leave me tied or I'll take a chair and brain that Chola what kicked Gentle Annie in the stummick this mornin'. He was goin' to milk her and I reckon she didn't like his looks. Anyhow, she laid him out with a kind of hind-leg upper-cut. When he come to, he set in to kickin' her. I got his picture and if I get me hands on him . . ."

Wingle cut the rope and Sundown stood up. "They swiped me gun," he asserted.

"Here's one I took off a herder," said Wingle. "if things get to boilin' over—why, jest nacherally wilt the legs from under anything that looks like a Chola. Jack's got the cards, all right—but I don't jest like the look of things. Loring's in the corner and he's got his back up."

As they came from the house, Loring was reading the papers that Corliss had handed to him. The old sheep-man glanced at the signatures on the documents and then slowly folded them, hesitated, and with a quick turn of his wrist tore them and flung the pieces in Corliss's face. "That for your law!

We stay!"

Corliss bit his lip, and the dull red of restrained anger burned in his face. He had gone too far to retreat or retract. He knew that his men would lose all respect for him if he backed down now. Yet he was unable to frame a plan whereby he might avoid the arbitration of the six-gun. His men eyed him curiously. Was Jack going to show a yellow streak? They thought that he would not—and yet . . .

Sundown raised his long arm and pointed. "There's the gent what kicked me cow," he said, his face white and his eyes burning.

The punchers of the Concho laughed. "Jump him!" shouted "Bull" Cassidy. "We'll stand by and see that there's no monkeyin'."

Corliss held up his hand. The Mexicans drew together and the age-old hatred for the Gringo burned in their beady eyes.

Sundown's thin lips drew tight. "I've a good mind to—" he began. The Mexican who had maltreated the cow mistook Sundown's gesture for intent to kill. The herder's gun whipped up. Sundown grabbed a chair that stood tilted against the house and swung it. The Mexican went down. With the accidental explosion of the gun, Mebby-So grunted, put his hand to his side, and toppled from the saddle. Corliss wheeled his horse.

"Don't shoot, boys!" he shouted.

His answer was a roar of six-guns. He felt Chinook shiver. He jumped clear as the horse rolled to its side. Sundown, retreating to the house, flung open the bedroom window and kneeling, laid the barrel of his gun on the sill. Deliberately he

Henry Hubert Knibbs

sighted, hesitated, and flung the gun from him. "God Almighty—I ought to—but I can't!" He had seen Corliss fall and thought that he had been killed. He saw a Mexican raise his gun to fire; saw him suddenly straighten in the saddle. Then the gun dropped from his hand, and he bent forward upon his horse, recovered, swayed a moment, and fell limply.

Bud Shoop, on foot, ran around to the rear of the house. His horse lay kicking, shot through the stomach. The foreman drew himself up under cover of the hen-house and fired into the huddle of Mexicans that swept around the yard as the riders of the Concho drove them back. He saw "Bull" Cassidy in the thick of it, swinging his guns and swearing heartily. Finally a Mexican pony, wounded and wild with fright, tore through the barb-wire fence. Behind him spurred the herders. Out on the mesa they turned and threw lead at the Concho riders, who retreated to the cover of the house. Corliss caught up a herder's horse and rode around to them. Shorty, one of his men, grinned, fell to coughing, and sank forward on his horse.

"Loring's down," said Wingle, solemnly reloading his gun. "Think they got enough, Jack?"

"Loring, eh? Well, I know who got him. Yes, they got enough."

Shorty, vomiting blood, wiped his lips on his sleeve. "Well, I ain't—not yet," he gasped. "*I'm* goin' to finish in a blaze of glory. Come on, boys!" And he whirled his horse. Swaying drunkenly he spurred around the corner of the house and through the gateway.

Corliss glanced at Wingle. "We can't let him ride into 'em by his lonesome," said Wingle. "Eh, boys?"

"Not on your fat life!" said Bull Cassidy. "I got one wing that's workin' and I'm goin' to fly her till she gits busted."

"Let's clean 'em up! Might's well do a good job now we're at it. Where's Bud?"

"He's layin' over there back of the chicken-roost. Reckon he's thinkin' things over. He ain't sayin' much."

"Bud down, too? Then I guess we ride!" And they swept out after Shorty. They saw the diminutive cowboy tear through the band of herders, his gun going; saw his horse stumble and fall and a figure pitch from the saddle and roll to one side. "And if I'm goin'—I want to go out that way," shouted Bull Cassidy. "Shorty was some sport!"

But the Mexicans had had enough of it. They wheeled and spurred toward the south. The Concho horses, worn out by the night-journey, were soon distanced.

Corliss pulled up. "Catch up a fresh horse, Hi. And let Banks know how things stand. If Loring isn't all in, you might fetch the doctor back with you. We'll need him, anyway."

"Sure! Wonder who that is fannin' it this way? Don't look like a puncher."

Corliss turned and gazed down the road. From the south came little puffs of dust as a black-and-white pinto running at top speed swept toward them. He paled as he recognized the horse.

"It's Loring's girl," said Wingle, glancing at Corliss.

Nell Loring reined up as she came opposite the Concho riders and turned from the road. The men glanced at each other. Then ensued an awkward silence. The girl's face was white and her dark eyes burned with reproach as she saw the trampled sheep and here and there the figure of a man prone on the mesa. Corliss raised his hat as she rode up. She sat her horse gazing at the men. Without a word she turned and rode toward the ranch-house. The Concho riders jingled along, in no hurry to face the scene which they knew awaited them at the water-hole.

She was on her knees supporting her father's head when they dismounted and shuffled into the yard. The old sheep-man blinked and tried to raise himself. One of the Concho boys stepped forward and helped her get the wounded man to the house.

Corliss strode to the bedroom and spoke to Sundown who turned and sat up. "Get hit, Sun?"

"No. But I'm feelin' kind of sick. Is the ole man dead?"

"He's hurt, but not bad. We want the bed."

Sundown got to his feet and sidled past the girl as she helped her father to the bed.

"I sent for the doctor," said Corliss.

The girl whirled and faced him. "You!" she exclaimed— "You!"

The rancher's shoulders straightened. "Yes—and it was my gun got him. You might as well know all there is to it." Then he turned and, followed by Sundown, stepped to the yard. "We'll keep busy while we're waiting. Any of you boys that feel like riding can round up the herd. Hi and I will look after—the rest of it."

"And Bud," suggested a rider.

They found Shoop on the ground, the flesh of his shoulder torn away by a .45 and a welt of red above his ear where a Mexican's bullet had creased him. They carried him to the house. "Sun, you might stir around and rustle some grub. The boys will want to eat directly." And Corliss stepped to the water-trough, washed his hands, and then rolled a cigarette. Hi Wingle sat beside him as they waited for dinner. Suddenly Corliss turned to his cook. "I guess we've won out, Hi," he said.

"Generally speakin'—we sure have," said Wingle. "But I reckon *you* lost."

Corliss nodded.

CHAPTER XXVII

"JUST ME AND HER"

Sheriff Banks tossed Corliss's note on his desk, reached in his pocket and drew forth a jack-knife with which he began to trim his finger-nails. He paid no apparent attention to the arrival of one of his deputies, but proceeded with his manipulation of the knife. The deputy sidled to a chair and sat watching the sheriff.

Presently Banks closed his knife, slid it into his pocket, and leaned back in his chair. "Lone Johnny gone back?" he queried.

The deputy nodded.

Banks proffered his companion a cigar and lit one himself. For a while he smoked and gazed at the ceiling. "I got two cards to play," he said, straightening up and brushing cigar-ash from his vest. "Last election was pretty close. By rights I ought to be at the county-seat. Got any idea why they side-tracked me here in Antelope?"

The deputy grinned. "It's right handy to the line. And I guess they saw what was comin' and figured to put you up against it. They couldn't beat you at the polls, so they tried to put you where you wouldn't come back."

"Correct. And there's no use running against the rope. Now I want you to call on every citizen in Antelope and tell every dog-goned one of 'em what Lone Johnny kind of hinted at regarding the Concho and Loring. And show 'em this note from Jack. Tell 'em I'm going to swear in each of 'em as a special. I want to go on record as having done what I could."

The deputy rose. "All right, Jim. Kind of late to make that move, ain't it?"

"I got another card," said the sheriff. "Tell 'em we'll be ready to start about twelve. It's ten, now."

With the departure of the deputy the sheriff reached in his desk and brought forth a book. It was thumbed and soiled. He turned the pages slowly, pausing to read a line here and there. Finally he settled back and became immersed in the perennial delight of "Huckleberry Finn." He read uninterruptedly for an hour, drifting on the broad current of the Mississippi to eventually disembark in Antelope as the deputy shadowed the doorway. The sheriff closed the book and glanced up. He read his answer in the deputy's eyes.

"'T ain't that they don't like you," said the deputy. "But they ain't one of 'em that'll do anything for Loring or do anything against Jack Corliss."

The sheriff smiled. "Public opinion is setting on the fence and hanging on with both hands. All right, Joe. I'll play her alone. I got a wire from Hank that he's got the herder, Fernando. Due here on the two-thirty. You hang around and tell Hank to keep on—take the Mexican along up to Usher."

"Goin' to go after the Concho boys and Loring's herders?"

"Sure thing. And I'm going alone. Then they won't make a fuss. They'll come back with me all right."

"But you couldn't get a jury to send one of 'em over—not in this county."

"Correct, Joe. But the county's paying me to go through the motions—don't matter what I think personally. If they've pulled off a shooting-match at the water-hole, the thing's settled by this time. It had to come and if it's over, I'm dam' glad. It'll clear the air for quite a spell to come."

"The papers'll sure make a holler—" began the deputy.

"Not so much as you think. They got one good reason to keep still and that's because the free range is like to be opened up to homesteaders any day. Too much noise about cattle-and-sheep war would scare good money from coming to the State. I heard the other day that that Sundown Jack picked up is settled at the water-hole. I took him for a tenderfoot once. I reckon he ain't. It's hard to figure on those queer kind. Well, you meet the two-thirty. I guess I'll ride over to the Concho and see the boys."

The Loring-Corliss case is now a matter of record in the dusty files of the "Usher Sentinel" and its decidedly disesteemed contemporary, the "Mesa News." The case was dismissed for lack of anything like definite evidence, though Loring and Corliss were bound over to keep the peace. Incidentally one tall and angular witness refused to testify, and was sentenced to pay a not insignificant fine for contempt of court. That his fine was promptly paid by Corliss furnished a more or less gratuitous excuse for a wordy vilification of the rancher and his "hireling assassin," "menace to public welfare," and the like. Sundown, however, stuck to his guns, even to the extent of searching out the editor of the "Mesa News" and offering graciously to engage in hand-to-hand combat, provided the editor, or what was left of him after the battle, would insert an apology in the next issue of the paper—the apology to be dictated by Sundown.

The editor temporized by asking the indignant Sundown to frame the apology, which he did. Then the wily autocrat of the "Mesa News," after reading the apology, agreed to an armistice and mentioned the fact that it was a hot day. Sundown intimated that he knew one or two places in Usher which he was not averse to visiting under the circumstances. And so the treaty was ratified.

Perhaps among Sundown's possessions there is none so cherished, speaking broadly, as a certain clipping from an Arizona newspaper in which the editor prints a strangely worded and colorful apology, above his personal signature, for having been misled temporarily in his estimation of a "certain person of warlike proclivities who visited our sanctum bent upon eradicating us in a physical sense." The apology follows. In a separate paragraph, however, is this information:

"We find it imperative, however, to state that the above apology is a personal matter and in no wise affects our permanent attitude toward the lawlessness manifest so recently in our midst. Moreover, we were forced at the muzzle of a six-shooter, in the hands of the above-mentioned Sundown, to insert that illiterate and blood-thirsty gentleman's screed in the MESA NEWS, as he, together with the gang of cutthroats with whom he seems in league, stood over us with drawn weapons until the entire issue had been run off. Such is the condition of affairs under the present corrupt administration of our suffering State."

Such advertising, Sundown reflected, breathing of battle and carnage, would obviate the necessity for future upholding of his reputation in a physical sense. Great is the power of the press! It became whispered about that he was a two-gun man of dexterous attainments in dispensing lead and that his mild and even apologetic manner was but a cloak. Accident and the tongues of men earned for Sundown that peace which he so thoroughly loved. He became immune to strife. When he felt his outward attitude sagging a little, he re-read the clipping and braced up.

Sundown rode to the Concho gate, dismounted and opened it. Chance ran ahead, leaping up as Corliss came from the ranch-house.

"Got them holes plugged in the tank," said Sundown. "Got the engine runnin' ag'in and things is fine. You goin' to put them cattle back on the water-hole range?"

"Yes, as soon as Bud can get around again. He's up, but he can't ride yet."

"How's Bull?"

"Oh, he's all right. Mebby-So's laid up yet. He got it pretty bad."

"Well, I reckon they ain't goin' to be no more fightin' 'bout cattle and sheep. I stopped by to the Loring ranch. Ole man Loring was sure ugly, so I reckon he's feelin' nacheral ag'in. He was like to get mad at me for stopping but his gal, Nell, she smoothed down his wool and asked me to stay and eat. I wasn't feelin' extra hungry, so I come along up here."

"I have some good news," said Corliss. "Got a letter from Billy last week. Didn't have time to tell you. He's working for a broker in 'Frisco. I shouldn't wonder if he should turn up one of these days. How would you like to drive over to Antelope and meet him when he comes?"

"I'd sure be glad. Always did like Billy. 'Course you don't know when he's comin'—and I got to do some drivin' meself right soon."

"So?"

"Yep. 'Course I got the wagon, but they ain't no style to that. I was wantin' a rig with style to it—like the buckboard." Sundown fidgeted nervously with the buttons of his shirt. He coughed, took off his hat, and mopped his face with a red bandanna. Despite his efforts he grew warmer and warmer. He was about to approach a delicate subject. Finally he seized the bull by the horns, so to speak, and his tanned face grew red. "I was wantin' to borrow that buckboard, mebby, Saturday."

"Sure! Going to Antelope?"

"Nope—not first. I got business over to Chico Miguel's place. I'm goin' to call on a lady."

"Oh, I see! Anita?"

"Well, I sure ain't goin' to call on her ma—she's married a'ready."

Despite himself, Corliss smiled. "So that's what you wanted that new bed and table and the chairs for. Did they get marked up much coming in?"

"The legs some. I rubbed 'em with that hoss-liniment you give me. You can hardly tell. It kind of smelled like turpentine, and I didn't have nothin' else."

"Well, anything you want—"

"I know, boss. But this is goin' to be a quiet weddin'. No brass-bands or ice-cream or pop-corn or style. Just me and her and—and I reckon a priest, seein' she was brung up that way. I ain't asked her yet."

"What? About getting married, or the priest?"

"Nothin'. We got kind of a eye-understandin' and her ma and me is good friends. It's like this. Bein' no hand to do love-makin' stylish, I just passes her a couple of bouquets onct or twict and said a few words. Now, you see, if I get that buckboard and a couple of hosses—I sure would like the white ones—and drive over lookin' like business and slip the ole man a box of cigars I bought, and Mrs. Miguel that there red-and-yella serape I paid ten dollars for in Antelope, and show Anita me new contract with the Concho for pumpin' water for seventy-five bones a month, I reckon the rest of it'll come easy. I'm figurin' strong on them white hosses, likewise. Bein' white'll kind of look like gettin' married, without me sayin' it. You see, boss, I'm short on the Spanish talk and so I have to do some figurin'."

"Well, Sun, you have come along a lot since you first hit the Concho! Go ahead, and good luck to you! If you need any money—"

"I was comin' to that. Seein' as you kind of know me—and seein' I'm goin' to git hitched—I was thinkin' you might lend me mebby a hundred on the contrac'."

"I guess I can. Will that be enough?"

"Plenty. You see I was figurin' on buyin' a few head of stock to run with yourn on the water-hole range."

"Why, I can let you have the stock. You can pay me when you get ready."

"That's just it. You'd kind of give 'em to me and I ain't askin' favors, except the buckboard and the white hosses."

"But what do you want to monkey with cattle for? You're doing pretty well with the water."

"That's just it. You see, Anita thinks I'm a rarin', high-ridin', cussin', tearin', bronco-bustin' cow-puncher from over the hill. I reckon you know I ain't, but I got to live up to it and kind of let her down easy-like. I can put on me spurs and chaps onct or twict a week and go flyin' out and whoopin' around me stock, and scarin' 'em to death, pertendin' I'm mighty interested in ridin' range. If you got a lady's goat, you want to keep it. 'Course, later on, I can kind o' slack up. Then I'm goin' to learn her to read American, and she can read that piece in the paper about me. I reckon that'll kind of cinch up the idea that her husband sure is the real thing. But I got to have them cows till she can learn to read."

"We've got to brand a few yearlings that got by last round-up. Bud said there was about fifteen of them. You can ride over after you get settled and help cut 'em out. What iron do you want to put on them?"

"Well, seein' it's me own brand, I reckon it will be like this: A kind of half-circle for the sun, and a lot of little lines runnin' out to show that it's shinin', and underneath a straight line meanin' the earth, which is 'Sundown'—me own brand. Could Johnny make one like that?"

"I don't know. That's a pretty big order. You go over and tell Johnny what you want. And I'll send the buckboard over Saturday."

CHAPTER XXVIII

IMPROVEMENTS

Out in a field bordered by the roadway a man toiled behind a disk-plough. He trudged with seven-league strides along the furrows, disdaining to ride on the seat of the plough. To effect a comfortable following of his operations he had lengthened the reins with clothes-line. He drove a team of old and gentle white horses as wheelers. His lead animals were mules, neither old nor gentle. It is possible that this fact accounted for his being afoot. He was arrayed in cowboy boots and chaps, a faded flannel shirt, and a Stetson. Despite the fact that a year had passed since he had practically "Lochinvared" the most willing Anita,—though with the full and joyous consent of her parents,—he still clung to the habiliments of the cowboy, feeling that they offset the more or less menial requirements of tilling the soil. Behind him trailed a lean, shaggy wolf-dog who nosed the furrows occasionally and dug for prairie-dogs with intermittent zest.

The toiler, too preoccupied with his ploughing to see more than his horses' heads and the immediate unbroken territory before them, did not realize that a team had stopped out on the road and that a man had leaped from the buckboard and was standing at the fence. Chance, however, saw the man, and, running to Sundown, whined. Sundown pulled up his team and wiped his brow. "Hurt your foot ag'in?" he queried. "Nope? Then what's wrong?"

The man in the road called.

Sundown wheeled and stood with mouth open. "It's—Gee Gosh! It's Billy!"

He observed that a young and fashionably attired woman sat in the buckboard holding the team. He fumbled at his shirt and buttoned it at the neck. Then he swung his team around and started toward the fence.

Will Corliss, attired in a quiet-hued business suit, his cheeks healthfully pink and his eye clear, smiled as the lean one tied the team and stalked toward him.

Corliss held out his hand. Sundown shook his head. "Excuse me, Billy, but I ain't shakin' hands with you across no fence."

And Sundown wormed his length between the wires and straightened up, extending a tanned and hairy paw. "Shake, pardner! Say, you're lookin' gorjus!"

"My wife," said Corliss.

Sundown doffed his sombrero sweepingly. "Welcome to Arizona, ma'am."

"This is my friend, Washington Hicks, Margery."

"Yes, ma'am," said Sundown. "It ain't my fault, neither. I had nothin' to say about it when they hitched that name onto me. I reckon I hollered, but it didn't do no good. Me pals"—and Sundown shrugged his shoulder—"mostly gents travelin' for their health—got to callin' me Sundown, which is more poetical. 'Course, when I got married—"

"Married!" exclaimed Corliss, grinning.

"You needn't to grin, Billy. Gettin' married's mighty responsible-like."

Corliss made a gesture of apology. "So you're homesteading the water-hole? Jack wrote to me about it. He didn't say anything about your getting married."

"Kind of like his not sayin' anything about your gettin' hitched up, eh? He said he was hearin' from you, but nothin' about Misses Corliss. Please to expect my congratulations, ma'am—and you, too, Billy."

"Thank you!" said Mrs. Corliss, smiling. "Will has told me a great deal about you."

"He has, eh? Well, I'm right glad to be acquainted by heresy. It kind of puts you on to what to expect. But say, it's hot here. If you'll drive back to me house, I'd sure like to show you the improvements."

"All right, Sun! We'll drive right in and wait for you."

They did not have to wait, however. Sundown, leaving his team at the fence, took a short cut to the house. He entered the back door and called to Anita.

"Neeter," he said, as she hastened to answer him, "they's some friends of mine just drivin' up. If you could kind of make a quick change and put on that white dress with the leetle roses sprinkled on it—quick; and is—is he sleepin'?"

"Si! He is having the good sleep."

"Fine! I'll hold 'em off till you get fixed up. It's me ole pal, Billy Corliss,—and he's brung along a wife. We got to make a good front, seein' it's kind of unexpected. Wrastle into that purty dress and don't wake him up."

"Si! I go queek."

"Why, this is fine!" said Corliss, entering, hat in hand, and gazing about the room. "It's as snug and picturesque as a lodge."

"Beautiful!" exclaimed the enthusiastic Margery, gazing at the Navajo rugs, the clean, white-washed walls against which the red ollas, filled with wild flowers, made a pretty picture, and the great grizzly-bear rug thrown across a home-made couch. "It's actually romantic!"

"Me long suit, lady. We ain't got much, but what we got goes with this kind of country."

Margery smiled. "Oh, Will, I'd like a home like this. Just simple and clean—and comfortable. It's a real home."

"Me wife's comin' in a minute. While she's—er—combin' her hair, mebby you'd like to see some of the improvements." And Sundown marched proudly to the new dining-room—an extension that he had built himself—and waved an invitation for his guests to behold and marvel.

The dining-room was, in its way, also picturesque. The exceedingly plain table was covered with a clean white cloth. The furniture, owing to some fortunate accident of choice, was not ornate but of plain straight lines, redeemed by painted ollas filled with flowers. The white walls were decorated with two pictures, a lithograph of the Madonna,—which seemed entirely in keeping with the general tone of the room, but

Henry Hubert Knibbs

which would have looked glaringly out of place anywhere else,—and an enlarged full-length photograph, framed, of an exceedingly tall and gorgeous cowboy, hat in hand, quirt on wrist, and looking extremely impressive. Beside the cowboy stood a great, shaggy dog—Chance. And, by chance, the picture was a success.

"Why, it's you, Sun!" exclaimed Corliss, striding to the picture. "And it's a dandy! I'd hang it in the front room."'

"That's what Neeter was sayin'. But I kind of like it in here. You see, Neeter sets there and I set here where I can see me picture while I'm eatin'. It kind of gives me a good appetite. 'Course, lookin' out the window is fine. See them there mesas dancin' in the sun, and the grass wavin' and me cows grazing and 'way off like in a dream them blue hills! It's sure a millionaire picture! And it don't cost nothin'."

"That's the best of it!" said Corliss heartily. "We're going to build—over on the mesa near the fork. You remember?"

Sundown's flush was inexplicable to Margery, but Corliss understood. He had ridden the trail toward the fork one night. . . . But that was past, atoned for. . . . He would live that down.

"It's a purty view, over there," said Sundown gently.

And the two men felt that that which was not forgotten was at least forgiven—would never again be mentioned.

"And me kitchen," said Sundown, leading the way, "is Neeter's. She runs it. There's more good eats comes out of it than they is fancy crockery in it, which just suits me. And out here"—and the party progressed to the back yard—"is me new corral and stable and chicken-coop. I made all them improvements meself, durin' the winter. Reckon you saw the gasoline-engine what does the pumpin' for the tanks. I wanted to have a windmill, but the engine works faster. It's kind of hot, ma'am, and if you'll come in and set down I reckon me wife's got her hair—"

"Wah! Wah! Wah!" came in a crescendo from the bedroom.

Sundown straightened his shoulders. "Gee Gosh, he's gone and give it away, already!"

Corliss and his wife glanced at their host inquisitively.

"Me latest improvement," said Sundown, bowing, as Anita, a plump brown baby on her arm, opened the bedroom door and stood bashfully looking at the strangers.

"And me wife," he added.

Corliss bowed, but Margery rushed to Anita and held out her arms. "Oh, let me take him!" she cried. "What big brown eyes! Let me hold him! I'll be awfully careful! Isn't he sweet!"

They moved to the living-room where Anita and Margery sat side by side on the couch with the baby absorbing all their attention.

Sundown stalked about the room, his hands in his pockets, vainly endeavoring to appear very mannish and unconcerned, but his eye roved unceasingly to the baby. He was the longest and most upstanding six-feet-four of proud father that Margery or her husband had ever had the pleasure of meeting.

"He's got Neeter's eyes—and—and her—complexion, but he's sure got me style. He measures up two-feet-six by the yardstick what we got with buyin' a case of bakin'-soda, and he ain't a yearlin' yet. I don't just recollec' the day but I reckon Neeter knows."

"He's great!" exclaimed Corliss. "Isn't he, Margery?"

"He's just the cutest little brown baby!" said Margery, hugging the plump little body.

"He—he ain't so *turruble* brown," asserted Sundown. "'Course, he's tanned up some, seein' we keep him outside lots. I'm kind o' tanned up meself, and I reckon he takes after me."

"He has a head shaped just like yours," said Margery, anxious to please the proud father.

"Then," said Sundown solemnly, "he's goin' to be a pole."

Anita, proud of her offspring, her husband, her neat and clean home, laughed softly, and held out her arms for the baby. With a kick and a struggle the young Sundown wriggled to her arms and snuggled against her, gravely inspecting the pink roses on his mother's white dress. They were new to him. He was more used to blue gingham. The roses were interesting.

"Yes, Billy's me latest improvement," said Sundown, anxious to assert himself in view of the presence of so much femininity and a correspondingly seeming lack of vital interest in anything save the baby.

"Billy!" said Corliss, turning from where he had stood gazing out of the window.

"Uhuh! We named him Billy after you."

Corliss turned again to the window.

Sundown stepped to him, misinterpreting his silence. He put his hand on Corliss's shoulder. "You ain't mad 'cause we called him that, be you?"

"Mad! Say, Sun,"—and Corliss laughed, choked, and brushed his eyes. "Sun, I don't deserve it."

"Well, seein' what I been through since I was his size, I reckon I don't either. But he's here, and you're here and your wife—and things is fine! The sun is shinin' and the jiggers out on the mesa is chirkin' and to-morrow's goin' to be a fine day. There's nothin' like bankin' on to-morrow, 'specially if you are doin' the best you kin today." And with this bit of philosophy, Sundown, motioning to Corliss, excused himself and his companion as they strode to the doorway and out to the open. There they talked about many things having to do with themselves and others until Margery, hailing them from the door, told them that dinner was waiting.

After dinner the men foregathered in the shade of an acacia and smoked, saying little, but each thinking of the future. Sundown in his peculiarly optimistic and half-melancholy way, and Corliss with mingled feelings of hope and regret. He had endeavored to live down his past away from home. He had succeeded in a measure: had sought and found work, had become acquainted with his employer's daughter, told her frankly of his previous manner of life, and found, not a little to his astonishment, that she had faith in him. Then he wrote to his brother, asking to come back. John Corliss was more than glad to realize that Will had straightened up. If the younger man was willing to reclaim himself among folk who knew him at his worst, there must be something to him. So Corliss had asked his brother to give him his employer's address; had written to the employer, explaining certain facts

Henry Hubert Knibbs

regarding Will's share in the Concho, and also asking that he urge Will to come home. Just here Miss Margery had something to say, the ultimate result of which was a more definite understanding all around. If Will was going back to Arizona, Margery was also going. And as Margery was a young woman quietly determined to have her way when she knew that it was right to do so, they were married the day before Will Corliss was to leave for Arizona. This was to be their honeymoon.

All of which was in Will Corliss's mind as he lay smoking and gazing at the cloudless sky. It may be added to his credit that he had not returned because of the money that was his when he chose to claim it. Rather, he had realized—and Margery had a great deal to do with his newer outlook—that so long as he stayed away from home he was confessing to cowardice. Incidentally Margery, being utterly feminine, wanted to see Arizona and the free life of the range, of which Corliss had told her. As for Nell Loring . . . Corliss sighed.

"It sure is hot," muttered Sundown. "'Course, you'll stay over and light out in the mornin' cool. You and me can sleep in the front room. 'T ain't the fust time we rustled for a roost. And the wimmen-folks can bunk in the bedroom. Billy he's right comf'table in his big clothes-basket. He's a sure good sleeper, if I do say it."

"We could have gone on through," said Corliss, smiling. "Of course we'd have been late, but Margery likes driving."

"Well, if you had 'a' gone through—and I'd 'a' *ketched* you at it—I—I—I'd 'a' changed Billy's name to—to somethin' else." And Sundown frowned ferociously.

Corliss laughed. "But we didn't. We're here—and it's mighty good to breathe Arizona air again. You never really begin to love Arizona till you've been somewhere else for a while."

"And bein' married helps some, too," suggested Sundown.

"Yes, a whole lot. Margery's enthusiasm makes me see beautiful things that I'd passed a hundred times before I knew her."

"That's correc'," concurred Sundown. "Now, take Gentle Annie, for instance—"

"You mean Mrs.—er—Sundown?"

"Nope! Me tame cow. 'Annie' is American for 'Anita,' so I called her that. Now, that there Gentle Annie's just a regular cow. She ain't purty—but she sure gives plenty milk. Neeter got me to seein' that Gentle Annie's eyes was purty and mournful-like and that she was a right handsome cow. If your wife's pettin' and feedin' somethin', and callin' it them there smooth Spanish names, a fella's wise to do the same. It helps things along."

"Little Billy, for instance," suggested Corliss.

"Leetle Billy is right! But he couldn't help bein' good-lookin', I guess. He's different. Fust thing your wife said wuz he took after his pa."

"You haven't changed much," said Corliss, smiling.

"Me? Mebby not—outside; but say, inside things is different. I got feelin's now what I never knowed I had before. Why, sometimes, when Neeter is rockin' leetle Bill, and singing and me settin' in the door, towards evenin', and everything fed up and happy, why, do you know, I feel jest like cryin'. Plumb foolish, ain't it?"

"I don't know about that, Sun."

"Well, you will some day," asserted Sundown, taking him literally. "'T ain't gettin' married what makes a man, but it's a dum' poor one what don't make the best of things if he is hitched up to a good girl. Only one thing—it sure don't give a fella time to write much po'try."

Corliss did not smile. "You're living the poetry," he said with simple sincerity.

"Which is correc', Billy. And speakin' of po'try, I reckon I got to go feed them pigs. They's gruntin' somethin' scand'lous for havin' comp'ny to our house—and anyhow, they's like to wake up leetle Bill."

And Sundown departed to feed his pigs.

CHAPTER XXIX

A MAN'S COUNTRY

"As for that," said John Corliss, gazing out across the mesa, "Loring and I shook hands—over the line fence. That's settled."

Sundown had just dismounted. He stood holding the reins of his old saddle-horse "Pill." He had ridden to the Concho to get his monthly pay. "And pore leetle ole Fernando—he's gone," said Sundown. "That's jest the difference between *one* fella doin' what he thinks is right and a *bunch* of fellas shootin' up themselves. The one fella gets it every time. The bunch, bein' so many of 'em, gets off. Mebby that's law, but it ain't fair."

"There's a difference, Sun. A fight in the open and downing a man from ambush—two mighty different things."

"Well, mebby. But I'm feelin' sad for that leetle Fernando jest the same.—That Billy's new house?"

"Yes. They expect to get settled this month."

"Gee Gosh! I been so busy I missed a bunch of days. Reckon I got to rustle up somethin' for a weddin' present. I know, be

Henry Hubert Knibbs

Gosh! I'll send 'em me picture. Billy was kind of stuck on it."

"Good idea, Sun. But I guess you'll miss it yourself."

"I dunno. Neeter ain't lookin' at it as much as she used to. She's busy lookin' after leetle Bill—and me. 'Course I can get another one took most any time."

"Make it two and give me one," said Corliss.

"You ain't joshin'?"

"No. I'll hang it in the office."

"Then she gets took—immediate."

Chance, who stood watching the two men, rose and wagged his tail.

Chance never failed to recognize that note in his master's voice. It meant that his master was pleased, enthusiastic, happy, and Chance, loyal companion, found his happiness in that of his friends.

"Well," said Sundown, "I reckon I got to be joggin'. Thanks for the check."

Corliss waved his hand. "I'll step over to the gate with you. Thought perhaps you'd stay and see Billy."

"Nope. I ain't feelin' like meetin' folks today. Don' know why. Sky's clear and fine, but inside I feel like it was goin' to rain. When you comin' down to see leetle Bill and Neeter?"

"Pretty soon. Is Billy well?"

"Well! Gee Gosh! If you could hear the langwidge he uses when Neeter puts him to bed and he don't want to go! Why, yesterday he was on the floor playin' with Chance and Chance got tired of it and lays down to snooze. Billy hitches along up to Chance, and *Bim*! he punches Chance on the nose. Made him sneeze, too! Why, that kid ain't afraid of nothin'—jest like his pa. I reckon Billy told you that his wife said that leetle Billy took after me, eh? Leave it to a woman to see them things!"

"Well, I'm mighty glad you're settled, and making a go of it, Sun."

"So be I. I was recollectin' when I fust come into this country and landed at that water-hole. It was kind of a joke then, but it ain't no joke now. Funny thing—that bunch of punchers what started me lookin' for that there hotel that time—they come jinglin' up last week. Didn't know I was the boss till one of 'em grins after sizin' me up and says—er—well, two three words what kids hadn't ought to hear, and then, 'It's him, boys!' Then I steps out and says, 'It is, gents. Come right in and have dinner and it won't cost you fellas a cent. I told you I'd feed you up good when I got me hotel to runnin'.' And sure enough, in they come and we fed 'em. They was goin' to the Blue. They bunked in me hay that night. Next mornin' they acted kind of queer, sayin' nothin' except, 'So-long,' when they lit out. And what do you think! They went and left four dollars and twenty-eight cents in the sugar-bowl—and a piece of paper with it sayin', 'For the kid.' We never found it out till I was drinkin' me coffee that night and liked to choked to death on a nickel. Guess them punchers ain't so bad."

"No. They stopped here next day. Said they'd never had a finer feed than you gave 'em."

"Neeter is sure some cook. Pretty nigh's good as me. Well, so-long, Jack. I—I—kind of wish you was buildin' a new house yourself."

Corliss, standing with his hand on the neck of Sundown's horse, smiled. "Arizona's a man's country, Sun."

"She sure is!" said Sundown, throwing out his chest. "And lemme tell you, Jack, it's a man's business to get married and settle down—and—raise more of 'em. 'Specially like *me* and *you* and Bud and Hi—only Hi's gettin' kind of old. She's a fine country, but she needs improvin'. Sometimes them improvements keeps you awake nights, but they're worth it!"

"Yes, I believe they're worth it," said Corliss, "So-long, Sun."

"So-long, Jack. I got to get back and milk Gentle Annie. We're switchin' Billy onto the bottle, and he don't like to be kep' waitin'."

Chance, following Sundown, trotted behind the horse a few steps, then turned and ran back to Corliss. He nuzzled the rancher's hand, whined, and leapt away to follow his master.

Choose from Thousands of 1stWorldLibrary Classics By

A. M. Barnard
Ada Leverson
Adolphus William Ward
Aesop
Agatha Christie
Alexander Aaronsohn
Alexander Kielland
Alexandre Dumas
Alfred Gatty
Alfred Ollivant
Alice Duer Miller
Alice Turner Curtis
Alice Dunbar
Allen Chapman
Alleyne Ireland
Ambrose Bierce
Amelia E. Barr
Amory H. Bradford
Andrew Lang
Andrew McFarland Davis
Andy Adams
Angela Brazil
Anna Alice Chapin
Anna Sewell
Annie Besant
Annie Hamilton Donnell
Annie Payson Call
Annie Roe Carr
Annonaymous
Anton Chekhov
Archibald Lee Fletcher
Arnold Bennett
Arthur C. Benson
Arthur Conan Doyle
Arthur M. Winfield
Arthur Ransome
Arthur Schnitzler
Arthur Train
Atticus
B.H. Baden-Powell
B. M. Bower
B. C. Chatterjee
Baroness Emmuska Orczy
Baroness Orczy
Basil King
Bayard Taylor
Ben Macomber
Bertha Muzzy Bower
Bjornstjerne Bjornson

Booth Tarkington
Boyd Cable
Bram Stoker
C. Collodi
C. E. Orr
C. M. Ingleby
Carolyn Wells
Catherine Parr Traill
Charles A. Eastman
Charles Amory Beach
Charles Dickens
Charles Dudley Warner
Charles Farrar Browne
Charles Ives
Charles Kingsley
Charles Klein
Charles Hanson Towne
Charles Lathrop Pack
Charles Romyn Dake
Charles Whibley
Charles Willing Beale
Charlotte M. Braeme
Charlotte M. Yonge
Charlotte Perkins Stetson
Clair W. Hayes
Clarence Day Jr.
Clarence E. Mulford
Clemence Housman
Confucius
Coningsby Dawson
Cornelis DeWitt Wilcox
Cyril Burleigh
D. H. Lawrence
Daniel Defoe
David Garnett
Dinah Craik
Don Carlos Janes
Donald Keyhoe
Dorothy Kilner
Dougan Clark
Douglas Fairbanks
E. Nesbit
E. P. Roe
E. Phillips Oppenheim
E. S. Brooks
Earl Barnes
Edgar Rice Burroughs
Edith Van Dyne
Edith Wharton

Edward Everett Hale
Edward J. O'Biren
Edward S. Ellis
Edwin L. Arnold
Eleanor Atkins
Eleanor Hallowell Abbott
Eliot Gregory
Elizabeth Gaskell
Elizabeth McCracken
Elizabeth Von Arnim
Ellem Key
Emerson Hough
Emilie F. Carlen
Emily Bronte
Emily Dickinson
Enid Bagnold
Enilor Macartney Lane
Erasmus W. Jones
Ernie Howard Pie
Ethel May Dell
Ethel Turner
Ethel Watts Mumford
Eugene Sue
Eugenie Foa
Eugene Wood
Eustace Hale Ball
Evelyn Everett-green
Everard Cotes
F. H. Cheley
F. J. Cross
F. Marion Crawford
Fannie E. Newberry
Federick Austin Ogg
Ferdinand Ossendowski
Fergus Hume
Florence A. Kilpatrick
Fremont B. Deering
Francis Bacon
Francis Darwin
Frances Hodgson Burnett
Frances Parkinson Keyes
Frank Gee Patchin
Frank Harris
Frank Jewett Mather
Frank L. Packard
Frank V. Webster
Frederic Stewart Isham
Frederick Trevor Hill
Frederick Winslow Taylor

Friedrich Kerst
Friedrich Nietzsche
Fyodor Dostoyevsky
G.A. Henty
G.K. Chesterton
Gabrielle E. Jackson
Garrett P. Serviss
Gaston Leroux
George A. Warren
George Ade
Geroge Bernard Shaw
George Cary Eggleston
George Durston
George Ebers
George Eliot
George Gissing
George MacDonald
George Meredith
George Orwell
George Sylvester Viereck
George Tucker
George W. Cable
George Wharton James
Gertrude Atherton
Gordon Casserly
Grace E. King
Grace Gallatin
Grace Greenwood
Grant Allen
Guillermo A. Sherwell
Gulielma Zollinger
Gustav Flaubert
H. A. Cody
H. B. Irving
H.C. Bailey
H. G. Wells
H. H. Munro
H. Irving Hancock
H. R. Naylor
H. Rider Haggard
H. W. C. Davis
Haldeman Julius
Hall Caine
Hamilton Wright Mabie
Hans Christian Andersen
Harold Avery
Harold McGrath
Harriet Beecher Stowe
Harry Castlemon
Harry Coghill
Harry Houidini

Hayden Carruth
Helent Hunt Jackson
Helen Nicolay
Hendrik Conscience
Hendy David Thoreau
Henri Barbusse
Henrik Ibsen
Henry Adams
Henry Ford
Henry Frost
Henry James
Henry Jones Ford
Henry Seton Merriman
Henry W Longfellow
Herbert A. Giles
Herbert Carter
Herbert N. Casson
Herman Hesse
Hildegard G. Frey
Homer
Honore De Balzac
Horace B. Day
Horace Walpole
Horatio Alger Jr.
Howard Pyle
Howard R. Garis
Hugh Lofting
Hugh Walpole
Humphry Ward
Ian Maclaren
Inez Haynes Gillmore
Irving Bacheller
Isabel Cecilia Williams
Isabel Hornibrook
Israel Abrahams
Ivan Turgenev
J.G.Austin
J. Henri Fabre
J. M. Barrie
J. M. Walsh
J. Macdonald Oxley
J. R. Miller
J. S. Fletcher
J. S. Knowles
J. Storer Clouston
J. W. Duffield
Jack London
Jacob Abbott
James Allen
James Andrews
James Baldwin

James Branch Cabell
James DeMille
James Joyce
James Lane Allen
James Lane Allen
James Oliver Curwood
James Oppenheim
James Otis
James R. Driscoll
Jane Abbott
Jane Austen
Jane L. Stewart
Janet Aldridge
Jens Peter Jacobsen
Jerome K. Jerome
Jessie Graham Flower
John Buchan
John Burroughs
John Cournos
John F. Kennedy
John Gay
John Glasworthy
John Habberton
John Joy Bell
John Kendrick Bangs
John Milton
John Philip Sousa
John Taintor Foote
Jonas Lauritz Idemil Lie
Jonathan Swift
Joseph A. Altsheler
Joseph Carey
Joseph Conrad
Joseph E. Badger Jr
Joseph Hergesheimer
Joseph Jacobs
Jules Vernes
Julian Hawthrone
Julie A Lippmann
Justin Huntly McCarthy
Kakuzo Okakura
Karle Wilson Baker
Kate Chopin
Kenneth Grahame
Kenneth McGaffey
Kate Langley Bosher
Kate Langley Bosher
Katherine Cecil Thurston
Katherine Stokes
L. A. Abbot
L. T. Meade

L. Frank Baum
Latta Griswold
Laura Dent Crane
Laura Lee Hope
Laurence Housman
Lawrence Beasley
Leo Tolstoy
Leonid Andreyev
Lewis Carroll
Lewis Sperry Chafer
Lilian Bell
Lloyd Osbourne
Louis Hughes
Louis Joseph Vance
Louis Tracy
Louisa May Alcott
Lucy Fitch Perkins
Lucy Maud Montgomery
Luther Benson
Lydia Miller Middleton
Lyndon Orr
M. Corvus
M. H. Adams
Margaret E. Sangster
Margret Howth
Margaret Vandercook
Margaret W. Hungerford
Margret Penrose
Maria Edgeworth
Maria Thompson Daviess
Mariano Azuela
Marion Polk Angellotti
Mark Overton
Mark Twain
Mary Austin
Mary Catherine Crowley
Mary Cole
Mary Hastings Bradley
Mary Roberts Rinehart
Mary Rowlandson
M. Wollstonecraft Shelley
Maud Lindsay
Max Beerbohm
Myra Kelly
Nathaniel Hawthrone
Nicolo Machiavelli
O. F. Walton
Oscar Wilde

Owen Johnson
P.G. Wodehouse
Paul and Mabel Thorne
Paul G. Tomlinson
Paul Severing
Percy Brebner
Percy Keese Fitzhugh
Peter B. Kyne
Plato
Quincy Allen
R. Derby Holmes
R. L. Stevenson
R. S. Ball
Rabindranath Tagore
Rahul Alvares
Ralph Bonehill
Ralph Henry Barbour
Ralph Victor
Ralph Waldo Emmerson
Rene Descartes
Ray Cummings
Rex Beach
Rex E. Beach
Richard Harding Davis
Richard Jefferies
Richard Le Gallienne
Robert Barr
Robert Frost
Robert Gordon Anderson
Robert L. Drake
Robert Lansing
Robert Lynd
Robert Michael Ballantyne
Robert W. Chambers
Rosa Nouchette Carey
Rudyard Kipling
Saint Augustine
Samuel B. Allison
Samuel Hopkins Adams
Sarah Bernhardt
Sarah C. Hallowell
Selma Lagerlof
Sherwood Anderson
Sigmund Freud
Standish O'Grady
Stanley Weyman
Stella Benson
Stella M. Francis

Stephen Crane
Stewart Edward White
Stijn Streuvels
Swami Abhedananda
Swami Parmananda
T. S. Ackland
T. S. Arthur
The Princess Der Ling
Thomas A. Janvier
Thomas A Kempis
Thomas Anderton
Thomas Bailey Aldrich
Thomas Bulfinch
Thomas De Quincey
Thomas Dixon
Thomas H. Huxley
Thomas Hardy
Thomas More
Thornton W. Burgess
U. S. Grant
Upton Sinclair
Valentine Williams
Various Authors
Vaughan Kester
Victor Appleton
Victor G. Durham
Victoria Cross
Virginia Woolf
Wadsworth Camp
Walter Camp
Walter Scott
Washington Irving
Wilbur Lawton
Wilkie Collins
Willa Cather
Willard F. Baker
William Dean Howells
William le Queux
W. Makepeace Thackeray
William W. Walter
William Shakespeare
Winston Churchill
Yei Theodora Ozaki
Yogi Ramacharaka
Young E. Allison
Zane Grey

www.ingramcontent.com/pod-product-compliance
Lightning Source LLC
Chambersburg PA
CBHW020556260626
47157CB00003B/725